Mister Rogers' Neighborhood

Mister Rogers' Neighborhood

Children, Television, and Fred Rogers

Mark Collins and Margaret Mary Kimmel, *Editors*

UNIVERSITY OF PITTSBURGH PRESS

The editors would like to thank Dean Toni Carbo Bearman, School of Library and Information Science, University of Pittsburgh, who was extremely supportive of this project, confident of its importance and contribution to the field. We would like to acknowledge the exemplary work of Lora Kohler in aiding in the completion of this manuscript. Other graduate students in the master of library science program, Jon Theisen and Mia Esserman, lent their support in tracking down endless bibliographic details.

Mister Rogers' Neighborhood is the registered trademark of Family Communications, Inc. and is used with their permission.

Published by the University of Pittsburgh Press, Pittsburgh, Pa. 15260
Manufactured in the United States of America
Printed on acid-free paper
Cataloging-in Publication data appears at the end of this book.
A CIP catalog record for this book is available from the British Library.
Eurospan, London

Grateful acknowledgment is made to the Vira I. Heinz Endowment for its generous support of this publication.

CONTENTS

Born Again in Rogers

My recovery began, ironically enough, as our whole family watched TV—right after *The Ren and Stimpy Show,* and it was as if a giant, leaded, dental X-ray apron had been peeled off my body. Suddenly I was unburdened. Life suddenly seemed more orderly and bearable. It was easier to walk downstairs to face the morning. Even food tasted better.

Day by day, over the years, the pressure had built—and not only in me. My wife, too, was full of conflicting emotions: pity, distrust, frustration, and plain incredulity that her husband could be such a man. We'd tried to protect the kids from my terrible secret, but of course they sensed something wasn't quite right. How could they not? They'd seen my mood suddenly darken. They'd seen the wincing expression of sheer revulsion. Maybe they knew everything—and maybe, at some subconscious level, I didn't care if they did. For the longest time, I refused to consider myself in any way afflicted. Sure, it was denial, but one can always rationalize. If I was so wrong, I'd ask myself, why weren't there encounter groups for like-troubled people? If compulsive shopping was deemed worthy of Thursday evening healing sessions, why no support group, no transdermal patch, no twelve-step program for me? And even if there were some sort of formal organization for my kind, what in the world could I say?

"Hi. My name is Bob, and Mister Rogers makes my flesh crawl."

My God. The shame.

But it's true. Over the course of twenty-five years, I'd come to detest Fred Rogers, along with everything and everyone around him. Twenty-five insufferably Pollyanna years of smiling, sharing, and reassuring. Twenty-five years of saccharine sincerity, of maddening beatificity, of low wattage. Twenty-five years of Mr. McFeely and his adult-size case of attention deficit disorder. Twenty-five years of folks just dropping in at eight o'clock in the morning and receiving a cheerful hello instead of the bum's rush they deserve. Twenty-five years of Henrietta Pussycat and meow meow damnedest speech meow impedi-meow you've ever meow heard. Twenty-five years of numbing repetition; of utter predictability; of purple cardigans matched with olive green trousers; of noxious Pittsburgh accents; of *extremely* unfortunate ball-handling skills; of the cheapest production values and, by orders of magnitude, the ugliest decor in the developed world; of Picture-Picture showing "Hi," instead of something cool, like brush fires being set with a magnifying glass; of nauseating sycophancy from Handyman Negri; of Lady Aberlin cooing at Daniel Striped Tiger with precisely the come-hither expression I'd fantasize about her bestowing on me. Twenty-five years, in short, of praying at the altar of wimpishness, to a piano accompaniment, day after day after damn beautiful day. Increasingly, over a quarter of a century, the whole thing made me want to puke.

Which is why we were watching *The Ren and Stimpy Show* in the first place. It was all my idea.

If, by some chance, you are not familiar with this cartoon, I can best describe it as thirty minutes of sadistic interplay between an oafish but guileless cat and a skittish, paranoiac chihuahua — an animal so malignantly self-absorbed he makes King Friday XIII look, comparatively speaking, like Lambchop.

A distinctive aspect of this cartoon show is the super-closeup, typically on facial pores, taste buds, carbuncles, bloodshot eyes, and lots and lots and lots of mucus, so that, in one episode, when Ren and Stimpy are space cadets driven crazy from boredom en route to the final frontier, their increasing insanity is communicated by ever-closer, ever-more-grotesque views of their every tortured grimace.

Naturally, the program is a big hit.

Thus, based on rave reviews and the personal recommendation of my big brother, *The Ren and Stimpy Show* became my choice for an evening of wholesome family togetherness. My wife at first resisted, but I presented a cunning argument for letting our eleven- and seven-year-old daughters tune in: that our scrupulous rationing of TV programming, intended to insulate them from sex, violence, and TV's generally empty intellectual calories, also shields them from the ironic, the irreverent, the satiric, the sardonic, and various other sensibilities we hold so dear.

"We can't let them grow up thinking 'The Berenstain Bears' constitutes cutting-edge comedy," I said. "Besides, the kids are on the playground every day. I'm sure they're very active participants in the free market of booger jokes. This is a very popular show. Let 'em watch."

That, as I say, was my argument. It was not necessarily everything on my mind, most of which, with more cunning still, I left unsaid. (Don't blame me for my thoughts; it was my sickness talking.)

"Let's cure these kids of Mister Rogers' brand of entertainment forever," I was thinking, "because *who needs him?!* To influence our precious children? If he is so influential, why does our second grader go to the bus stop every day to be systematically assaulted by little boys dressed in Teenage Mutant Ninja Turtle regalia and performing reptilian martial arts? Why aren't they wearing little zipper cardigans and singing 'It's You I Like'? Some influence. Didn't yesterday's Mister Rogers' kids ripen to become a generation of teenagers that is impregnating, shooting, and selling drugs to one another in unprecedented numbers? Didn't millions of others sit watching him on TV day after day to derive from the experience — above all else — the capacity to sit watching TV day after day? If we are to evaluate his legacy based on the test scores of his alumni, we will see only a generation at risk of crashing, having veered out of control on a treacherous, severely declining curve.

"They've sat wide-eyed for those idiotic puppets in the Neighborhood of Make-Believe plenty long enough," I ranted to my tortured self, "and they damn well are going to get the antidote."

Whereupon, verily, they did: twenty-five minutes of nihilistic Ren and Stimpy madness, punctuated by yet another cartoon hero called Powdered Toast Man. As a notable part of our wholesome family evening, Powdered Toast Man bravely saved the President of the United States from the agony of getting himself caught in his own zipper. Then, taking off Superman-like for his next adventure, he propelled himself by breaking wind.

And they say wit is dead.

It won't surprise you to know that our sophisticated, public-TV bred little girls were plenty stunned by the whole thing, especially the toast flatulence. They shouted "Oooh, grossssssssss!" again and again. They did not, however, exactly run from the room in disgust. What they did was laugh — no, *howl* — like children possessed.

It was the scariest thing I'd ever seen in my life.

It was also the moment of my conversion. Like a flash from heaven, my recovery began. In this moment of epiphany, I understood that there need be no antidote for Mister Rogers. In my blindness and cynicism, I had failed to realize that Mister Rogers *is* the antidote for everything else. He isn't the disease; he's the remedy. He isn't the problem; he's the solution. He isn't the devil in sneakers. He's an angel of God.

My name is Bob, and I want to be your neighbor.

Born again in Rogers. You might wonder how such things can so suddenly occur. The answer is knowing, just *knowing*, something that your whole life before was obscured by the inconclusive reckoning of relative merits. There are times when debate is rendered irrelevant; one simply knows — just as one knows love, just as one knows a force greater than self, just as one knows King Friday needs to have his thyroid medication adjusted.

Indeed, in the case of my epiphany, what I spontaneously knew was that Mister Rogers is not the puppet king's insufferable wimp alter ego. He's an endocrinological wonder drug, restoring metabolic balance to our entire culture.

This realization dawned as I stared in abject horror at my kids, who cackled and hooted at the puerile, scatological humor of Ren and Stimpy. I'd been looking at everything backward: while it may be true that the first generation weaned entirely on Mister Rogers is the most dysfunctional in American history, there's no telling how much worse off things might have been without him.

What would have happened to my sweet little daughters, for instance, had their morning TV programming been flatulent-intensive from the get-go? The thought made me queasier than Handyman Negri ever did on his most obsequious day.

Until my conversion, I'd been crediting the girls' generally docile demeanors and the pristine condition of our furniture to the lovely pairing of X chromosomes, the bane of reupholsterers everywhere. When I grew up with my two brothers, emergency-room visits and the occasional arson were a way of life, but my own children have had no casts, no fireworks accidents, not so much as a suture. It seemed like a simple matter of my

kids being — in the most politically correct phrasing I can think of —
testicularly challenged.

Yet I could hardly ignore the evidence of my own eyes. Halfway
through "Powdered Toast Man," it was as though they'd been on an intra-
venous testosterone drip. Limbs were flailing. Otherworldly noises were
coming from their mouths. A small davenport was toppled. How could
I fail to contrast this experience to the transcendent civility of Mister
Rogers? If twenty-five minutes of sick cartoon could so profoundly drug my
kids, how could I discount the effect of Mister Rogers' twenty-five years?
How could I hold him in such contempt for the very characteristic that, all
at once I just knew, is the heart and soul of his civilizing influence?

Yes, I admit it. At a visceral level, my beef with the guy had a lot to do
with the conviction that *he* was testicularly challenged, that his gentility
was unmanly, that he was just too sensitive to bear. But that, too, was my
sickness speaking. Part and parcel of my recovery is the sobering understanding of what I'm recovering from, of why I hated Fred Rogers for
twenty-five years, of why the man threatened me so. It was all revealed in
my Ren and Stimpy epiphany: It's not just that he counterbalances other
media influences. It's not just that he cancels out Marky Mark. There is
also the fact of my own glandular excesses.

My name is Bob, and I have testosterone poisoning.

Shameful, but true. Mister Rogers may have a very serious wardrobe
disorder, but he has never once neglected my children in favor of house-
work, tax preparation, or the Redskins-Eagles game. He has never reneged
on a promise; when he says they're going to the sneaker factory, by God
they're going, and right now. He has never exploded like flash powder
before their eyes, causing them to literally shudder at the suddenness and
excessiveness of the fulmination. He has never made Mommy cry — and, if
he had, he wouldn't have subtly shifted the blame to her.

In short, he is a totally dependable adult. If not a male ideal, necessarily, he's nonetheless a certain kind of prototype, living evidence that
the Mom-and-Dad-established rules of conduct have some basis in grown-
up reality. So, yes, among the problems he is the antidote for is the problem of me, and for that I am most grateful.

Or put another way, the man is a saint — something I've discovered lately and four-year-old kids have known all along. When you are four, and you are a little steel ball in the pinball machine of life, landing if only by gravity against an innocuous-looking bumper and being instantaneously propelled — "DON'T TOUCH THAT!" — full speed and out of control to another apparently safe port, only to be jettisoned again — "NO! YOU MAY NOT DO THAT!" — to subsequent sudden and stunning reactions, careening every which way without the slightest idea how or where to alight, there is something to be said for utterly predictable, low-wattage, numbingly repetitive, overly solicitous pabulum. There is something to be said for reassurance and security and unequivocal kindness and patience. For decency. For eminent fairness. For drapes that hideously defy grown-up convention by being colorful for colorfulness' sake. For the rare expression, in a world of harried and jaded adults, of the presumption of innocence.

Okay, it's true that the little boys at our bus stop don't collect Sensitive Adult action figures, but what of it? If that depresses public broadcasters and sociologists, it needn't — no more than it should depress the clergy that the children in their churches and synagogues sit inattentively week after week, apparently wholly unengaged by the liturgy, the mythology, or the moral substance of the religious experience. In fact, millions of children are oblivious to the proceedings *because* they are preoccupied with their Turtles, trolls, Flutter Ponies, baseball cards, and you name it. Yet that preoccupation is transitory; the religious experience, in varying degrees, tends to endure.

Maybe the Holy See and WQED would like the instant gratification of seeing their creed, canon, and rituals spontaneously capture the childish imagination in the manner of Leonardo, Rafael, and the rest. They'll have to be satisfied instead with something slower to take root, but more resonant and lasting.

Indeed, Fred Rogers may be a genuinely messianic figure. His personal life, from all available evidence, is as impeccable as his TV one, and he has gone to astonishing lengths never to exploit his media value for financial gain. For instance, though you may search in shoe store after shoe store, you will never find a pair of Official Mister Rogers Keds. But his true nature isn't particularly relevant. He could be as cynical and embittered as Krusty the Clown, the character from *The Simpsons* whose on-air persona is a giddy lie. Irrespective of whether the medium is actually the message, undeniably the broadcast signal is the reality. His lifestyle, his motivations, his character, his convictions are at most side issues to his product. And the product—cloyingly cheerful, reassuring and 100 percent carbuncle-free—speaks for itself.

So, yes, I say it without reservation: Mister Rogers is a national treasure.

The problem, the scourge, the *blight on our cultural landscape*, is Barney, the high-fructose reptile in the purple suit.

My name is Bob, and Barney makes my flesh crawl.

Bob Garfield

Bob Garfield is a columnist and critic for Advertising Age. *He has been a commentator and roving features correspondent for National Public Radio's* All Things Considered *since 1986 and is a contributing writer for the* Washington Post Magazine. *He has written for many newspapers and magazines, including* USA Today, The New York Times, Civilization, Playboy, Sports Illustrated, *and* Psychiatry. *He occasionally wears a cardigan.*

PREFACE

"The Chinese word [for] crisis," John F. Kennedy once said, "is represented by two characters — one signifying danger, the other, opportunity."

In that sense — in every sense — we stare now at the crisis of the future: the crisis of childhood, and what we plan to do about it. Unless you reside in a salt mine (a very specific salt mine without newspaper delivery or cable access), it's impossible to miss the endless stories of kids in trouble. Kids with guns. Nine-year-olds in gangs. Fourteen-year-old girls pregnant with their second child. On a recent weekend evening in Pittsburgh, a pizza delivery man was gunned down in cold blood by a fifteen-year-old boy, who happened to be finishing the pizza when the police arrived.

We tell ourselves that it's not us, it's "them," and in doing so ignore the truth: that we all share complicity. We know the statistics — more children in single-parent homes, more children living below the poverty line than at any time in history, more children raised by other children — but we fail to see our role in any of this. And because we can't see what happened, we cannot see a way out. So instead of investing in possible solutions that offer admittedly few guarantees, we invest in more and better deadbolt locks, in pepper spray and car alarms, in guns. We circle the wagons in ever-tighter orbits, hoping to keep out the intruders, the Others, who lurk just beyond the shadows.

In the face of such fear, it's easy to succumb to the detached and faultless logic of cynicism and hopelessness. We ask ourselves: What can one person do? What can *anyone* do?

And so, a choice. We can choose resignation — a defensible and reasoned response — or we can choose action, which is far more problematic. To choose to act, to participate, requires trust — the faith necessary to believe that one can make a difference; the confidence needed to lift the lid off our airtight defenses. And taking action requires creativity — not just accepting how things are, but imagining what might be.

What's ironic is that this triumvirate — hope, trust, and imagination — is not only what we need but what our children need, have always needed. Fred Rogers has recognized that need and has spent more than forty years of his professional life trying out answers. And in more than twenty-five years of *Mister Rogers' Neighborhood,* in a slow voice and dead-on stare, Fred Rogers has spoken to unseen millions of children about self-respect and respecting others. It's a deceptively simple message about tolerance and self-respect that's been honed from a complex life, fully and generously lived.

Such simplicity isn't easy. Simplicity is nature's complex economy of effort and focus. Polymer crystals are "simple." So are electrons. The primordial soup that first breathed life into this planet was pathetically simple. Simplicity isn't failure but something to be sought. " 'Tis a gift to be simple, 'tis a gift to be free," the Shaker hymn begins, " 'tis a gift to come down where you ought to be." It's the clarity Thoreau spoke of — not an easy life but one that edges toward the core of existence, one that sheds the layers of possessions and prepossessions. It's an omnipotent simplicity that looks past our material accoutrements to our true mettle, the stuff that makes us who we are.

The following fourteen essays document Fred Rogers' lifelong mission to children. We chose this format so that Fred Rogers' recurrent themes of hope and trust and creativity and acceptance could be sung by a diverse chorus, rather than a single voice. Each essay documents a different aspect of the complex and intricate nature of Fred Rogers' simple art.

And most of all, each essay documents the choices Fred Rogers and others from *Mister Rogers' Neighborhood* present each day to 10 million households. Trust and hope and creativity, it turns out, are not bestowed upon us. We make an active, conscious choice to witness and respond to the world around us — or not.

"I've been thinking about the kinds of choices we make each day," Fred Rogers said recently. "What is it — *who* is it — that enables us human beings to make choices all our lives? What choices led to 'ethnic cleansing'? What choices lead to healing? What choices led to the chipping away of the Berlin Wall? What helped those students to choose to lie down in front of the tanks in Tienneman Square?"

This is a book about choices. It's about Fred Rogers' choices, about our own, about what we plan to do for our lives and the lives of our children. Like a sailor's lighthouse, this collection signals the attainment of a milestone, a cause to celebrate a fruitful twenty-five-year journey. But beacons also serve as a warning of the jagged shoreline ahead — a passage that requires prudent navigation and careful, careful choices.

Mark Collins and Margaret Mary Kimmel

Mister Rogers' Neighborhood

Our first story begins . . . well, with a story. George Gerbner explores the deep-rooted human penchant for telling tales — an innate drive that, Gerbner maintains, is our species' most distinctive trait. Although uniquely innovative, television programming, Gerbner says, is just the latest step in the development of storytelling. Like people who listened to ritualized storytelling of the preindustrial age, modern TV viewers "absorb" their programs at a certain time, in a certain place. With the television turned on an average of seven hours a day in most homes, programs are digested without even acknowledging their presence: "It is like wallpaper: you are born into it; you absorb its patterns without knowing."

By itself, Gerbner says, television is not evil, and does, in fact, perform important cultural functions. But its ceaseless presence in our lives means that the values of our cultural stories may be filtered through a gauze of rote plots, commercialism, and advertising. Through the lens of this "historic if not cosmic" perspective, Gerbner sees Fred Rogers as something of a subversive, whose alternate view "counteracts the unwitting absorption of what is seen elsewhere."

Dean emeritus of the Annenberg School of Communications at the University of Pennsylvania, Gerbner has written numerous books and articles in the field of communications and was editor of the Journal of Communication. He has served on a number of national councils and commissions, including the National Commission on Aging, the White House Office of Telecommunications Policy, the Surgeon General's Science Advisory Committee, the National TV Cable Association, and the U.S. Commission on Civil Rights. He is founder of the Cultural Environmental Movement.

George Gerbner

Fred Rogers and the Significance of Story

There is a story about a mother who said to her child, "I wish you would change your behavior." The child said, "That's all right, Mother; Mister Rogers loves me as I am."

Forty years in children's television — with an approach that is so different from so many other programs — is an event of historic significance. Forty years as a gentle provocateur and a counterpoint clearly is more than a story of quick success. If you are trendy, you will last as long as a trend does. If you are going along with convention you will quickly get used up by television.

So what is it about *Mister Rogers' Neighborhood* that's outside convention or trend? My purpose is to try to place this program in a historic if not cosmic perspective.

If I ask you what is the unique or the most distinctive aspect of human life or the human species, what would you say? There have been many answers to that question. *Homo sapiens* is the tool-making animal, the social animal, the language-using, communicating animal. All are true but I don't think any of those is *the* most distinctive characteristic of our species. Other creatures do some of each of those things. But there is one thing that no other species does: tell stories.

Our ability to tell stories is important not only because we live by storytelling, but also because we erect a world that is constructed from the stories we hear and tell. Most of our reactions are *not* in response to the immediate physical environment, which is what most other species do most of the time. We are not on this planet just to look at our immediate environment or to experience reality. We are here in a very general but very real way to exchange stories. We are here to contribute to that reality (or should I say that fantasy we call reality). Each of our stories contributes to a larger context, a larger environment, a larger world in which we live — most of which we have acquired not through direct experience but through stories we hear and through stories we tell. To each story we adjust our everyday experience; by each story we judge and measure our everyday experience and even ourselves.

So it is the stories that animate the human imagination — the stories about how things work, what they are, and what to do about them — that provide the most distinctive and characteristic aspect of human life. And as Fred Rogers wisely notes, each of us is capable of contributing; each individual viewer creates his or her own exciting, vital story.

In theory, there are three kinds of stories. In reality they are all mixed up; there are few pure stories, but for the sake of analysis, the pure types can be reduced to three categories.

The first kind of story illuminates one of the most important aspects of human life: invisible relationships. It reveals how we relate to each other — the hidden dynamics of the network of relationships in which we live. By such revelations, these stories tell the truth about how things *really* work, because how things *really* work is not apparent, is not visible. It is something behind the scenes, and the only way to make it apparent is to make us see something that we otherwise cannot see. The way to do that is fiction and drama, or as Fred Rogers calls it, make-believe. "Make-believe" is the construction of a story that allows us to see what is usually covert. It depends on characters and actions that we invent in order to tell the truth about how things really work or might work or should work or should not work. (When Lady Elaine challenges a pronouncement of King Friday, it is really an inquisitive child insisting one more time, "But *why*, Mom?") These kinds of stories — what we usually call fiction, drama, and fairy tales — are often dismissed as unreal or fantasy when they are in fact the unique and indispensable ways of illuminating not that which *is* but that which shows *how things work*, or what's behind the scenes.

The second kind of story is that of factual explanation and explication. Histories, documentaries, the news of today — these are all examples of this second brand of story. By themselves, these stories are meaningless. A news story — a story of a fact — acquires significance only as it is fitted into a framework that is erected by the first kind of story of how life really works behind the scenes where we can't see. Once we understand that —

and we all acquire some understanding of it as we grow up in a culture — *then* we can use the facts, *then* we can fit in the facts to confirm the fantasy we call reality and say, "Yes, that is real." If it doesn't fit, we discard it, or we say it is biased or false or invalid.

The third story is a story of value and choice. This type of story asks, "Well, if this is how things work and this is how things are, then what are we going to do about them?" These are the sermons, the instructions — today most of them are commercials — that present a little vignette about a style of life that says, "This is how things work, this is how things are, and this is a desirable outcome for us to attain (or an undesirable thing that you want to avoid), and therefore you should choose this particular direction, product, or service." It is an enormously important cultivation and reinforcement of a framework of life, of what is desirable, of what are the values and choices of what to select, and how to select from them. Mister Rogers' reiterative theme of recognizing the worth of the individual echoes and re-echoes in the lives of the children who watch.

These three kinds of stories have always been interwoven, and together they provide the fabric and context of what we call the culture. (I am defining "culture" here as a system of stories that regulates human relationships, into which we are born and which we absorb and acquire as we grow and become socialized into our place in a social structure.) They have been woven together in very different ways at different times in history.

In the first (and longest) historical period, the preindustrial period of many tens of thousands of years, storytelling was oral, handcrafted, and infinitely adjusted to time, place, and circumstance. An oral story is always a play or production or dramatic interpretation. As Shakespeare said, "The play's the thing." It is in the *telling* — infinitely adjustable, always interruptable and transformable, depending on the listeners' reactions. Such oral narrative — usually called mythology and later on religion — requires a great amount of human resources. Pretechnological men and women needed much more talent, needed much bigger and better memories, needed much greater skill in order to live as they did in a world of stories. They had to carry with them and in them most useful knowledge that had to be remembered and memorized. Education in a preindustrial age consisted of aphorisms and folk tales and stories and memorization of instructions about the seasons and about how to handle the land and the animals. The older you were the more valuable you became because you experienced more and remembered more and could contribute more.

In order to accumulate this knowledge, this reservoir of human resources, "primitive people" developed *ritual* — a ritualistic repetition and reiteration of the stories, of the songs, of the dances, of the celebrations. Most celebrations had to do with a sort of rehearsal about what is tried and true and established and valid. And that ritual encompassed all three kinds of stories — about what the world is like and how it works and what is the nature of the universe and meaning of life, and what are the facts of life presumed to be true and untrue, and what to do about them. In other words, these rituals were embodied in the mythologies of all communities and of all tribes, and it was only when certain tribes explored and found that there were other people who had other mythologies that the notion of religion arose. All the great religious teachers — Buddha, Jesus Christ, Mohammed — were storytellers. They said to their people, "Listen to me. I know this; believe it." And the people listened and believed.

Then came a major transformation in the storytelling process: the printing press allowed the first mechanical reproduction of stories in a book. This began the industrialization of the story-telling process, and remains one of the most profound transformations (if not the most profound transformation) in the way human beings live their lives. It had a direct impact on the mind; once stories were recorded and printed and later distributed, there was an immediate connection with the world that we erected and the way in which we lived through our stories.

The coming of printing broke up the ritual. You could look it up; you didn't have to remember it all. It broke up the centralized ministration of stories by the priests, the interpreters, the storytellers. You didn't have to have somebody to interpret a book — for instance, in the Western world, the Bible. You could read it yourself, or take it with you. This was the beginning of the Reformation. The Reformation would have been inconceivable without printing because it was based on the possibility of a diversity of explanation instead of a grand interpreter of the book. It is the beginning of the notion that a community can exist with more than a single philosophy, more than a single interest, more than a single perspective. Printing helped establish the right of different classes, regions, ethnic and religious communities to tell unique stories from their own points of view. With print, the storyteller was out of view, and could no longer look at the crowd and cry, "Believe me; I know." As receivers of story, we lost an absolute faith in the storyteller alone. The story was there, but we gained time and perspective. We could *choose* to say, "Yes, I've read this and I believe and I have faith" — or choose to reject that story in favor of another one.

To tell stories that illuminate the interest and perspective of a particular subculture and to permit the publication, dissemination, and analysis of those stories was a revolutionary development. Publication invented a new form of social enterprise called *publics*. Without printing and publication, the concept was unthinkable, because a "public" is a community who have something in common but who may never meet. Before the printing press, the territory in which a community could be governed was the area that its most distant citizens could reach in a short period of time, perhaps one or two days. Citizens had to meet to discuss matters face to face. The larger communities of the so-called ancient empires were really not communities but tribute-collecting organizations. You sent out the legions when the roads hardened in the spring to collect the taxes. Only since the coming of printing has it been possible through publication to enlarge the community's reach to what we today call a "public," which extends beyond all impenetrable barriers of time, space, class, and language, because print can be translated, disseminated, and preserved.

This theory of community — where competing interests can live more or less peacefully side by side, freely pursuing their conflicting interests by virtue of their power to tell stories from their own points of view — is only a few hundred years old, yet it has transformed the basis of our political, cultural, social, and religious life. So the notion of public, on which all modern theories of government and education and communication are based, is itself a product of the printing press. It broke up the ritual; it decentralized and pluralized communication; it gave rise to the notion of mass publics and, therefore, to a plurality of perspectives in modern society. But to participate fully in this pluralized society, to participate in the changed ritual of story, the individuals in the community must be literate. Without literacy human beings are without the story that is literature. We have always asked that literature turn statistics into human beings. We have story to guide us and illuminate our thoughts and behaviors.

Now comes the present age, the telecommunications age, whose flagship is television. Despite other technological developments, television will, I think, dominate our culture for a long time to come. Television has certain unique and very specific characteristics that no other medium has.

The first and most important characteristic is that television is a ritual. Most people watch television by the clock and not by the program. Its true predecessor is not radio or film, but preindustrial religion. Children today are born into a home in which the set is on an average of seven hours a day. That means that in half of our homes it is put on in the morning and turned off in the evening. It is like the wallpaper: you are born into it; you absorb its patterns without knowing; and you learn a great deal about your surroundings.

We know from research that by the time children are five or six years of age — about when they first encounter the outside culture, either by going to school or by going to church or both — they have already lived in an informative, intensive, ever-present televised environment in which all the stories are told and retold but with very little variety. The same basic patterns are told in endless repetition but are disguised by what appears to be the novelty of the plot. Forget the plot — the plot is there to conceal what is really going on and to give the appearance of novelty. Look at the casting, look at the relationships, look at the fate of different social types in these stories. Whether it is news or drama or talk shows, you'll find great similarity in the basic constituents of storytelling among all these forms.

For the first time in human history the storyteller who tells most of the stories to our children, and at the same time to our parents and grandparents, is not the church or the school. It is a small group of distant corporations with purposes of their own that have great virtues and great weaknesses. They are the storytellers that in many ways have taken over and given us a world into which our children are born and in which we all live.

Let me tell you a few things about what kind of a world that is, both good and bad. Remember the positive things as well as the negative.

For the first time in human experience, the poor share a great deal of cultural content with the rich. Isolation and parochialism are no longer a given condition of poverty. Because of television, a child from the farm may know just as many sophisticated brands and practices as the aristocracy. You are no more out in the sticks; you are part of the mainstream. You have been brought into it. You are no longer politically uninformed; you have been brought into a national flow of social, political, and cultural current. The great names and celebrities of our age, the beautiful and the ugly, the famous and the infamous, come into your homes every day, and provide an unprecedented social cohesion between otherwise very different and heterogeneous groups of people. This has never before happened.

Such a normative standard erodes traditional differences among human beings in our society. They get absorbed by a form of "cultural mainstreaming," which is very different from its namesake, educational mainstreaming. In cultural mainstreaming, groups who are divergent from the great national mean—divergent in their points of view, in their philosophies and standards by which they measure how things work and what to do about them—are divergent only as long as they are "light" viewers of television. Being a light viewer doesn't mean that one doesn't like television, but that one watches more selectively and may engage in a variety of other cultural pursuits. Such viewers tend to have higher incomes, be more educated, have many more cultural opportunities available to them, and have more diverse tastes.

The heavy viewers are those groups who are otherwise divergent from the mainstream but tend to converge upon the mainstream. Television tends to erase cultural differences, and by doing that presents a kind of homogenized standard for response for action and reaction that is national, almost international, in scope.

What kind of a world does this mainstream present? We have a group of maybe 40 or 50 million Americans who had very little before television but a lot of boredom—who are not book readers, who have never been book readers. Television has monopolized the lives of people who have had little cultivation of diversified tastes. Television has become all of culture for them. It has become, in the lives of people less culturally privileged, the most interesting thing going on any time of the day or night, and that is a tremendous attraction. Instead of being automatically critical of television and everything it stands for, we should try to understand what is going on; we should examine the kind of world it presents, become more active citizens in constructing that kind of world, and appreciate the few historical phenomena such as *Mister Rogers' Neighborhood*.

I'm going to pick out some results of our research on the TV world and its basic story-making elements. This "mainstream" television world is a place where men outnumber women across the board at least three to one. Starting out with that kind of cast, what can you get that is really accurate and valid? There is a basic flaw in almost every play, in most of our news, in most of our formula-bound children's programs (where the disproportion is even greater). Representation is not only a question of numbers, but also a question of the range of opportunities one sees a significant majority element of human beings pursue. If you are underrepresented in the culture in which you grow up, you see yourself limited in the number of life's opportunities. You see yourself undervalued, underendowed, overvictimized, less powerful, and more vulnerable. That is the true meaning of representation and its distribution in the world in which our children become encultured.

It works the same way with age. Young people are vastly underrepresented, less than one-third of their true proportion of the population. Likewise, people sixty-five and older are portrayed on TV in less than one-fifth of their true numbers. They are practically invisible. And when either group *is* visible, they play the obligatory parts that are the most stereotyped — a romantic partner, a grandmother baby-sitting, or a child who is either overly charming or overly abused.

The most victimized populations on television are young boys and adolescent girls. One way to measure victimization is not to simply calculate the sheer number of "violent acts" but to construct a ratio of the frequency of someone asserting his or her will over an unwilling person — which creates a good definition of violence with someone subjecting another to that kind of violation. That "violent/victim" ratio establishes a gauge for measuring *relative power*. In that sense, young boys are the most victimized, young girls are the second most; in general women are more victimized than men, and minorities more so than majorities. If you are a white male in the prime of life, although your chances of getting into a violent situation are frequent on television, your chances of getting away with it, of being the winner rather than the victim, are the greatest.

Violence is being shown on television an average of five times per hour in prime time; twenty-five times per hour in children's weekend prime time programming. It has become a cheap industrial ingredient to hype otherwise lagging interest in relatively poor programs (most of the highly rated programs tend to be the least violent), and it has become a great exercise and demonstration of power in our society. This role of violence on television is subtle, unrecognized, unwitting, and certainly unacknowledged.

The ratios between the violent and the victimized reflect the hierarchies of power in our social structure. If you get ten violent perpetrators on a television show, the overall average number of victims is about twelve. But for every ten women written into the scripts (women who are able to enforce their own will), about sixteen women will be victimized. For older women, this "victimization ratio" is one to thirty-six. And so on with nonwhites, with boys, with girls, and other cultural minorities.

Violence is essentially a demonstration of power — the very thing that perpetuates the underrepresentation of women and minorities. The frequency of violence enforces the kind of cultural colonization of our people that takes place in the world of television. What really counts in violence is not only the *possibility* of imitation (although that is a price we pay for maintaining the structure of power), but who can get away with what against whom most frequently. Television violence is simply a convenient dramatic shorthand for this kind of power equation.

The occupational distribution in the world of television is peculiar because of this power play. Prime time is essentially devoted to a world of power, where power plays are dominant. Daytime TV is maybe artistically less pleasing, but at least it's a world of more equitable, *internal* turbulence rather than external power.

Children's commercial programming involves an extended combination of both. It is not muted. Everything in terms of stereotyping and violence — and in terms of the imbalance found in prime time and daytime programming for relatively mature and sophisticated tastes — takes on its crudest and most exploitative aspect in children's programming. This is not just a little aberration. It is a world-class scandal.

Children are also viewers of prime time. Four-fifths of children's viewing time goes into prime time. The average viewer of prime time sees a cast of about three hundred characters week in and week out. The single

highest occupation on television is law enforcer; about forty-four characters enforce the law per week, and about twenty-three criminals violate
the law. There are about twelve nurses, ten doctors, six lawyers, and three
judges. The intimate glimpses of how law-and-order and medicine work
are mostly untrue but very realistic. Thanks to television, who doesn't
know what a courtroom or an operating room looks like from the inside?
And every child has an image of what a police station looks like, and an
executive boardroom. Most children today have a better understanding of
these types of occupations than they do of what their mothers and fathers
do at work each day.

Television culture presents to our children and to all of us a world
of manufactured, assembly-line, mass-produced, high-pressure daydreams.
They are dreams that scare, that shame, that hurt too many.

Mister Rogers explores the very stuff of this world. In one episode (one
of many examples), he goes behind the scenes of a scary television show,
The Incredible Hulk. He shows all of us how this is made. In a single stroke
he achieves the shift from attribution to inference. "Attribution" is a kind
of childish way of looking at a story as something natural arising out of the
natural world — in other words, attributing meaning to something that's
merely an image. "Inference" is when you can get behind the scenes and
know there is a script, an actor, a camera, and make-up. Infer from what
you see. You are in control. And as soon as you do that, it becomes an
enriching experience no matter how bad the program may be. Rogers
allows a young audience to make this crucial shift.

In this world of too many manufactured dreams, Fred Rogers is hand-
crafting — for us as well as for our children — the dreams that heal. Just
how does Fred craft these dreams? First, he always has something to tell,
rather than something to sell. He has a purpose, a message that respects
the viewer and what the viewer may need, rather than what the viewer
may be induced to buy.

His perspective on life's needs, problems, and conflicts does more than
help the child. It confers a measure of immunity from other programs that
may be damaging. Knowing that there is another way of looking at things
counteracts the unwitting absorption of what is seen elsewhere.

His dreams, his stories, offer ways to control the chaotic life of the
streets and neighborhoods in which many children live. Children are

starving for story, the kind that builds on hope, the kind that echoes for a lifetime. We need story in our lives, not dreams based on greed. Mister Rogers turns to the viewer and says quietly, "Believe *you*. It is *your* story that is important. It is *your* mind and heart that can make things possible — just because of who you are."

Jeanne Marie Laskas's highly personal look at Fred Rogers traces the businessman's-son-turned-icon from his roots in Latrobe, Pennsylvania, to his days as floor manager on NBC's Kate Smith Hour to joining WQED, the nation's first public broadcasting station. Acknowledging both the frustration and rewards of interviewing a legend ("him on one end of the couch, me on the chair, he so skillfully dodging all direct questions about himself, me frustrated by that skill yet moved by his words"), Laskas lets Fred Rogers' own words trace a complex self-portrait. What emerges is ironic: a complicated personality whose many layers form a seamless coat of simplicity.

"Like your first hero, your first psychotherapist, and your first-grade teacher, anything that inspires that much awe becomes just that: a thing," Laskas writes. "I think Fred is often regarded this way, certainly by the media, by scholars who study his work, by museum curators like the ones who put his sweater in the Smithsonian Institution as a permanent piece of Americana. . . . It's the hidden human, the Fred of Mister Rogers, whom I hope to uncover, at least for a glimpse."

Laskas is a columnist for the Washington Post Magazine, where her personal essays column, "Uncommon Sense," appears weekly. Her first collection of stories is The Balloon Lady and Other People I Know. Laskas's essays and profiles are featured in GQ, Life, Allure, Health, Philadelphia Inquirer Magazine, Good Housekeeping, Reader's Digest, and others. Formerly a writing instructor at the University of Pittsburgh, she has an MFA in nonfiction writing.

Jeanne Marie Laskas

"What Is Essential Is Invisible to the Eye"

Something you said a little while ago triggered something that I think is very important. And that is the whole business of, when you're with somebody, trying to be present in a moment. I think there are many people who bring a whole lot of baggage from their past and a whole lot of anxiety about the future to the present moment.

What's so great is that people can be in relationship with each other for the now. If we can somehow rid ourselves of illusions. The illusion that we are greater or lesser than we are. The illusion that we're going to save the world. There are a lot of illusions that people walk around with.

I would love to be able to be present in every moment I have.

Fred Rogers talked this way, his usual way, during an interview in his office. I had joined him in numerous such conversations over the years, many of these documented in a series of magazine articles I wrote about him.

When our time together was nearing an end, we marveled at the number of times we'd been thrown together this way, him on one end of the couch, me on the chair, he so skillfully dodging all direct questions about himself, me frustrated by that skill and yet moved by his words in ways that words had never moved me. Fred said he thought we were bound to meet like this in heaven, too. I said the heaven idea was good. I said the way my luck was going I'd surely be getting a call from the Big Editor in the Sky asking me to do a story on Fred Rogers for *Heaven Today*.

He cracked up laughing. Then he said, "In Heaven, I'll be interviewing *you*."

And so, a moment. I'm searching for one single scene that will best introduce the Fred Rogers I know. Would it be this delightful and generous exchange? Would it be a scene of him working the puppets in Studio A, or sitting at Johnny Costa's piano surrounded by the people who have worked with him for some thirty years? Would it be a quiet moment in his writing room, or a day at his favorite place on earth, Nantucket, with his favorite person on earth, Joanne, his wife? Or maybe it would be an interchange with Jeff Varion, the guy who works in the locker room at the pool where Fred takes his daily swim. Perhaps something more dramatic is in order, like the time Fred reluctantly agreed to say a prayer at a fund raiser for then-president George Bush, or any of the times he got dressed up in fancy graduation robes and was awarded one of 26, 27, 28 — Fred is now up to 29 — honorary doctorates.

I consider myself enormously privileged to have spent so many moments over so many years with Fred Rogers. For one, he is not what you'd call an eager man when it comes to press coverage. He goes into interviews with all the enthusiasm of a child learning to swim: Nose held, head down, head up, cough, cough, can I go home now? It's even more agonizing to watch him get his picture taken. Fred does interviews and photo shoots mostly because David Newell, his good friend, PR man, and the actor who plays Mr. McFeely, is begging him to. And I'm begging David. And some editor is begging me. It's a chain reaction that finds Fred and me connected, and I'm careful to remember where Fred believes the links extend: From some hidden place in the universe where God has His office, to some hidden place inside some heart somewhere down here on our humble planet Earth.

Interviewing Fred about Fred can be a technically difficult challenge since he has a way of turning the conversation on you and away from him. In this way, he is hard to get to know. You think you're learning about him, but all of a sudden you realize you're learning about yourself. That, of course, is fascinating. So you stay with it. And pretty soon Fred is invisible; it's just you in the room, facing you.

I remember one of our early interviews when I was just trying to say good-bye and thank him for passing on his thoughts.

I think it's very important to learn that you get that largely because of who you are. I could be saying the same words and giving the same thoughts to somebody else who could be thinking something very different. The receiving in life to me is one of the greatest gifts that we give another person. And it's very hard. Because when you give you're in much greater control. But when you receive something — you're vulnerable.

I think the greatest gift you can give someone is an honest receiving of what they have to offer.

At times like this I would shake my head, walk out, and conclude that Fred Rogers wasn't a person at all, but a godlike figure, a holy man put on this earth with the singular task of making me feel good.

Wearing my journalist hat presented me with some conflict. I wanted to write about a man, a human being, warts and all, and instead I kept writing about a saint. My stories all centered on the same point of focus: Here is one of the most powerful figures of our time. You hear him satirized on television sometimes, and you may at first be threatened by his slow, deliberate style. But take a moment and listen to this man. Listen, for instance, to the way he addressed Boston University's class of 1992 at their baccalaureate service. "L'essentiel est invisible pour les yeux," he said, quoting from one of his favorite sayings from one of his favorite books, *The Little Prince*, by Saint-Exupéry.

"What is essential is invisible to the eye." It's not the honors and the prizes and the fancy outsides of life which ultimately nourish our souls. It's the knowing that we can be trusted, that we never have to fear the truth, that the bedrock of our very being is good stuff.

What is essential about you that is invisible to the eye?

He paused for a long time. That question seemed to grip many in the audience, even the president of the university sitting there in his tassel cap and fancy gold medallion. Then Fred recited a version of "It's You I Like," a song he often sings on his television program.

It's you I like. It's not the things you wear. It's not the way you do your hair, but it's you I like. The way you are right now. The way deep down inside you. Not the things that hide you — not your diplomas, they're just beside you. But it's you I like. Every part of you.

A stillness fell over the crowd. The people sat in silence, thinking about some part of themselves that they had long since forgotten, or some part they had not yet found. Or something else entirely. Whatever it was, a lot of them cried.

The power of Fred's message is so simple and yet so strong, anyone who gets it for the first time usually feels bowled over. You feel uplifted. You feel strengthened from some deep place within.

And, inevitably, you want more of this. You want more of Fred. You want to put him in your pocket or have him on your shoulder as you go, then, about your business of braving the harshness of your real world.

Like your first hero, your first psychotherapist, and your first-grade teacher, anything that inspires that much awe becomes just that: a thing. An object to be treasured, but an object nonetheless. I think Fred is often regarded this way, certainly by the media, by scholars who study his work, by museum curators like the ones who put his sweater in the Smithsonian Institution as a permanent piece of Americana. A great honor, to be sure, to have yourself remembered in a museum, or your picture in a magazine, or your life's work analyzed as literature. But then again museums are places for things called exhibits, and magazines are places for things called articles, and academic journals are places for things called ideas. I've often wondered if Fred ever feels like an exhibit, an article, an idea, a thing any which way we look at him.

It's the hidden human, the Fred of Mister Rogers, whom I hope to uncover, at least for a glimpse, in this essay. My motivation is not born of an urge to snoop into the dark corners of some private place, but instead to simply touch the truth of a life being lived.

My dad was pretty much Mr. Latrobe. He worked hard to accomplish all that he did, and I've always felt that that was way beyond me. And yet I'm so grateful that he didn't push me to do the kinds of things that he did, or to become a miniature version of him. It certainly would have been miniature.

Boy, am I glad that I've been able to do what I've done and not been sidetracked all along the way.

Dr. Orr calls it guided drift. Isn't that wonderful? You're drifting and yet you've got a rudder. I've always known who was in charge, but then, I've told you that.

The story of how young Fred Rogers became the Mister Rogers of public television has been told enough times now to be part of American folklore.

He was born in Latrobe, a small industrial town in western Pennsylvania, also the home of Arnold Palmer and Rolling Rock beer. He lived in the great big red brick house on Weldon Street. The Rogerses were a very wealthy family; his father was president of the McFeely Brick Company, one of the largest employers in the area.

A smart young man, gifted at piano, Fred planned to be a musician, or a minister, or both. He went to Rollins College in Florida to study musical composition and by his senior year he was accepted at Pittsburgh Theological Seminary.

That was 1951. Fred was home for Easter vacation when he saw television for the first time.

And I just hated it. I looked at these people on television, throwing pies into each other's faces. And I thought: I'm just going to go into television! And everyone was so flabbergasted. Because literally, I was supposed to start in the seminary in September.

So he didn't go to seminary, but instead to New York. He got a job working on the *NBC Television Opera Theatre*, then on *Your Lucky Strike Hit Parade*, and *The Kate Smith Hour*. He moved up the ladder, got promoted to network floor director. Then, in 1953 Fred startled everybody once again by deciding to leave NBC and move back to Pittsburgh to take a job with the nation's first community-supported public television station, WQED.

And the people at NBC said, "You're out of your mind! That place isn't even on the air yet!" And I said, "Well, something tells me that's what I'm supposed to do." And that was it.

He left New York. In Pittsburgh, the show he helped develop was called *The Children's Corner*, which he wrote, produced, and performed in partnership with his friend Josie Carey. Fred worked the puppets — the same characters on today's program — and was not seen on camera. Meantime, he finally began his studies at Pittsburgh Theological Seminary. His education there included training in child psychology at Pittsburgh's Arsenal Family and Children Center, founded by Benjamin Spock and Erik Erikson. He was ignited by these studies, particularly by noted child psychologist Margaret McFarland. It was she who taught him about the inner-workings of a child's mind. He went on to consult with McFarland almost daily until she died in 1987.

> One day she told me that she remembered the time when I seemed to find my focus. She said when I first came to her she knew I was interested in theology and music and writing and all these different things. And she said, "I remember the day, Fred, when all of those things seemed to come together for you and you called it: the desire to work with children." So that was the integrating force. And it came largely from my being able to work with Margaret McFarland.

In the end, it was the marriage of television, psychology, and theology that provided the atmosphere in which Fred Rogers thrived. When he was ordained a Presbyterian minister in 1963, he was given the charge of ministering to children through television.

The earliest prototype of *Mister Rogers' Neighborhood* was a fifteen-minute program called *Misterogers*, produced by the Canadian Broadcasting Corporation, which resembled the Neighborhood of Make-Believe segments of today. It was revamped and extended to a half-hour format incorporating visits with Mister Rogers in his living room, and next seen on local Pittsburgh TV. In 1967 the Sears Roebuck Foundation agreed to fund the program and make it available to all public television stations nationally. Today, *Mister Rogers' Neighborhood* is broadcast on 290 stations and watched by more than 8 million people a week.

Such is the official Fred Rogers résumé.

It was only after I knew Fred for years that he began telling me the history not just of his career but of his heart. It was interesting to see how tightly the two were intertwined.

With Fred everything is so simple and yet everything is so complex. Just as on television, in real life he has a way of zooming through life's most complex situations and reaching the simplest truths. He speaks a language that is understood by children and by the child within all of us. Perhaps because he is so well acquainted with the child in himself. Fred's gift for communicating lies somewhere in this puzzle, I think, and certainly the keys to the whole kingdom lie in Fred's own childhood.

One day he opened up and presented me with a marvelous gift: stories of his childhood told in rich detail.

> My parents presented to me whatever material things I needed as far as learning and growing were concerned. That's a given. My dad, you know, my dad was a wonderful person. He was the kind of person who would leave pennies on window sills in New York City. One day I said, "Dad, why do you do that?" And he said, "It gives me such pleasure to think of those who are finding them."
>
> In a way it was awful nice.
>
> In his later life he spent probably between 80 and 90 percent of his time listening to people in his office. The minister in Latrobe, Bob Vogel, he told me that my mother and father were the parents that he never really had.
>
> You get such a much better view of your own parents from other people who love them, other people who haven't had to go through the whole oedipal phase, the whole business of the necessary separation, individuation phase.
>
> My parents were greatly loved.

It was with reverence and a slight distance that he spoke of his parents, as if these were honored guests kept, in the tradition of the day, at arm's length.

> I think I told you that my father and I had a major separation each year when my mother and my grandparents and I would go to Florida for three months, January, February, and March. And I think in a way that was tough. When I would leave at Christmas time then I'd know that I wouldn't see my Latrobe friends until probably the first of April. I don't know how it was. I just think that

I felt I had to get back in the swing somehow all over again. And so much happens in three months. It's one-third of the school year.

But the biggest issue of all was leaving my father. I can remember the joy of talking to him on the phone. And then he would come to visit once or twice in Florida. But you see my grandfather McFeely would be there in Florida. So that was a connection with the other important man in my life.

And that was the key. Fred's maternal grandfather was the one person who would come up again and again whenever Fred talked about his boyhood. Fred would get excited talking about him.

He was a character. Oh, a lot of me came from him. I think so. Oh, he was a real pioneer. He really helped start Latrobe. The fascinating thing about him was that he loved to do things so much that every time he would get something started, a company started, he'd sell his entire interest in it to be able to start something else. So when he died I think he had all of twenty-five or thirty dollars. After all that. He started something like four companies in Latrobe. My dad bought the last one, the McFeely Brick Company. But then my grandfather retired and he went out to the country and he always wanted some chickens so he bought five thousand chickens and then he got rid of them, that was too much trouble, and he bought 150 head of cattle, and then he got rid of them and he bought a whole lot of pigs. And then he had a slaughter house and they made sausage and they evidently didn't make a penny. The last thing he bought was a little coal mine, and then he sold that when he went into a nursing home.

But the thing that impressed me was that he was not interested in amassing stuff; that wasn't any fun. What he wanted to do was work. He certainly was not retentive. And I wonder if it's unconscious with my mother that she would have named me for my grandfather. His name was Fred Brooks McFeely.

As a small child Fred called him "Ding Dong," after the nursery rhyme that his grandfather would read to him. He was, certainly, the brightest spot in young Fred's life. Fred was sickly. His was a solitary childhood. He was an only child until he turned eleven, when his parents adopted a baby girl. His mother, known for her enormous generosity, doted on him, fearing always for his safety. He was not allowed to play outside by himself. She tried to cure him of his hay fever by providing him with an air-conditioned room where he spent an entire summer, day and night.

Paul [a young boy who had asthma] is the one I was cooped up with the air conditioner with. That was the first air conditioner unit in Latrobe. The family doctor and my parents went together and bought it, put it in Paul's room, and then I went to live there all summer. They thought that's what you do with kids who have hay fever. Put them in there and just get them through.

Paul was probably sixteen. I was probably ten.

Now that I think about it, I think how he must have hated that. He was an only child, I was an only child, and here's this kid invading his space. Because they would say that when we would go to an ice cream parlor or something he would order something and then I would order the same thing, of course; being that much older he was a real hero. And then he would whisper to the person who was making the things to change the order — so that when his would come, mine would be different, and I would be disappointed.

But I see now that I was this sibling that he never had to take things out on before.

No, we rarely left that room. We had our meals there.

After that we got an air conditioner at our house.

Fred describes himself as a lonely boy, overweight, and sickly. He worked life's traumas out through his puppets, through music; and he drew a strength from his grandfather that he would take with him throughout his adult life.

In the summer they used to let me visit with my grandfather for a week or so, and I had a good time. He had an old horse, it was so old nothing could have happened to you. Sally. And he taught me all kinds of really neat stuff. And I think maybe that's who I am to the kids on the "Neighborhood." I don't know. I'm always bringing stuff to show them. I'm always welcoming neighbors. I always think of myself as a neighbor or an uncle or somebody who has time to spend with them. I think that was who my grandfather was to me.

Listening to these stories, you begin to realize the depth of conviction that is the foundation of *Mister Rogers' Neighborhood*. People often remark that Fred in real life is just like Fred on camera. Because Fred isn't acting. He will never use the word "show" to refer to his program. There is no showmanship here. *Mister Rogers' Neighborhood* is Fred through and through. He writes all the programs, does the voices for most of the puppets, composes all the music.

> I started playing piano at five. I would just go and pick out things I learned on the radio — before any lessons at all. But Nana McFeely, she bought me my first piano, my first organ. I wanted an organ very badly. No, she didn't buy the first one, no, that was a pedal organ. And it was about this big. And it was in the Schwartz catalogue. And for staying in that air-conditioned room that whole summer with Paul, the boy with asthma, they told me I could get anything I wanted out of that Schwartz catalogue.
>
> Isn't that interesting; it just dawned on me, there was something else that I had to do that was unpleasant, and that was I had to take worm medicine when I was real young and they told me that I could have a dog for doing that. And after I took it, I mean I was so young, and after I took it, I said, well, where's the dog?
>
> It was a Sunday and there wasn't any place to get one. And I said well, I want one, I want it now, I mean I did this, where is the dog? This is family lore; I mean I don't remember this at all, I think I was three.
>
> And finally they looked in the newspaper and saw that there were some people who were giving away these mutts, and we went and got one. That was Mitzy. She lived to be eighteen. So I was about twenty-one when Mitzy died.

It was fun to watch his mind go into free fall like this. It was so rare for Fred to present himself this way. When he talked about television, or psychology, or theology, his thinking was disciplined and deliberate and mannered. But when he talked about his youth he seemed to be dancing free. It was as if he knew how to suddenly become a child again, as if he could turn a youth-adult switch on and off at will. And over and over again he would recall a story about being with his grandfather.

> Oh, I would have such a good time when I would visit him. And he'd even let me send away to Sears for things. At the beginning of my visit we would send away and invariably the things would arrive just before I would leave.
>
> I remember one day my grandmother and my mother were telling me to get down or not to climb, and my grandfather said, 'Let the kid climb on the wall! He's got to learn to do things for himself!' I heard that. I will never forget that. What a support that was. He had a lot of stone walls on his place.
>
> And you can understand my mother and grandmother, they didn't want a scratched-up kid. They didn't want somebody with broken bones. No. But he knew there was something beyond that. He knew there was something more important than scratches and bones.

He knew something about freedom. About permission. About allowing a kid to simply be a kid. About allowing a boy to *be* himself rather than just *behave* himself.

Fred will tell you today that that feeling is the one he hopes through his work to help others know. His ministry is not, after all, about preaching, not about trying to get people to behave or act a certain way.

It is about permission. It is about providing an atmosphere for people where they are allowed to be simply and purely themselves.

> I climbed that wall. And then I ran on it. I will never forget that day.

I have in my possession about two dozen photographs of myself, all taken by Fred Rogers. This is an interesting little personality quirk of his. Well, once you know him you realize it isn't a quirk at all but the perfect metaphor for how he sees himself in relation to others. He would often say that nothing in life matters so much as people in relationship to other people.

He goes in and out of the picture-taking stage. It works this way: Fred keeps a miniature automatic Olympus camera in his jacket pocket. He will pop this out without warning, greet you, and snap away. "He wants *my* picture," you think, and you feel special. It makes no matter that he is taking pictures of virtually every human being with whom he comes into contact that day. He picked you, and somehow you feel lifted up.

Then, approximately two weeks later, you get a card in the mail from Fred. Inside the envelope will be one or two or perhaps half a dozen pictures of yourself. On the backs of some he may make a comment, like, "I like this one a lot," or, "You look surprised here." The card, by the way, will never be signed. Instead, Fred will put his message on a yellow Post-it note and affix that to the card. That is so you can use the card again.

You are left in a most unusual and private moment. You are standing there flipping through images of yourself, given to you by Fred. "Yep, here I am," you think. You wonder what in the heck you are supposed to do with these pictures of yourself, and under the best of circumstances, perhaps you get a moment to view yourself anew. Here you are, alive and well in the twentieth century.

Lately when I see Fred come at me with that camera, I've said, "Why do you do this?" But he has a way of avoiding the question. I always wonder how he finds the time to do this, to write all the cards to all the people whose photos he has taken. Fred spends an enormous amount of time each day writing to people and remembering people. He lives by his little blue calendar book in which every anniversary, birthday, and special day of every person close to him is carefully monitored. In this way, and in many others, he is, perhaps, the most disciplined person I have ever known. His day is tightly scheduled, up at 5:00, swimming at 6:00, weighing in at precisely 143 pounds after the swim, then the writing room, then business as usual at the Family Communications offices. He doesn't go out at night, doesn't watch any TV, is a strict vegetarian, doesn't drink or smoke, reads voraciously, and is in bed by 9:30.

People think he is a slow and wishy-washy man. He is the opposite. He is focused, directed, and swift. Taking a stroll with Fred Rogers requires extra little skips on the part of the walker if the walker has even a prayer of keeping up.

The brisk walking thing was, in fact, how we all lost him at the George Bush fund raiser.

You need to understand that Fred did not, first of all, want to be at that fund raiser. This was a difficult predicament he had found himself in. This was during the 1992 presidential campaign.

It was one of those luncheons where you pay a thousand dollars to sit and eat and be in the presence of the president. Fred wasn't at all sure he wanted to do it. A pacifist, he thought about how much he opposed Bush's decision to go to war in the Persian Gulf. An artist, he thought about how he opposed Bush's educational policies — no money for the arts. He thought about all the reasons he shouldn't go.

And in the end, he went.

The function was held at Duquesne University in Pittsburgh. Fred arrived late, skipping the cocktail party. He was escorted by a throng of beefy Secret Service men up to a private room where President Bush was to be waiting. As we walked, I asked Fred how he felt on the occasion of meeting the President of the United States.

> I just don't know what to expect. You know, that's why I sing that song "Children Like to Be Told." When a child is being taken some place new it may seem like nothing to the grown-up, but to the child it is so very frightening. If the grown-up could just explain what to expect. That's why I sing that song.

Fred was escorted to a make-shift room that was basically a big blue curtain standing up with a couple of plants inside. President Bush was in there. Fred looked at him. "Oh, aren't you nice to be here?" the president said to Fred, excitedly. "Thank you for coming, oh, thank you for coming, I am so sorry Barbara isn't here, she is a real fan of yours."

"Thank you," said Fred and moved along, rejoining Bill Isler, friend and general manager of Family Communications. Bill made perhaps the most astute observation of the day: "My God, Fred and George shaking hands! You guys looked like you were part of a wax museum in there!" Fred laughed but offered no further comment.

The opening ceremonies began. Down in the banquet room, Fred Rogers was announced. He stood at the podium, facing all the fancy and excited Republicans, flanked by George Bush on one side, and Senator Arlen Specter on the other. Everybody looked important and serious and heavy with political agendas.

Standing behind that podium, Fred looked . . . skinny. He didn't fit in. He could have been a six-year-old kid. He cleared his throat.

I know of a little girl who was drawing with crayons in school.

He paused. The Republicans looked at one another. Was this . . . appropriate?

The teacher asked her about her drawing and the little girl said, "Oh, I am making a picture of God." The teacher said, "But no one knows what God looks like." The little girl smiled and answered, "They will now."

He asked each member of the crowd to think of his or her own image of God, and that's who he prayed to. He asked that all the politicians listen to the cries of despair in our nation and help turn those cries into actual rays of hope. He never did actually mention George Bush's name.

And when his short speech was over, he stepped off the podium. He darted out of the room. Fred has a habit of doing this. "Okay, now where the hell is Fred," said Bill. Bill couldn't find him. The beefy Secret Service men couldn't find him. We climbed the stairs and combed the building and the Secret Service men talked into their secret little walkie talkies. The lunch was about to be served and Fred was . . . missing.

Finally, we found him. He was standing outside alone, by an oak tree. "Can we leave now?" he said.

A priest came running up. "Mister Rogers! Where are you going! We are just about to start the lunch!"

"Oh, I have to go back to work now," he said. And then he was gone.

Fred did not want to be a part of that event. But he would say a prayer with those people or any other people. He was not put on this earth to snub anyone, that's how he saw it.

I wasn't about to participate in any fund raising or anything else. But at the same time I don't want to be an accuser. Other people may be accusers if they want to; that may be their job. I really want to be an advocate for whatever I find is healthy or good.

I think people don't change very much when all they have is a finger pointed at them. I think the only way people change is in relation to somebody who loves them.

I am often stricken by how many people have a distorted view of Fred Rogers. I was marveling over this fact as I sat in the office of my editors at *Life*. This was a unique situation for me; I actually had to convince a magazine editor that a story about Fred Rogers could be a good one. These were tough-guy, cynical editors, as editors sometimes are, who couldn't quite grasp why I felt so strongly about the power of Fred Rogers. "Isn't he, like, gay or something?" one editor said to another. I rolled my eyes and told them they needed to get out more. They agreed that Fred was a well-known public figure, there was no denying that. Perhaps they could put him on the cover. Perhaps he could sell magazines.

I got the go-ahead to write the story, a typical day in the life of Studio A in the WQED building in Pittsburgh where *Mister Rogers' Neighborhood* is produced. I spent a lot of time there. One exchange between Fred and a little boy was particularly moving.

"Hey, you're the real Mister Rogers!" a young boy named Brian cried out one day, on seeing his hero walk into the studio. Nearly every morning of taping there were kids running through Studio A. They came to meet Mister Rogers. Many were fans who had written letters — Fred receives about a hundred a week and responds to each one personally — and children with special needs are often invited to come visit the Neighborhood.

"And you're the real you," Fred said, bending down. He shook Brian's hand. "You're so brave to shake my hand," he said. Brian, eleven, was a plump boy, somewhat awkward in his own body. He had Williams Syndrome, a condition that causes mild mental retardation and congenital heart failure. He'd come all the way from Arlington, Texas, to meet Mister Rogers.

"I am special," Brian said, "aren't I, Mister Rogers?"

"Yes, you are."

"You know what, Mister Rogers?" Brian said. "You are my friend." With that, the boy started singing a song from the Neighborhood. "You are my friend, you are special. . . ." Fred put his arm around him and sang along quietly. The crew in the studio grew silent.

"Good for you, Brian," Fred said when the song was over. "Good for you!"

"Can I give you a big hug, Mister Rogers?" Brian asked.

Fred Rogers opened his arms and Brian Campbell fell inside.

"I love you, Mister Rogers," Brian said.

Brian's mother was completely undone by this exchange. "This is, like, the highlight of my life," she said.

Fred and young Brian continued playing. Brian made the trolley go, then fed the fish, while Fred followed along, trying to crouch down to the boy's height. Eventually, the producer came over, hoping to turn this studio back into a place of work. "Come on, Fred," she said. But Fred had one more thing to say to Brian.

He got on his knees. He looked the child square in the eye. "You blessed my space today, Brian," he said.

Brian considered this. "Well, I'm glad you're here, Mister Rogers," Brian said. "But we'll probably never see each other again after today, will we?"

"We can still be television neighbors," Fred said. "Can't we?"

"Okay," Brian said, adding, "I am special, Mister Rogers, aren't I?"

"Yes, you are."

This exchange, which I documented in the piece for *Life*, was the one that got my editors at *Life* to thoroughly soften up. The toughest of all called after he read it to tell me he had cried. I had never experienced such a genuine human exchange with that editor. Usually, in our work relationships, we're spending our days competing and negotiating. But suddenly, thanks to the parables of Fred, it was as if we suddenly had permission to strip ourselves of our masks and our armor and our weapons and be, for a moment, just plain old human beings.

I'm sure Fred has no idea how far and wide his message is transmitted.

I got letters from all sorts of unlikely folks — business executives and plumbers and hairdressers and car salesmen — telling me of their tears, having read about the Fred and Brian exchange.

And yet really it was nothing so out of the ordinary. You experience a lot of warm and fuzzy moments if you spend any amount of time with Fred Rogers. These aren't sappy moments of sugary good will. These are intense moments of heart-to-heart contact. Perhaps it's his training that enables him to zoom to a needy child like this, but more likely, I think, it's Fred's power of extraordinary empathy — a kind fully understood, perhaps, only by a sickly, lonely boy who found safety in the arms of a cherished grandfather.

You know, if I knew how to paint I could paint you a picture of my grandfather's house in Florida and his house in New Florence. I still think about that house. I long to have that place. My dad sold it for twenty-five thousand dollars after my grandfather died. And there was an electric company that wanted the property to put their wires through, so it just kind of little by little disintegrated. But I realized the only thing I really longed for was to have my grandfather back.

It was greatly anticipated. He was in a nursing home for over two years. I was in New York by then. Nineteen fifty-one. The year before Joanne and I were married. I was working at NBC and I was floor managing *The Kate Smith Hour* every afternoon and I had three days in a row that I could go home. I went home that night and I went to see him. He was in a nursing home in Butler. And he didn't know me. And he introduced me to a picture of myself. He said, "I'd like you to know my grandson." The picture of me that he had in his room. And he said, "He works with Kate Smith." He watched Kate Smith every afternoon. Well, I hadn't known that. And so when I went back to do that program, well, I knew that he was watching.

And it wasn't very long after that he died.

And that was a really wonderful tie that television gave me.

In the end, I suppose the truest glimpse of Fred I ever got was in Nantucket, at his small summer house there. Nothing extraordinary happened. Fred wasn't "on." He wasn't being all brilliant or generous and he wasn't zooming into anybody or touching anybody's soul. He was just Fred: man on vacation.

The thing that struck me was that Fred being just Fred was so very Fred-ish. He was still the curious, delighted child. And still the star. And still somewhat the outsider. He spent long hours in his study, reading and playing his piano. He went to the pool every day. He kept his schedule and Joanne kept hers. She is a good match for him. A concert pianist and mother to their two grown children (John Rogers lives with his wife in Topeka, Kansas; James Rogers lives with his wife and son in Pittsburgh), Joanne is forthright, full of humor, and fully present in the moments of the day.

Also along that weekend was my friend Lynn Johnson, a photographer for *Life*. In the morning we all walked on the beach. Fred was dressed in the rattiest old blue jacket. He kept finding stuff: a washed-up beach chair, a hat, a towel. He would pick these things up, saying, "Now what could I use this for?" and shake the sand off and carry them along toward home. How odd to discover Fred Rogers, the scavenger.

When we got near the house he found a dirty old sheet that had just tumbled in from some faraway sea port. He lifted it into the air, shook it, and laid it down flat on the ground. "Now, what size is our bed, Joanne?" he asked.

Joanne, Lynn, and I exchanged glances.

"Fred, I think that really might be too disgusting to bring home," I said. Joanne shook her head back and forth. Lynn did too. Fred seemed awfully disappointed by the consensus. He was at that moment a little boy with three stern mothers.

We got back to the house. "The Crooked House" it is called. It is a spectacular place in that it is entirely ordinary. Fred and Joanne have had the house for thirty years, and for thirty years it's looked the same: old, beat-up, furnished entirely with stuff they've picked up in thrift shops. We're not talking delicate antiques here. This is the functional furniture of young starving artists. Fred was particularly enamored of a little ceramic deer he had just gotten at a flea market. He kept attending to the deer and requested several times that Lynn get the deer in her pictures.

In the kitchen, Fred reached into the cupboard to show off some aqua-blue plastic plates he had recently bought. "It's my new pattern," he said, flipping the plate over, and reading the back. "It's called 'OTHER.'"

"Oh, that is wonderful!" Joanne said. "Just wonderful!" She let loose a hearty laugh. "This place has known so much laughter," she said, fixing some lunch. "But like I always say, 'This is the closest I'll ever get to camping.'"

"This is *nothing* like camping!" Fred said, then asked for the butter, which turned out to be margarine.

"Oh, I can't *believe* it's not butter!" Fred said, reading the package labeling, waiting for a laugh.

"You say that every single time, Rog," Joanne said.

"Do I?"

"Yes, you do."

They shared a meal in this ordinary kitchen; they could have been any old couple, anywhere in America, eating in a trailer. Joanne served locally baked "Portuguese bread," and dished out some tomatoes and coleslaw to put on top. I asked her if she always cooked simple meals when in Nantucket.

"I don't believe I've ever made a fancy meal anywhere," she said, laughing, and her husband laughed along.

"I can't *believe* it's not butter," he said again, reaching for the margarine.

"Oh, Rog."

Later, we went back out to the beach. Joanne didn't particularly like the beach, and kept reminding us all of that fact. Lynn wanted pictures, however. She asked Joanne and Fred to climb into a large hole dug into the sand, sit in there, and hug. Joanne did this in the comic tradition of Lucille Ball, hobbling and tumbling, reminding us of how ridiculous this moment was. And Fred was laughing so hard he was practically crying. The laughter grew and grew and became a contagious flu we all caught, standing in the wind, unable at that moment to contain the hilarious joy for living that Joanne and Fred screamed out to sea.

By the time we left Nantucket I was convinced that Fred Rogers was a contented man, having thus far lived a life vastly enriched by his work — a true ministry — and by all the people who have helped him do his work. It certainly has been a life that would have made his grandfather proud.

Fred Rogers' trademark message, "I like you just the way you are," is practically a direct quote taken from his grandfather.

> I think it was when I was leaving one time to go home after our time together that my grandfather said to me, "You know you made this day a really special day. Just by being yourself. There's only one person in the world like you. And I happen to like you just the way you are."

Well, talk about good stuff. That just went right into my heart. And it never budged.

And I've been able to pass that on. And that's a wonderful legacy. And I trust that he's proud of that. I could have walked into some positions that were already set. I could have walked into an office that was already furnished for me.

But I would much rather have done what I have done.

David Bianculli's view of Mister Rogers is seen through one of those museums that Laskas talks about — specifically the Museum of Television & Radio, where Bianculli unearthed early footage of Mister Rogers' Neighborhood and its predecessor, The Children's Corner. In tracking the evolution of a small, local kids' show to a nationally known program, Bianculli traces the early formation of the set, the format, and the puppets (some brought onto the studio as an afterthought — one of which is still around after thirty years).

Bianculli's detailed exploration leads to an ineffable conclusion: "The slow pace, the dead-on-look-into-the-camera gaze, the activities, the songs, the puppets, reassuring messages . . . all of these have a lot to do with making the show what it is. But much of it, I suspect, is less clinical and identifiable. Instead, it comes from Rogers himself. He doesn't go through the motions; he may not know how to feign anything. He sincerely enjoys and believes in what he's doing. And that sincerity is largely why his young audience responds so strongly: while we grown-ups may wonder if anyone can be that genuine, children — the ultimate connoisseurs of candor — recognize his honesty immediately."

Bianculli is currently the TV critic for the New York Daily News. He has been associated with NPR's Fresh Air since 1985 and has syndicated stories and reviews in most major newspapers. He is the author of Teleliteracy: Taking Television Seriously, a 1992 publication of Continuum. Over the years, he has written articles about television for such publications as Rolling Stone, Film Comment, Washington Journalism Review, TV Guide, Channels of Communication, Electronic Media, and the London Independent.

David Bianculli

The Myth, the Man, the Legend

Fred Rogers and I got started in children's television at the same place, and about the same time.

His career as a children's TV personality began in Pittsburgh, Pennsylvania, in 1954, as puppeteer, musician, producer, and cocreator of *The Children's Corner*, a local TV show on WQED. I had begun in Pittsburgh a year earlier — as a child.

More specifically, as a child of television.

So when Rogers and his partner, Josie Carey, first served up their programs, I was in the right place at the right time to be one of their young viewers. Along with *The Mickey Mouse Club* and *Captain Kangaroo*, two influential national children's TV series that started the year *after* Rogers' local show, *The Children's Corner* was one of my earliest exposures to the world and wonders of television.

By the time I met Fred Rogers, more than thirty years had passed. Thanks to PBS's *Mister Rogers' Neighborhood,* on which he was on-camera star as well as off-camera guiding force, Rogers had become a TV institution. So, during his visit to Philadelphia to address a group of kindergarten students, the *Philadelphia Inquirer* sent their TV critic (me) to interview the legend.

I spent an hour with Rogers. I left utterly beguiled.

Perhaps, deep down, many of us harbor a hidden, deviant suspicion that the Fred Rogers of "real life" is slightly, or even shockingly, different from his quiet and deliberate persona on PBS. It's our imagination's equivalent of Baby Herman in the movie *Who Framed Roger Rabbit?* — adorable while the camera rolls but a leering, cigar-smoking oaf the moment he strides off the set. My brief meeting with Rogers dispelled any such fears or fantasies. Not only does the "private" Fred Rogers speak with the same quiet, molasses cadence as on TV, but he has the same gaze and manner that make you feel he is concentrating completely and solely on you. Which, of course, he is.

Further proof of Rogers' sincerity came during the same meeting, when ABC's *Nightline* called to offer Rogers a coveted spot on their program. The topic was children's fears, yet Rogers declined the invitation. He had come to town to address a kindergarten class, Rogers explained, and he felt that those children deserved his full and rested attention. The speed with which the decision was reached — as well as the decision itself — indicated just how different a TV animal Fred Rogers was — and is.

Other essays in this collection address the particular traits that make Fred Rogers so mesmerizing and soothing a TV personality. The slow pace, the dead-on-look-into-the-camera gaze, the activities, the songs, the puppets, reassuring messages . . . all of these have a lot to do with making the show what it is. But much of it, I suspect, is less clinical and identifiable. Instead, it comes from Rogers himself. He doesn't go through the motions; he may not know how to feign *anything*. He sincerely enjoys and believes in what he's doing. And that sincerity is largely why his young audience responds so strongly: while we grown-ups may wonder if anyone can be that genuine, children — the ultimate connoisseurs of candor — recognize his honesty immediately.

My own contact with Rogers has been so limited and brief over the years that I make no claims to know the man at all. But my impression of him, after a handful of telephone interviews and one in-person meeting, is of a man who is both committed and cautious when it comes to his image and his audience. Of all the people I interviewed for my book *Teleliteracy: Taking Television Seriously* — including the likes of Bill Cosby, Peter Jennings, Kurt Vonnegut, David Attenborough, and Ken Burns — only Fred Rogers requested a written synopsis of the project before agreeing to take part. I took that not as an insult, but as an indication of how protective he is about what he says, and where and how he says it.

Perhaps he is so protective of himself because he *is* so aware of what his image on television can provide: immediate legitimacy to any theme or message. During the Gulf War, Rogers was reluctant to fulfill a request to create and appear in a series of public-service announcements aimed at children, talking to them about their war-related questions and fears. "I didn't want to get involved and get in the fray of the whole thing — but when I heard that kids were really scared, then I felt, 'Put those feelings aside, Rogers, and do what you can.' That's when television can be at its best."

By being so shielding of his straightforward image, Rogers has preserved his multigenerational allure. Asked about the secret of his own appeal to his young audience, Rogers says simply that children, like adults, are hungry for the truth.

"Every one of us longs to be in touch with honesty," he says. "I think we're really attracted to people who will share some of their real self with us."

So how did Rogers' "real self" develop, as refracted through the prism of television? How soon did he adopt, then adapt, his now-familiar persona? The answers are hidden in surviving tapes from *The Children's Corner*, and from subsequent early episodes of what was then called *Misterogers*. I viewed random samples of them recently, courtesy of the archives at New York's Museum of Television & Radio, and learned a lot — beginning with why I remembered, from my own earliest viewing, Daniel Striped Tiger and the other hand puppets, but not Rogers himself.

On *The Children's Corner*, he wasn't there; not on camera, anyway. But he figures handily in the show — literally, in the hand puppet sense. The wall behind hostess Carey features the crudely painted "homes" of Daniel Striped Tiger, Henrietta Pussycat, and "X" the owl. (The exact same configuration would continue on *Misterogers*.) In a 1956 episode of the local Pittsburgh TV show, Rogers, through the voice and movements of Daniel Striped Tiger, already is engaging in conversation with the viewer out there in television land.

"Welcome to *The Children's Corner*," the tiger puppet says. "How are you today?" Then, after a pause, "I'm just fine, thank you." (Even at this early juncture, Rogers is beginning to hone his dead-on, wait-for-his-viewers'-unseen-response-look that would become a staple of his on-air personality.) "Today's a very special day on *The Children's Corner*," Daniel continues, "and we're glad you could be with us."

The human hosting chores are delegated to Carey, who, among other duties, sings songs obviously written by Rogers, with the same gaze-into-the-camera approach. In this example from another show during the same period, she addresses the young viewer directly in song:

> Why, hi, don't I know you?
> Why, hi, I'm sure I do.
> Why, hi, you know me, too.
> Why, hi, how do you do?

One surprising element of these mid-fifties *Children's Corner* shows is their playfulness with TV technology, which at times reveals the young Rogers as an artistic cousin, as well as contemporary, of Ernie Kovacs. In musical sequences set in *The Children's Corner* attic, formerly inanimate objects — telephones, doors, lamp shades — ring, slam, and shake, respectively, in tune to the music. And while such set pieces are similar to the kind Kovacs staged so regularly and inventively, the fanciful names given the objects — Gramma Phone, Lawrence Light — echo a much older, less visual influence: namely, the 1930s and 1940s radio show *Vic and Sade,* which Rogers says inspired him as a child. "I loved *Vic and Sade,*" he recalls, fondly remembering such playful puns as "The Ohio Home for the Bland." Rogers adds, "I just love whimsical stuff," as if there's some surprise in that.

Another "Kovacsian" element of *The Children's Corner* was the playfulness of the people making the show. In one episode from 1957, there's some good-natured bantering between hostess Carey, who wants to recite a particular poem, and Daniel Striped Tiger, who would rather she didn't. Looking back on this show as an adult, and hearing the crew's appreciative laughter in the background, it's obvious there is some truth behind the jokes being tossed around. (It may even be the closest documented evidence of anything resembling tension on the set of a Fred Rogers program.)

The poem Carey wishes to perform, she announces, is "Poor Lady" — news of which doesn't exactly excite the normally affable Daniel Striped Tiger. "Ladies and gentlemen, you're in for it," the puppet growls. And the more she pouts and protests about Daniel's lack of enthusiasm, the more sarcastic he gets. "The volume control on the television set is *soooo* handy," he purrs, and suggests to his human hostess, "You might try to warn them not to eat dinner during the poem, Josephine."

The tiger flees the scene, the crew laughs, and Carey seizes the opportunity. "Poor Lady," it turns out, is the old I-know-an-old-woman-who-swallowed-a-fly poem, which apparently has been heard often enough on *The Children's Corner* to become a source of good-natured irritation among the regulars. And on this occasion, we learn just how busy the unseen Rogers was on those old shows: as soon as he exited the scene as Daniel Striped Tiger, he ran off-camera to sit at the keyboard in his added duty as music director. We know this because of Carey's next comment.

"I could recite it right *now*," Carey says enthusiastically, and more than a little threateningly. "There's nobody around really to stop me — except Mister Rogers at the organ. He could play loud and sort of drown me out." And Mister Rogers does just that.

By the time the musician-puppeteer moved in front of the camera as on-air host of *Misterogers*, the program was a more recognizable ancestral cousin to its present incarnation. The new opening song was of Rogers' invention and choosing — and though it was different from the now-familiar *It's a Beautiful Day in the Neighborhood*, it, too, mentioned neighborhoods and neighbors, and addressed viewers in the second-person singular:

> Right in the middle of the alphabet,
> There's a friendly neighborhood
> Where a king is in charge of the calendar,
> And the rockets are made of wood . . .
>
> So if you may, just come and stay,
> And we'll be neighbors here,
> Because you make each day a special day,
> By just your being here.

And there's Fred Rogers, introducing the show by initiating a quiet, one-on-one conversation. In this vintage 1964 edition of *Misterogers*, he's wearing a coat and tie — not yet adorned in his trademark sweater — but both his approach and his appeal are, by this point, clearly evident.

Rogers starts by asking, "How are you today?" — opening this particular show with the same words Daniel Striped Tiger used to kick off *The Children's Corner*. Then Rogers introduces the day's topic.

"Did you ever have a baby-sitter? Or *were* you ever a baby-sitter? What do you *do* when you have a baby-sitter, or *are* a baby-sitter?"

Then: "Do you ever make any crayonings? Do you? Here's some for you to see . . . and thank *you*, Joseph, for the turkey with the fancy plumes."

The trolley to the Neighborhood of Make-Believe is a two-dimensional cut-out in the opening credits of this version, rather than the brightly colored, fully working miniature trolley of *Mister Rogers' Neighborhood*. But the mewing Henrietta, "X" the wise owl, and good-natured Daniel Striped Tiger look pretty much the same.

"I don't growl any more, I'm tame, I'm tame," Daniel sings happily. "I don't prowl any more, I'm tame, I'm tame." But in a later episode of *Misterogers*, Daniel is dealing with a different set of feelings. "I'm orange and black outside," he confides, "but a little blue inside."

And in a different episode in 1964, King Friday XIII is making plans to write a play that, in effect, predates postmodern. It's a two-character play called "The King and the Donkey," and all the actors do during the play is sleep. "Isn't it original?" the King asks. The nonsensical *Vic and Sade* influence is clear, too, when the King invites a guest to tea and offers directions, which are, in both spirit and voice, equally traceable to Rogers. "The tea room," the King reminds his subject, "is just down the hall from the 'S' room."

There are, and always have been, critics who feel watching Fred Rogers, at whatever stage of his career, is about as enthralling as watching a puppet and donkey sleep. But the appeal of Fred Rogers, to his target age group, is genuine, potent, and nothing new. On a show broadcast two weeks before Christmas in 1964, the host of *Misterogers* holds up a large, handwritten thank-you card from youngsters at a kindergarten in nearby Dorseyville, Pennsylvania. Rogers holds it up only briefly, and the camera doesn't linger on it. But isolating the image in freeze-frame, all these years later, shows that oversize card to be a clear indicator of the depth and breadth of Fred Rogers' appeal to his loyal preschool audience.

"We like your show," the poster announces. "We like you. We like your puppets." Then the litany gets longer and more specific, showing the individualized, precise nature of the show's appeal: "Dennis likes the dog. Patti likes the cat, and Ernie likes the owl. Mike and Kathy like King Friday. Amy likes the mouses. Johnny likes to hear the Captain sing." And then, at the end of the card, simply this: "Thank you for putting on the show."

It's a little difficult, from an adult perspective, to look at *Mister Rogers' Neighborhood* and not think of the various parodies aimed at him over the years—from Johnny Carson on *The Tonight Show* to Eddie Murphy on *Saturday Night Live.*

Fred Rogers has become so much of a cultural icon that "Mister Rogers" is its own individual entry in Jane and Michael Stern's *Encyclopedia of Pop Culture*, sandwiched alphabetically (and perversely) between "remote control" and "Rolling Stones." Rogers himself takes the spoofs in stride, and even tells warm stories about some of the comics who poke fun at him.

Johnny Carson, Rogers says, once defended his impersonation by saying, "Fred, first of all, we'd never do these if people didn't know who we were talking about. And second of all, it's done with a certain affection."

That's why, and how, Johnny Carson and Robin Williams can isolate Rogers' questioning, conversational, talk-to-the-camera style and distill it into the comedic "Can you say *entropy*, boys and girls?" as Williams asks his audience in one routine. It's also why, and how, Eddie Murphy eagerly played his own wicked variations on the *Mister Rogers* theme song in the parody *Mister Robinson's Neighborhood* ("I've always wanted to live in a house like yours, my friend / Maybe when there's nobody home, I'll break in").

Yet when Rogers visited the *Saturday Night Live* studios years ago, neither the imitator nor his subject bore any malice. Rogers says Murphy came out of one room, threw his arm around the object of his good-natured ridicule and said, "The *real* Mister Rogers!"

It's interesting that Rogers enjoys telling those stories, and not because they contain a message of validation from those who have both acknowledged and lampooned his particular style. They suggest Rogers is well aware he is made fun of in some quarters but is self-assured enough not to let it bother him. The attitudes and opinions of his young viewers—the kids who watch each day, the ones who write the giant cards and send the little drawings—are all that count. And though that audience often quickly grows out of its *Mister Rogers* phase, it's an audience that is constantly replenished by fresh, equally eager sets of eyes.

A glimpse at some of the more modern installments of *Mister Rogers' Neighborhood* show how things have improved over the years, but not substantially changed. Yes, the supporting cast, both human and puppet, has grown a bit, and Rogers is more likely to take viewers along on more exotic field trips—like the time in 1981 he took them into an underground mine used to cultivate mushrooms. And even in that dark, dank environment, dealing with bulbous clumps of fungi, Rogers finds something nice and bright to say. "Every mushroom is different," he marvels, holding up a few freshly picked ones to the camera. "Like people."

But after all these years, the puppets remain defiantly simplistic in their stylization. (It's not for nothing it's called the Neighborhood of Make-Believe.) The background music remains chipper, fluid, and soothing; musical director Johnny Costa, after all those years at the Neighborhood keyboard, may as well be credited as the grandfather of what's now called New Age music. Creativity and self-image remain at the core of every show. And whether Rogers and company are dealing with going to school for the first time or confronting the difficult concepts of death and divorce, the approach and style remain constant. The direct, slow, and soothing manner of the newest episodes of *Mister Rogers' Neighborhood* are mirrored by the same attributes found in the earliest extant copies of *The Children's Corner*.

Those kids to whom Fred Rogers first spoke via television in his puppet guises on *The Children's Corner* are approaching forty, or on the other side of it, and even those who didn't catch his act until public television acquired *Misterogers* are now old enough to have weaned their own kids on the quiet style of Fred Rogers. He takes more field trips now, and in the nonrepeat shows, looks less parental than grandparental; the trolley is a little grander, as are the show's aspirations and achievements. But King Friday and the rest haven't aged, and *Mister Rogers' Neighborhood* remains one of the first, best, and safest programs through which preschoolers should be introduced to the medium of television.

In one way, it's not surprising that Fred Rogers found his voice so early, and came to television with his puppets, puns, and guileless musical compositions already aimed and ready. Like Samuel Clemens, whose earliest sketches for newspapers (written as a teen) revealed the writing talent he would eventually display as Mark Twain, Rogers knew what he was doing — and had an innate sense of how to do it — at a very early age. Rogers tapped into something very basic, speaking to viewers in a tone that implies private conversation and that, despite its deliberate cadence and basic vocabulary, never suggests condescension. Even when Rogers sits there folding a paper fan out of construction paper or using safety scissors to cut out something, he acts like he's doing something for himself as well as the viewer — as though, on a rainy day, he might amuse himself the same way even if there were no cameras to record his actions.

Nor is he above making himself look bad to make a larger, more important point. An example of this, from the early eighties, has Rogers singing the opening song, changing into a blue cloth coat (he doesn't *always* wear that sweater), and excitedly grabbing a squirt bottle and a flashlight. He's all set to mount an experiment and make a rainbow, so he dims the lights, turns on the flashlight, squeezes the bottle and shines a beam through the mist.

"You see that?" he asks, as Costa's tinkling piano notes emphasize every squirt. "Do you see a rainbow?"

Well, no. Not really. And after what seems like an eternity of TV time, Rogers admits defeat — his experiment didn't work, and he doesn't know why. For a second or two, but only for a second or two, Mister Rogers pouts. Then, rising above his disappointment, he decides to call his old friend Mr. McFeely (played by David Newell, a dedicated backstage and on-camera veteran of Rogers' TV activities) for help. With typical Speedy Delivery, Mr. McFeely drops by with a prism, explains the principle of refraction, and sets up a projector so that the beam can serve as the sun, and his prism as a raindrop. Presto: a beautiful spectrum of rainbow colors is projected onto Rogers' refrigerator door. But that scene isn't a lesson only about how lights and prisms work together; it's a lesson about how people do too, and how collaboration can turn defeat into victory and sadness into happiness.

"I'm mighty glad to have a friend like Mr. McFeely, who knows so many things," Rogers says, looking, as usual, directly into the camera. "Like, I just wasn't able to make that [rainbow] myself. People can help each other."

In every phase of Rogers' TV career, there are the same elements — puppetry, simplicity, camaraderie, and musicality — that critics love to ridicule and youngsters love to watch. The reactions, in both cases, are somewhat understandable. Because Fred Rogers is one of the first TV personalities children encounter, he is also, naturally, one of the first ones they outgrow. But their little brothers and sisters flock to him just as readily and enthusiastically, and while Rogers' spell may last only a while, it's not broken — only dormant. In millions of households, adults who long ago had "outgrown" the Neighborhood of Make-Believe delight in returning to it as parents, carrying on what has become a multigenerational TV tradition by introducing *Mister Rogers' Neighborhood* to children of their own.

And what they find, if and when they make that return journey to the Neighborhood of Make-Believe, is the same seamless magic spell. The lyrics and music to Rogers' songs may be different, but the messages are the same. In most popular music, according to sociologists who track such things, the word most frequently used is "I." Were a concordance of the music of Fred Rogers to be compiled, it's a good bet the word used more than any other would be "you." He always has, and presumably always will, put the viewer first. Here's a sample lyric, from 1982, that amply illustrates the point:

> Sometimes you feel like holding your pillow all night long.
> Sometimes you hug your teddy bear tightly;
> He's old, but he's still strong.
>
> And sometimes you want to snuggle up closely
> with your own mom and dad.
> At night, you even need the light sometimes,
> but that's not bad.
>
> Please don't think it's funny
> when you want an extra kiss.
> There are lots and lots of people
> who sometimes feel like this.
>
> Please don't think it's funny
> when you want the ones you miss.
> There are lots and lots of people
> who sometimes feel like this.

Jaded adults might find that message and sentiment a walk on the hokey side — but if you're a small child watching TV, and Mister Rogers both acknowledges and soothes a secret fear with such a song, what's happening is more miraculous than mawkish.

"I have watched kids watching *Mister Rogers*," says Roger Desmond, a postdoctoral fellow in media literacy at the University of Pennsylvania's Annenberg School of Communications, "and they're *rapt*. . . . Fred Rogers' style is paced at a pace that four- and five-year-olds just love."

According to Desmond, there are other reasons, too, for Rogers' appeal and longevity. "The kid who's a preschooler is developing a sense of self," Desmond says. "Most television doesn't even address that. 'Who am I? Why am I here?' — that kind of stuff."

That kind of "stuff," combined with Rogers' success at what Desmond calls "breaking the fourth wall" (talking directly to the audience), makes *Mister Rogers' Neighborhood* ready-made for young viewers — and for proponents of quality children's television as well. "If we took all the indictments against TV for young kids," Desmond notes, "*Mister Rogers* embodies their opposites." Which, when you think about it, may be another reason *Mister Rogers' Neighborhood* has such a relatively brief window of interest for young viewers: The program has the approval of too many authority figures.

"It's so easy to satirize," Desmond says. "All this sincerity. It's everything big kids like to make fun of little kids for." Desmond's research reflects that the passage of young viewers through the Mister Rogers "phase" has to do with child development. Young fans of the series are in the "preoperational" stage, and learn all manner of information about the world and themselves. When they become "operational" and want to explore things with even more complexity, they often move on. "They've built another identity," Desmond says; "one that says, 'I'm not *that* any more, so now I can *reject* that and make fun of it." But like children's songs and fairy tales, which are similarly bypassed at about the same age, the influence of Fred Rogers carries on into adulthood — and is passed on to the next generation of receptive viewers.

"He's done something right," Desmond says. "I'm surprised he hasn't had more imitators."

Frankly, I'm not. Style can be imitated and approximated, but commitment and credibility cannot.

"Fine art, civilized speech, thoughtful ways of interacting with people — children's introduction to such things can come early, on television," Fred Rogers once said. "Some children wouldn't have the opportunity of some of those cultural riches — even to know what an opera or a symphony or a cello was — if not for television." .

And, it should be added, if not for *Mister Rogers' Neighborhood*.

Bill Cosby says that he considers *Mister Rogers' Neighborhood* to be among those few children's shows that "were and are very, very important." Even the Yale research team of Dorothy and Jerome Singer, whose opinions seem diametrically opposed to mine when it comes to most issues of children's TV, find common ground when it comes to the efforts of Fred Rogers. In their 1990 book *The House of Make-Believe*, the Singers write, "One TV program that is especially sensitive in helping the preschool child make sense out of a confusing world is *Mister Rogers' Neighborhood*. The host, Fred Rogers, acts as a surrogate parent, explaining through verbal repetition, music, puppets, special guests, and trips to various locations some of the confusing elements in a child's environment. . . . He can help a child deal with a first day at school, a visit to the doctor, or a stay in the hospital." Coming from Jerome Singer (who once suggested completely denying children access to television until their reading and writing habits were established), that ranks as high praise indeed.

Yet the best words on the subject come, not surprisingly, from Rogers himself. In a recently published essay, Rogers writes:

"Just like a refrigerator or a stove, television is seen by children as something that parents provide. In a young child's mind, then, parents probably condone what's on the television set, just like they choose what's in the refrigerator or on the stove!"

He goes on to warn, "That's why we who make television for children must be especially careful with what we produce, with the people we present, and with attitudes we show in television relationships — attitudes of respect, kindness, healthy curiosity, determination, and love . . . just as parents would want for their children."

I don't remember whether, as I watched *The Children's Corner* back in the 1950s, I presumed that my parents approved of what I was watching —

any more than they did when I watched Bob Keeshan's *Captain Kangaroo* or Don Herbert's *Mister Wizard*. What I do remember about TV, back then, is a feeling TV was talking to *me*, even if my name wasn't called out that often when the hostess "looked out" into the audience during *Romper Room*. And when, a generation later, I held my children on my lap and watched them watching *Mister Rogers' Neighborhood*, I saw in them a little bit of myself, back when TV, Fred Rogers, and I were all a lot younger. We were friends then. We are friends still.

Nancy Curry, a former colleague of Fred Rogers at the Arsenal Family and Children's Center, combines stories about her friendship with Fred with a theoretical look at play versus reality.

In exploring theory, Curry examines the value of a "transitional object" — a beloved doll or blanket that serves as a child's bridge between reality and fantasy. Such bridges are part of the work between parents and children — the child works at making sense of everyday reality, while caring adults help to interpret for the child. ("That roaring noise scared you? It's the blender that I'm using to fix your orange juice. Watch how I turn it on.") "If all goes well developmentally," Curry says, "children come to recognize the differences between real and pretend and to relish both the cognitive and affective aspects of their world."

Ironically, it was Fred Rogers' son Jamie who taught Curry the value of a transitional object. While working at the Arsenal Family and Children's Center, Curry says she "quietly discouraged children's bringing their blankets or soft animals, with the rationale that if they accidentally left them at school, they would be too distressed at home without them. But Jamie's parents knew better . . . [and] I learned a valuable lesson. . . . Fred's intuitive knowledge about the usefulness of the transitional object became further elaborated on and translated into his masterful use of transitions on his program."

Curry is professor emerita in the Child Development and Child Care program in the School of Social Work, University of Pittsburgh. She held joint appointments with the Schools of Health Related Professions, Medicine, and Education at the university, where her research interests included affective and social development of young children. The former associate director of the Arsenal Family and Children's Center, Curry also coproduced more than twelve films on children's play, was editor of The Feeling Child, and coauthored Beyond Self-Esteem: Developing a Genuine Sense of Human Value. She is currently in private practice as a child and adult psychotherapist and psychoanalyst, as well as a consultant in child development and play therapy.

Nancy E. Curry

The Reality of Make-Believe

> And on the basis of playing is built the whole of man's experiential
> existence. No longer are we either introvert or extrovert. We
> experience life in the area of the transitional phenomena, in the
> exciting interweave of subjectivity and objective observation, and in an
> area that is intermediate between the inner reality of the individual
> and the shared reality of the world that is external to individuals.
> — Donald W. Winnicott, *Playing and Reality*

The importance of pretend play and reality is at the heart of Fred
Rogers' work. Daily he invites children to enter his play space, and
together they confront both the inner reality of imagination and the
shared reality of the world that Winnicott so poetically describes. As a
classmate, colleague, and observer of Fred Rogers, I have been "Fred-
watching" for nearly three decades. In that time, I have come to understand why his blend of reality and fantasy is so important in a child's
development and how his program aids in the vital developmental task of
resolving subjective and objective reality.

I first met Fred when I was a nursery school teacher and he was an
eager student, combining child development with his theological training.
We still share memories of the times he spent in my preschool group, first
as a participant-observer and later as the gifted performer, testing himself
on the children in my class.

Both of us trained under Margaret McFarland, a woman deeply committed to the emotional development of children and to the theoretical
understandings of such development. She taught us to be careful observers, to use our empathy and our own experiences as children to understand the child we were observing, to relate these observations to psychodynamic theory, and then respond with clinical insights to children in our

care. This method of teaching made working with and learning about children enriching and exciting. It has become a lifelong way of learning for me as I became a professor and psychoanalyst and certainly for Fred as the most outstanding producer, writer, and performer of children's programming in our country.

Normally Margaret McFarland was kind, insightful, and even-tempered; behind the wheel of a car she was something else. The staff at the Arsenal Family and Children's Center did not always agree with Margaret's policy of keeping the center open during severe weather. To prove her point she would forge in from her distant suburban home on very snowy days and put to shame those of us who lived in the city and griped about having to drive a few blocks to work. One especially bad storm kept the city snowbound for three days. I felt guilty staying home, even though the city was virtually shut down, and on the third day drove my intrepid Volkswagen to the center. (It was the 1960s; *everyone* had a VW.) The parking lot had still not been plowed, but two cars had blazed a trail already. I climbed the stairs and saw in Margaret's office Fred and a fellow seminary student sitting side by side, knees-to-chin on a Victorian love seat, assiduously taking notes while Margaret calmly taught, parable-fashion, about child development. Just another day in the snows of Academe.

One of my fondest memories was of Fred accompanying our class on a field trip to a wooded area that was beloved by Margaret from her own childhood. Fred arrived in his yachting whites and agreed to drive half the children in his car while Margaret drove the others. Once on the parkway we were amazed to be in the wake of a transformed Margaret who drove at such a speed and took such risks that Fred and I were both breathless and not a little terrified. Our relief at arriving became tempered by the daunting task of scaling an almost perpendicular hill in search of the waterfall where Margaret promised the children a surprise. The woods were dank and dark, and one emotionally disturbed child who had been "mainstreamed " into the class became terrified. All along the path he kept crying, "How can we see the mushroomed-shaped cloud through all these trees if we are bombed?" Fred's white outfit soon was besmirched with mud and leaves. Margaret's "surprise," as it turned out, was some lovely wildflowers; of course, they could only be reached by fording a waterfall. I left Fred to comfort and contain the terrified and now deeply disappointed child whom we had kept going with the promise of the surprise. (He had thought our surprise would be discovering a train, something that he talked about obsessively.) As we were driving back to the center, still unable to keep up with Margaret's speedway driving, I murmured to Fred that the little boy now was lying on the back seat, sucking his thumb . . . and clutching his penis. Fred, exhausted and rumpled, muttered, "Leave him alone. It's probably the happiest he's been all day."

When he wasn't driving, white-knuckled, behind Margaret, Fred had a wonderful sense of humor and a deep appreciation of the absurd. We took our child development classes seriously, but both of us felt bombarded at times by the numerous theoreticians whose names were tossed around as authorities. It was hard to keep all the experts and their theories straight, so we invented an imaginary expert, "Orvetta Wells," a universal child theoretician to whom we could turn when we forgot to attribute some bit of wisdom: "As Orvetta Wells would say . . ." we would mutter when a teacher would drop one too many names.

It was Fred's son, Jamie, who taught me directly about the transitional object, a Winnicott concept about the child's first bridge between reality and fantasy. Before Jamie's attendance in our center and not having yet read Winnicott, I had quietly discouraged children from bringing their blankets or soft animals, with the rationale that if they accidentally left them at school, they would be too distressed at home without them. But three-year-old Jamie's parents knew better. He had his beloved stuffed dog, Ann, and brought it to school as a matter of course. I felt slightly intimidated by having Fred Rogers' son as a pupil and did not feel I could prohibit his bringing the dog, which was clearly of great comfort to him. Once Jamie's Ann arrived, it was as if transitional objects came out of the woodwork, for every child who had one felt freed up to bring it. I learned a valuable lesson, for children did not forget to take them home, and the soothing they provided made the transition between home and school much smoother. Fred's intuitive knowledge about the usefulness of the transitional object became further elaborated on and translated into his masterful use of transitions on his program.

Prior to his child development studies, Fred had been the coproducer and behind-the-scenes puppeteer for an early TV show called *The Children's Corner*. There his humor and whimsy shone through in the creation of his puppet characters, some of whom are still part of his repertoire. This fantasy world of personalities portrays, then and now, the range of human foibles and individuality that are part of every child — for example, King Friday's omnipotence, Lady Elaine's troublemaking, Daniel's fearfulness, Henrietta's shy inarticulateness, and Cornflake's naïveté. But Fred was behind a screen with his puppets and served as a diffident counterfoil to Josie Carey, the onstage mistress of ceremonies. His creativity in his original music scores and in the puppets made the show unique for its time, but the Fred Rogers we now know was still in the background, hard working, inventive, and ever learning.

Fred began to test himself in direct work with children at the Arsenal Family and Children's Center. He would bring his puppets to the center and engage the children in dialogues with the various characters. His interactions were not for entertainment; he used the puppets to communicate with the children about their concerns and interests. Each puppet had a different appeal. I watched Fred blanch when the children would attack the nose of "X" the Owl, as if that protuberance were fair game for little boys very aware of their own extensions. King Friday — in spite of, or maybe because of, his omnipotence — was a great favorite. One child called out one day, "Bring out the father of them all!" referring to the king. And the same little boys who tweaked "X" the Owl's beak, one day rebelled at King Friday's dictatorial ways and turned their backs on him. Later they capitulated and showered the king with gifts of pictures and other homemade crafts in what seemed to be recompense for their anger at the authority represented in "the father of them all." Another time, a little girl who had just lost her pet bird told each puppet in turn with intense affect the story of the loss; her obliviousness to Fred's control of the puppets and her awareness of the distinct personality of each puppet were remarkable.

Fred used not only his puppets to relate to the children's emotional concerns but also his music. We were privileged to hear his old songs and the steady stream of new ones he was creating. The children listened to and sang the songs; they also danced to the improvisations he developed to their rhythms. One child, whose father was killed that year, turned to music and dancing for relief and for expression of the deep emotions that were tugging and pulling at her. Often Fred would take special time to match his music to her whirling and twirling, in recognition of the inarticulate nature of her feelings.

Then Fred left us for his year in Canada, a year that continued to shape and form *Mister Rogers' Neighborhood*. It was then, Fred said, that he came in front of the camera at the insistence of Fred Rainsberry, head of children's programming for the Canadian Broadcasting Corporation who said, "I've seen you talk with kids. Now I want you to try to do it to the camera."

Once again I was privileged to watch Fred perform, this time in front of the camera; I was struck by the glow that came over him as he greeted his unseen audience. It was indeed as if he were looking at and speaking to each child, just as he had at the nursery school. Later back in Pittsburgh one of my pupils said proudly, "Mister Rogers talks to me every day on TV."

(I have since learned of the importance of eye gaze in early parent-child contacts — the unspoken dialogue that goes on between infant and parent and that conveys a myriad of meanings. Daniel Stern, in *Diary of a Baby*, points out the importance of mutual gazing, not just in infancy, but all through life at moments of intense emotionality, such as lovemaking or anger. Somehow Fred knew this intuitively and has used his intense gaze to engage his child audience and the guests on his show.)

Fred's use of "real" and make-believe began in Canada. (The original *Children's Corner* was *all* make-believe.) He found the weaving of reality with fantasy to be a large challenge. He developed the show, he says, with the underlying philosophy that "Reality is the stuff dreams are made of. The more hints you can give to the child in reality, and the greater elaboration of those hints in make-believe, the more fun it is." As a creator, Fred gives us a glimpse of one of the many elements that make his show work — his joy in teaching and in pretending, which models for the children that it's fun, important, and essential to work *and* to play.

In his own childhood, Fred was an only (and probably lonely) child until age eleven. Because of this, he became a strong fantasy player. He used stuffed toys, but he especially relished a lead soldier-making kit from which he made and used soldiers and other figures. He also suffered from a wide range of childhood illnesses, including scarlet fever, a disease that (in those days) forced a child to be quarantined for a month or six weeks. The Robert Louis Stevenson poem "The Land of Counterpane," which begins,

"When I was sick and lay abed," had special meaning for him. Reflecting on those times, Fred has noted, "Nobody would wish a child to have that many illnesses, but who knows what adversity might force out of somebody." Already he was beginning to understand the therapeutic nature of fantasy.[1]

Once the format of the program had been fully developed, Fred and the other creative talent in the Neighborhood began crafting "theme weeks," where a full five-day cycle would be devoted to a single topic, such as competition, divorce, sharing, or learning, which is then interwoven into every aspect of the programs. In the old days such planning was not as premeditated — "It has gotten more and more conscious as I have grown more and more facile," he says now. "Something will pop up in fantasy that I dealt with in reality. It's like variations on a theme; the more that you live with something, the more varied you can make it. If you live with it long enough, you can find things that you never expected to find." If this sounds like psychoanalysis — another kind of journey of self-discovery — I don't think it's an accidental comparison. In helping children discover the fullness of their self-development, Fred has been discovering and sharing his own self in ever-evolving higher levels of sophistication and artistry.

After our nursery school year together, when Fred and I went our separate professional ways, I followed his career with interest and respect. I saw how he used Margaret's mentoring while deepening his child development insights on his own. Occasionally, I would watch his program to catch up on where *he* was developmentally, but also to monitor his impact on a growing horde of nieces and nephews, and now grandnieces and grandnephews, as well as on the children and grandchildren of my friends. When my grandnephew was diagnosed with a brain tumor, Fred responded to my anguish by setting a time to call Ian with whom he talked — or rather Ian talked to Fred — for over forty-five minutes. It was as if Fred were a member of the family with whom the child could confide and share the important news of his life — not the tumor, but about his sister's broken leg, the new baby who had just arrived, and the sheep that grazed in the backyard of his country home. Fred Rogers always practiced what so many development specialists never seemed to grasp: yes, children *are* endlessly fascinating research subjects, but first and foremost they deserve to be treated not like rats in a Skinner box, performing at will to prove our academic theories, but as unique and gifted individuals.

British child development theorist Donald W. Winnicott has written extensively about playing and reality, creativity, and the role of parent-child relationships. Winnicott suggests that early interactions between parent and child call for a "holding environment" in which the child develops a sense of the dependability of the outside world embodied in "good enough" parenting.[2] In having her needs met, the baby can begin to move toward separation.

> In the experience of the more fortunate baby (and small child and adolescent and adult) the question of separation in separating does not arise, because in the potential space between the baby and mother there appears the creative playing that arises naturally out of that relaxed state; it is here that there develops a use of symbols that stand at one and the same time for external world phenomena and for phenomena of the individual person who is being looked at.[3]

In this concept of *shared space*, babies and mothers together create what Winnicott calls *transitional objects* (a beloved blanket, diaper, scarf) that has attributes of each, but is separate from both. Winnicott believes that this is the first true act of creativity on the baby's part and leads the child into the symbolic world of play. Later this shared space includes play with other objects and people.

It is presumptuous to try to analyze a person in an attempt to understand the creativity that Fred has demonstrated over the years, but we can speculate that his early experiences as an only child with a mother clearly invested in the world of music and drama gave him the necessary "shared space" to create musically and playfully. Now he encourages *all* viewers to be in tune with their childlike natures, to be open to new experiences, to try out new ways of looking and doing, to suspend belief at times and join in a fantasy world made manageable by his preparations and mediations, to use pretend play for problem solving, to test out hypotheses (What will happen if . . . ?) and to appreciate the creative efforts of others. These are building blocks for creativity and learning.

In addition to helping children learn and be in tune with their feelings and to move comfortably between the worlds of play and reality, Fred Rogers uses his own immense wellsprings of creativity that make his show unique. His musical talent spills over into every aspect of the show and is so much of the background that it could get overlooked. It is mind-boggling to think that he writes the songs and the scripts and performs in front of the camera as well as supplying most of the puppet voices. The show appears to be low-keyed and relaxed, and its pace does not reflect the tremendous energy its creation requires. His early interest in music, spawned by his parents, is shared with his audience through his guests (opera stars, famous instrumentalists like Van Cliburn and Yo-Yo Ma, dancers). He has probably done more to introduce music to children than any other performer.

Through this space shared by Fred Rogers and his parents—indeed, between all parents and children—the child works at making sense of everyday reality. Caring adults interpret and narrate the child's common encounters. ("That roaring noise scared you? It's the blender that I'm using to fix your orange juice. Watch how I turn it on.") They enter into the child's more subjective experiences around reappearances and disappearances with games of peek-a-boo and around feelings of engulfment and abandonment through games of looming and distancing. ("I'm coming . . . I'm gonna get you . . . I got you!") Such facilitations help the child move back and forth between highly idiosyncratic thinking called primary process thinking toward secondary process thinking, which reflects the child's increasing experiences with and understanding of reality. At the same time, children are building internal working models of these interactions with the meaningful people in their lives. These models will come to guide all human interactions.[4]

So—if all goes well developmentally—children come to recognize the differences between real and pretend and to relish both the cognitive and affective aspects of their world. Once this milestone is achieved, children can use their knowledge to develop and enhance their play. The creativity, problem solving, and hypothesis testing—all integral to pretend play—are essential to cognitive development and to emotional growth.

As one example, *Mister Rogers' Neighborhood* spent a week on the topic of growing. (This is at the heart of Fred's messages to children—his oft-repeated confidence that they can and will grow, that it can be painful but rewarding, and that he and other grown-ups are there to support and enhance their growth.) Fred's treatment of this subject illustrates his understanding of reality versus fantasy. Here he creates the "shared space" Winnicott describes where children play about their subjective/pretend/affective world *and* their objective/real/cognitive world.

During the week's episodes, Fred interweaves into every segment the concept of growing. He starts the week off in the "real" neighborhood with a small model car and a set of blocks, which he uses to make a road. He tells of his own pretending as a child that he could drive a car just like his father and of his wish to be big like his father. This wish is mirrored in the Neighborhood of Make-Believe by Prince Tuesday who, yearning to be big like his father, King Friday, chafes at how long it takes to grow. An atmosphere of tension is created by the rumor of an amorphous menace, the "Big Thing," who is nearing the Neighborhood.

Back in his "real" living room, Fred resumes his play with the car and blocks, saying, "Only living beings like you and I grow. Other things like models and blocks don't grow because they aren't alive. We human beings grow because we are alive." He tops the program off with a video of the making of these tiny cars in a factory. The photography of the cars suspended on hooks and being spray-painted is breathtakingly beautiful; the ordinary is transformed into a visual work of art. Fred concludes the program with a heartfelt commentary, "I hope you feel good about the ways you are growing inside and out. We all need to feel good about growing."

The remainder of the week's programs provide variations on the theme. In the "real" world he plants a bean that sprouts toward the end of the week; he visits a flower conservatory; he does exercises to help with his growing; he brings in a fully grown cat and shows us a video of that cat as a kitten; he shows an album of baby pictures and later shows us these babies as grown-ups; he has a little girl demonstrate her beginning reading skills; he has his hair cut; and he introduces the Harlem Spiritual Ensemble, which has grown from a pair of singers to a group which perform around the world. In each of these visits he emphasizes and expands on the concept of growing, always ending by feeding his fish who, of course, are growing too.

On the set of Make-Believe, the theme gets played out with Prince Tuesday still railing against how slow his growing is proceeding. On a more metaphoric level the wish-fear around growing is exemplified by the tension continuing to build around the unknown Big Thing, which finally arrives. It frightens everyone because of its inexplicable nature and motivations. The characters act in their unique ways with the king announcing pontifically that "You are not to be afraid of anything" and the others hearing in that message sung by Handyman Negri that there must be something to be afraid of. In the end Bob Trow can understand the Big Thing's communication that it is harmless and needs to be nurtured; when that happens, it produces a shoot and a lovely flower.

There is a moving scene when King Friday addresses firmly and compassionately his son's wish to be big like him. "I happen to like you exactly as you are, Tuesday. You are growing every day, son. You are growing just right without any magic stuff. You are growing with just the right stuff already inside you — the same kind of stuff that's inside me. You are growing royally." In this dialogue he allies himself with his son by conveying his love and approval with warmth and dignity. It is touching (and amazing) to see how Fred depicts the small boy's patent relief through this father-son puppet episode.

Throughout the program he continues to maintain a steady stance of pretending by stating after each Make-Believe segment that what is happening in that neighborhood is pretend just as his set is real. (In another episode, King Friday gets the idea to build a pretend bubble all around the castle. When he asks Joe Negri to do the job, the handyman claims he can't: "The bubble you're talking about is just pretend." The King leans close to Negri and whispers, "So are we.")

On the affective level, Fred masterfully helps children confront their ambivalences around growing. In several episodes he plays games of disappearance and reappearance, through a jack-in-the box, hide-and-seek, and even a cognitive game of removing objects (plastic vegetables, model buildings) of the structures in the Neighborhood of Make-Believe. These age-old games help children deal with their wishes and fears around the inevitable separation from loved ones that is a part of growing up and away. By "playing out" these anxieties in familiar games, Fred dissects their fear into something manageable. For instance, he demonstrates to youngsters that having one's growing hair cut doesn't hurt in spite of the look of the barber shears and the sound of the electric razor. He talks of things growing youngsters can do that babies can't, and he sings several songs that consider the many aspects of growing: "Children Can," "You Are Special," "You're Growing," "I'm Taking Care of You," "Everybody Has a History," "I Like to Be Told," "I'll Think of You." Even King Friday's song of denial, "You Are Not to Be Afraid of Anything," offers Fred the opportunity to say that it is really okay to talk about being afraid.

In his final words to the children every day, he further explains the concept of growing — that it takes place inside and out little by little, that growing is learning to take care of yourself, that it feels good to grow, that everybody all over the world grows in similar ways, as well as in some particular ways. In the last episode of the week on growing, he summarizes enthusiastically, "Isn't it great to know we are alive and real and we can grow and grow and grow! Everybody you see is growing in some way."

While the week on growing demonstrates the way Fred comfortably creates the space to allow children to integrate concepts and feelings, there are other aspects to his artistry. Throughout his programs he models for children both the seriousness and joyfulness of the playful person. Jerome and Dorothy Singer, in *The House of Make-Believe*, recently compared the memories of childhood play as revealed in the writings of famous authors. The Singers conclude, "Memories of pretend play are often associated with a special person who encouraged play, told fantastic stories, or modeled play by initiating games, who perhaps had a flamboyant personality that inspired imitation or gave wonderful gifts of puppets and picture books or shared exotic travel adventures–who above all showed a trusting, loving acceptance of children and their capacity for playfulness." This description could well be of Fred Rogers and what he does, not just for one child, but for the millions of children who have viewed him over the years.

Helping children recognize the value (and necessary distinction) in play and reality requires an excellent play facilitator. Good players have had adults who have facilitated their play from infancy. Caregivers begin a play dialogue very early in their playful encounters — during feeding, diapering, and soothing. They make pretend gestures, change their voices in mock surprise, loom and distance themselves from the baby's view. Fred does this so unselfconsciously that it is sometimes missed — for example, when he zips up his sweater, he plays around with the speed of the zippering. He sometimes addresses inanimate objects such as the trolley, and he uses the word "pretend" as a matter of course, very unselfconsciously.

As children grow older, good facilitators supply time and a play space. Fred's set is designed to encourage make-believe play. He paces the program to the tempo children need to integrate rich stimuli. His voice is deliberately slow and if something happens too quickly in the Neighborhood of Make-Believe, he carefully explains it later, much like adults may need to see a fast-paced movie several times to catch the nuances that have flashed past the first time.

Good caregivers also narrate their own and their children's activities, thereby highlighting their unique qualities. While he cannot observe his child audience, Fred draws on his own recall of childhood interests and shares them with the children. In the week on growing, he talks of his love of miniature cars and his wish to drive a real one like his dad, a wish of most small boys. He tells of the first time he was allowed to feed the fish in his childhood home and of his mother's pride in his growing so that he could feed them just the right amount. He even states directly to the audience that the things he recalls liking to do as a little boy help him know what they might like to do. He narrates to the child what he, his visitors, and the puppets in Make-Believe are doing. The play themes and the actors' motivations give the children the message that play is important and serves a vital purpose. The sometimes spoken invitation is "Come play with me!" — the most potent form of play facilitation.

In exemplifying what the developmental literature says about the importance of caring adults in a child's life, Fred also models for parents the essential roles of *integrator* and *synthesizer*. Just as a good parent or teacher introduces concepts to children in a variety of contexts, Fred does this daily. When, for example, he is presented with a spray plant mister from someone at the conservatory, he uses it for the rest of the week on his sprouting bean plant and names it as he uses it. Further, when he gets his hair cut, he comments on the sprayer the barber uses and likens it to his plant mister. Finally, on the pretend episode of the Big Thing he has Purple Panda spray the Big Thing's emerging flower with a magic growing solution. This helps the child integrate the concept by encountering it in a multiplicity of contexts. He not only interweaves the broader concepts, such as growing, but also blends even the simplest concepts, adding pattern and variety to the final creation.

The program's context, as well as its content, helps children organize their understanding of the television world. Mister Rogers' creation of the "shared space" makes it possible for children and beloved adults to test out the meaning of inner and outer reality. The format of the program is almost invariant: from Fred's singing the same unchanging song as he enters the set, taking off jacket and shoes and putting on sweater and sneakers, and introducing some of his corps of regulars, such as Speedy Delivery McFeely, François Clemmons (the former Officer Clemmons, now leader of the Harlem Spiritual Ensemble), or even Maggie Stewart. To these he adds new neighbors such as his barber and Dale Lignoski of the Phipps Conservatory. Like a good parent Fred relates to these new people as familiar friends who, of course, are no threat to his child friends. Usually these visits take place at the beginning of the program and lead into the Neighborhood of Make-Believe, which echoes the visit in one way or another. For example, in the first growing episode, he and Mr. McFeely are taught exercises by Marilyn Barnett. Later in Make-Believe, Neighbor Aber, Prince Tuesday, and King Friday do the same exercises to help Tuesday in his search for ways to speed up his growing. The final segment may summarize the theme or add more information by way of a video. Then Fred feeds his fish, may remove a prop he has brought, like the jack-in-the-box, to take to his "real" home (even there he points out the different worlds he lives in), and sings an appropriate song to tie the program together. His final song is always the same, with the reassurance that he'll be back next time.

Young children like and need ritual, to know what to expect, and in a sense to be "in the know." (As Fred has said often, "The knowable is manageable.") Fred's format allows for this with its invariant structure into which variety can be added. Cognitive psychologists know that children learn best and attend more closely to stimuli that are familiar, yet have variety enough to be intriguing. Fred Rogers, like a good intuitive parent, knows this too. By organizing his television world, he helps children organize what they see. This is in marked contrast to many children's shows that consist of quick, unrelated episodes leading to fragmented understanding and behavior. In an era of fast food and fast imagery, both of which may be indigestible, *Mister Rogers' Neighborhood* stands out as an island of peace and coherence leavened by humor and a gut-level sense of how children come to understand and master the awesome developmental tasks.

We are left, then, with a man whose professional goal is to create a space where children can be comfortable about who they are, what they can do, and how they feel. He gives them the tools to navigate through the "neighborhoods" of reality and pretend, and the permission to use these tools to confront their own internal and external worlds. He models the use of these tools with a faithful stance of respect and decency for his fellow men and women.

The paths Fred and I have traveled both together and apart began in our own "shared space," learning and growing along with the children we studied. Would that we all could utilize our "internal working models" as Fred Rogers has for two generations of children. Even Orvetta Wells would be proud.

In "Fred's Shoes," Roderick Townley examines the format of the show itself: the setup and delivery of each week's themes. Despite the diversity evident in thousands of shows, one central element remains: Fred Rogers' use of transitional devices. Although humble objects in themselves — toy trolleys, for instance — these devices are deeply meaningful to children. They are, in fact, a fitting equivalent to the kind of "transitional objects" (teddy bears and such) seen in Nancy Curry's classroom.

The ultimate example of such a transitional device is Fred Rogers' shoes. "After so many years, it's hard to realize how oddly daring that little business with the shoes is," Townley says. "Even CBS's Dan Rather, who for a time seemed willing to try on every kind of sweater his producers could find in an effort to appear at ease on camera, never thought of taking off his shoes. A young viewer watching Mister Rogers change into his playtime sneakers," says Townley, "cannot help sensing that here is a man who's willing to meet the child halfway."

Townley received his Ph.D. from Rutgers and taught in South America on a Fulbright before turning to writing full time. His books include a critical study of William Carlos Williams, a novel, two volumes of poetry, and several nonfiction books. His poems, stories, and articles have appeared in The Paris Review, The North American Review, The New York Times, Western Humanities Review, and many other publications. He recently moved from New York to Kansas with his wife (writer Wyatt Townley), his daughter, and his cat.

Fred's Shoes

The Meaning of Transitions in *Mister Rogers' Neighborhood*

In the Fauvist paintings of Maurice de Vlaminck, there is always a pathway leading the eye safely through the fields and foliage of his color-splashed world. An analogous path can be found in the world Fred Rogers creates on *Mister Rogers' Neighborhood,* the longest-running program on public television. There's always a way for the child to get smoothly from one part of the program to the next.

Does the comparison with de Vlaminck seem far-fetched? Many people don't associate children's television (or *any* television) with "art." But no one who seriously examines the work Fred Rogers has done over three decades can doubt his artistry, unpretentious and understated though it may be. A central element of that artistry is his use of transitional devices. They consist of humble objects — shoes, for example — but humble as they are, the uses he puts them to are often complex and deeply meaningful to children.

The program always begins the same way: a delicate slither on the celesta to announce our entrance into a gentler world. The TV camera begins panning over a strangely traffic-free town — obviously a toy model — until it finds a familiar house. An upward scurry of piano music brings us inside the house, our eyes moving past the living room's whimsical traffic light, past the closet and the curtained window to an obviously lockless door. A crescendo of arpeggios climbs a seventh chord just as our eyes reach the door and our familiar friend walks in, singing, "It's a beautiful day in the neighborhood."

The opening of *Mister Rogers' Neighborhood* may be reassuring and nonthreatening, but it is also dramatic. In his quiet way, Fred Rogers makes an entrance worthy of a movie star, delighting children to the point of squeals because he appears at the culmination of a careful visual and musical buildup.

Once inside, Mister Rogers proceeds to bring the viewer in. "Won't you be my neighbor?" his song continues, as he hangs his jacket in the closet and slips on a comfy sweater. He shucks off his shoes and laces on sneakers as the song concludes: "Won't you, please? Won't you, please? Please, won't you be my neighbor?"

After so many years, it's hard to realize how oddly daring that little business with the shoes is. Even CBS's Dan Rather, who for a time seemed willing to try on every kind of sweater his producers could find in an effort to appear at ease on camera, never thought of taking off his shoes.

A young viewer watching Mister Rogers change into his playtime sneakers cannot help sensing that here is a man who's willing to meet the child halfway. That one action tells him that Rogers has a grown-up life of his own somewhere else, but that he has set aside this time to pay full attention to the child's concerns. By the time the sneakers are laced, the first cluster of transitions is complete. Mister Rogers has invited and welcomed the child into a safe, familiar, and caring world.

Rogers himself has said that "the matter of transitions is one of the most important aspects of the whole thing." But "the whole thing" here refers not only to the Neighborhood, but to the cycles of life. He defers to the late Margaret McFarland—his longtime mentor and psychological consultant to the program—who considered transitions as one of "the most important aspects of people's lives."

The problem, Rogers says, is that many people don't seem to believe that. We tend, he says, "to hurry through transitions and to try to hurry our children through them as well. We may feel that these transitions are 'nowhere at all' compared to what's gone before or what we anticipate is next to come."

Children's television programmers apparently share that feeling. Recall, for instance, the quick-cutting visual chaos of *Peewee's Playhouse*. *Sesame Street* provides an even more influential example of this quick-cut approach. Bert and Ernie, the letter J, a film clip of lions, and Oscar's trash can come zinging past the child's consciousness without any time provided to make connections, if indeed the connections exist. It is as if programmers were afraid to slow down the action, lest the child become bored and reach for the channel-changer.

Defenders of *Sesame Street* argue that, despite the instant switches, the show uses recurring characters and similar situations in many episodes (sometimes within the same episode), providing a sense of continuity. Time and again, for instance, the preschooler gets to see Kermit the Frog in his fearless reporter trench coat putting some adult twist on a childhood fairy tale. If the child misses the jokes about Rapunzel one week, he can catch the parody of Cinderella the next.

But such recurrent modules, popping out of the visual maelstrom at unpredictable moments, hardly add up to a sense of continuity. Such an approach encourages children to accept disorder as a representation of the way the world really is.

Without clear transitions, it is difficult for a young child to sustain concentration. After all, no one can concentrate if he is constantly interrupted, even by creatures as universally beloved as Grover or Big Bird. It's hard, therefore, to see the advantage of teaching preschoolers letters and numbers if one is ultimately compromising their ability to concentrate.

Several studies of preschoolers reveal that children shown episodes of *Mister Rogers' Neighborhood* were better able to concentrate and stick with an activity than were children who had been shown high-action cartoons. In part, this may be attributable to the overt messages of the Rogers shows (including supportive songs such as "Children Can" and "You've Got to Do It"). But another cause may be the fact that Rogers never breaks the child's concentration. There is always a neural pathway to follow from one activity to the next.

Looking back, Rogers identifies *Laugh-In* as the program that introduced the pseudopsychedelic quick-cut to the TV lexicon. In the late 1960s, the device was effective in shocking adults into laughter. It was never intended as a tool for early childhood development. But imitation, we know, is the sincerest form of television, and before long it seemed you couldn't have a program without finger-snapping quick-cuts from scene to unrelated scene.

"I've resisted that," says Rogers. "I'm interested in continuity. There's something that goes against my existential being to have things cut up like that."

Although Rogers consults with child psychologists before adding new elements to the program, he also relies a great deal on instinct. For instance, he says he can't recall how he first thought of changing his shoes on the program. "As I come to think about it, maybe it was just to set the tone. There is so much that's so fast about television. Wherever you're placed on the television schedule you know very well there's going to be some hyper thing before you, and it goes off in a very hyper way, so we have some music and movement right away to help make the transition."

Longtime associate producer Hedda Sharapan confirms that transitions on the program often come from hunch and instinct. Even the trolley that takes us from the "real" living room to the Neighborhood of Make-Believe originated in a personal feeling, she says. Really any vehicle, from skateboard to rocket ship, might have served as a transition object for that part of the program. "But Fred wrote me a note saying he remembered coming into Pittsburgh as a child and riding the trolleys," she recalls. "There was something fascinating about it for him." Such personal connections, she thinks, result "in the best kind of creative work."

The shoes, the sweater, and the trolley, says Rogers, are the "three major symbols" on the program; and they are all transitional devices. They ease the child into the next segment, or the next idea. They get him around the set.

Other transitional objects are perhaps less obvious. The character of Mr. McFeely, the Speedy Delivery postman, is himself a walking, talking transitional device, a liaison from the outside world to the intimate domain of the show. On one level, he serves to deliver props to the set. Things don't just appear in *Mister Rogers' Neighborhood:* They are brought by a trusted person.

Often Mr. McFeely (played by David Newell) brings little video documentaries to play on the Picture-Picture machine, and he usually stays to narrate them. Of course, the documentaries all lead directly into the day's theme. On one of Fred Rogers' hour-long home videos (*Music and Feelings*), Mr. McFeely brings in a documentary about the manufacture of bass violins. Later in the program, Fred Rogers visits cellist Yo-Yo Ma at Negri's music shop. And during the make-believe segment, King Friday orders everyone to participate in a bass violin festival (even though he's the only one who can play the instrument). The child is treated to a medley of interconnections.

The metaphor of music is particularly apropos to the topic of transitions. "The insides of me," says Rogers, "from the very beginning, have been connected to music." He composes the songs used on the show, and he tends to think of transitions in musical terms. "I've always had the analogy of moving from one key to another in the program," he says. In order to "modulate" from the living room to the Neighborhood of Make-Believe, for instance, "you want to find as many notes in the new key that are the same as the notes in the old key. And you play with those and almost imperceptibly get into the new key." In the modulation from C to F, he says, only the B-flat is new. "There are a lot of notes you can play as if you were playing in both keys. So little by little you get into F."

He gives a homely example: "If you're taking a child to a new school for the first time, it's very helpful for that child to see the mother and the teacher together and to know that they have good feelings about each other. That's a little like playing in both keys at the same time for a while."

This gradual extension of the child's world is crucial to the development of trust, and it goes back to earliest childhood. In his book *Mister Rogers' How Families Grow*, Rogers talks about "a child's transition from the oneness with the mother to relationships with a world full of people — first other people in the family, and then all those people beyond." In the neighborhood represented on the program, Mister Rogers is the primary figure, analogous to the parent. Through carefully built transitions, the child is helped to branch out to Mr. McFeely, Betty Aberlin, Joe Negri, and "other people in the family"; and finally to nonregulars (drop-in guests like Julia Child or Tony Bennett) — "all those people beyond."

These modulations are often quite complex. An episode about talent, for instance, begins with Mister Rogers demonstrating a couple of exercises he learned over at the Neighborhood gym. He tells his "television neighbor" that a friend of his, Hindu dancer Via Vetra, is rehearsing at the gym right now, and suggests they visit her.

The Neighborhood itself serves transitional functions. It's a friendly neighborhood, for one thing. It's not a jungle out there. If Mister Rogers goes to visit someone at the gymnasium, the camera watches him wave and walk out his door, then follows his route along the streets of the model village, finally zooming in on the model of the gym. Only then do we see Mister Rogers entering a real-looking gym. And of course, wherever he goes, he introduces each new person to "my television neighbor." At every point the child sitting at home is included, acknowledged, treated as a collaborator.

Like the mother paving the way with the new teacher, Mister Rogers talks with the unusual-looking Ms. Vetra and asks her to show his television neighbor a Hindu dance. She explains a number of hand gestures, or *mudras*, and Mister Rogers tries them out, inviting the child at home to do the same. Then Ms. Vetra performs a story dance, bringing together the gestures for deer, lotus, waterfall, and so on.

About to leave the gym, Mister Rogers runs into Betty Aberlin, who has come by to show him a pastel drawing by singer Tony Bennett, another old friend. Mister Rogers muses that people can be good at more than one thing, then he heads back to his house, while the camera follows his route through the model town.

Once home, he proposes a little trip to the Neighborhood of Make-Believe. "We could make believe that Tony Bennett visits Lady Elaine's Museum-Go-Round television station," he tells the viewer, thus signaling that fantasies don't just happen to people. We are in control of the contents of our own make-believe.[1]

In this episode, Mister Rogers forgoes the trolley and uses an alternate means of transportation. He takes out models of the principal Make-Believe buildings, including Lady Elaine's Museum-Go-Round. The camera focuses on the spinning museum, then dissolves to the Neighborhood of Make-Believe, where a nervous Lady Elaine is getting ready for the appearance of Tony Bennett on her TV show.

When the singer saunters in carrying a sketch pad, Lady Elaine doesn't recognize him. She's expecting a person who sings, not a person who draws. He begins to sketch Lady Elaine and sings the Rogers song, "Sometimes Isn't Always" ("Sometimes I feel like . . . sometimes I don't"), reinforcing the point that people don't always have to do what others expect.

The scene dissolves to the spinning model of the Museum-Go-Round, and we are back in the living room, where Mister Rogers talks about what we've just seen. He takes out a sketch pad and draws a few lines, strengthening the transition from the visit with Tony Bennett. Then we see that Mister Rogers has drawn a stylized deer. The lines correspond to the deer gesture that Via Vetra taught us earlier. Mister Rogers puts his hand into the same gesture and asks if the child at home remembers how to do it. He then makes the lotus flower gesture, and (as he passes the fish tank) the fish gesture. Every element in the program is sewn together in a subtle fabric, stitched with a single needle.

Even his farewell song, with the lines, "I'll be back when the day is new, and I'll have more ideas for you," comprises a transition of its own, setting up anticipation for his next visit. Issues of disappearance and reappearance are very important to young children, who want to be reassured that when parents go away they will return. In fact, the trolley itself addresses this need: After it takes us to the Neighborhood of Make-Believe, it always brings us back to Mister Rogers' living room.

The tooting, smooth-rolling trolley is a particularly reassuring element on the show. Physical movement is a subject of great interest to kids just learning to crawl or walk. Children, Rogers once wrote, are "so intensely involved in learning how to get around that anything suggesting mobility can captivate them. Things on wheels, like trucks, can hold special delight for a toddler because they roll along with such ease."

It's true that Mister Rogers, not the child, controls the trolley's arrival and departure schedule, but in every other way the child's collaboration is essential. For one thing, the trolley is empty. It takes the child's own vision to fill it with people.

And when the trolley pulls up in front of the castle, the first-time viewer may be disappointed to find that all the inhabitants of the Neighborhood of Make-Believe have immobile, impassive faces. Lady Elaine's face seems actually crude. There's not a soft, expressive, high-tech, Muppetlike creature in the lot. They are, in a sense, projective devices onto which the child casts his own meanings. It is the child's power of visualization that helps the puppets make the transition to "reality," just as, in the classic tale *The Velveteen Rabbit*, it is a child's love that allows an old tattered bunny to come to life.

It may be accurate to call *Mister Rogers' Neighborhood* a travel program. In the first part of the show, the viewer gets to walk a mile in Mister Rogers' shoes as he goes about the neighborhood visiting and learning. For the make-believe section, the trolley becomes the vehicle of choice, and the journey is no longer from one neighbor to another, but from the outer world to an inner world, or from the waking world to dream.

The form of the show, says Rogers, is usually A-B-A-C-A, like the theme-and-variation form of a musical composition. "We start in my room [A], and from there go to some place like Brockett's Bakery [B], as a way of collecting things for the dream. Then we come back [A] and talk about what we have just seen, and then we introduce this dream and go into it [C]. And when we come back [A], we reflect on it."

In some ways, he notes, the transition from reality to make-believe resembles the film version of *The Wizard of Oz*. Once Dorothy has ridden her whirlwind to the technicolor world on the other side of the rainbow, Kansas farmhands turn into the Scarecrow, the Tin Man, and the Cowardly Lion. Similarly, says Fred Rogers, "the inhabitants of the Neighborhood become part of the dream. For instance, Maggie Stewart, who is someone who lives in my [television] neighborhood, becomes Mayor Maggie when we make believe. Betty Aberlin, who has a little theater in the Neighborhood, becomes the niece of King Friday XIII in the Neighborhood of Make-Believe."

In *The Wizard of Oz*, the changes in appearance reflect aspects of Dorothy's transformation. The same can be said of Fred Rogers' program, only here the person being transformed, or at least helped, is the child viewer. For instance, the fears he may have of abandonment are often addressed by Daniel Striped Tiger (a sort of Cowardly Lion) in the make-believe segment. A child's proud reluctance to share toys may be dealt with through the egotistic antics of Lady Elaine. Then, after the make-believe segment is over, Mister Rogers is there to look the child in the eye as only he can and talk the issues over some more.

It's natural to think of the passage from reality to make-believe in terms of the transition from wakefulness to dream. But there's also an archetypal dimension to all this. The soul's journey from the secular world to some celestial or infernal counterworld has been a staple of mythology since primitive times. The Greco-Roman model, as most of us learned in grade school, showed the newly deceased entering a cave and descending to the River Lethe, River of Forgetfulness, where they proceeded to board Charon's ferry for the trip to Hades.

In the Christian schema, one finds similar migrations from here to eternity. Bunyan's seventeenth-century account depicts the journey of a weary pilgrim named Christian from the City of Destruction to the Heavenly Gates. Adding a little whimsy to that story, Nathaniel Hawthorne came up with a nineteenth-century update, "The Celestial Railroad": "Not a great while ago, passing through the gate of dreams, I visited the region of the earth in which lies the famous City of Destruction. It interested me much to learn that by the public spirit of some of the inhabitants a railroad has recently been established between this populous and flourishing town and the Celestial City." Add yet more whimsy and a touch of warmth to Hawthorne's account, and we find ourselves in a landscape in which Fred Rogers' trolley might safely operate.

The point is not that Rogers consciously considered such paradigms when he came up with the idea of the trolley. The trolley is no more a refurbishing of Charon's ferry than King Friday is a reimagining of the king of the underworld — or the King of Heaven, for that matter. But in Western culture such paradigms underlie much of our moral and aesthetic thinking, whether we're aware of the fact or not. They provide preexistent patterns that shape the way we picture ourselves. Even the most imaginative, avant-garde artists make use of such patterns. Jean Cocteau's film *Orfée* owes much of its power to the superimposition of ancient myth onto modern life.[2] Cocteau's crossbreeding of pagan and Christian symbolism, fertilized by modern dream psychology, is no doubt anathema to many theologians, but it resonates deeply. I suspect that is because myth, Christianity, and psychology are structurally similar. They fit over one another like a grid.

And so, as Mister Rogers invites his television neighbor to take the trolley to the Neighborhood of Make-Believe, he is in a sense reenacting a process as ancient as mankind. With no theological overlay, he is helping children to feel comfortable making interior journeys from the visible to the invisible and safely back again. It is the same migration they take each night as they clutch their teddy bear and go off to sleep. And it is the same route they may someday use to find their way into prayer and meditation.

And always there is the kind, quiet figure of Mister Rogers to help them on their journey. He plays the role of Virgil to the viewer's Dante, Heurtebise to Orpheus, Moses to the Israelites. Like Moses, he does not enter the Promised Land of the child's imagination — we never see him in the Neighborhood of Make-Believe — but his presence is everywhere. Rogers provides the voices for King Friday XIII, Queen Sara, "X" the Owl, Daniel Striped Tiger, and most of the other puppets. They are all, he says, aspects of his own personality. He is the Prospero in his own television *Tempest*.

It is in this role that we see Rogers' true generosity. He is always seeking to empower children, encouraging them to make up their own stories, imagine their own make-believe kingdoms. His intention is not to rule over those kingdoms, but to pass the magic wand to the children watching at home. Everything he does gives the same message: The world doesn't need more viewers, it needs more Prosperos. That is Rogers' greatest ambition — to invest each child with power over his own inner life.

In this essay, renowned cellist (and Neighborhood guest) Yo-Yo Ma and flutist-writer Eugenia Zukerman discuss the role of music in Fred Rogers' programs. In the free-flowing interview below (edited for brevity), Ma commends Rogers and musical director Johnny Costa for including elements of jazz, classical, folk, and dance music into the show's repertoire. Such openness to diverse tastes are crucial for children, Ma says, especially when art is often parsed, separated, and categorized: This is my music; that's your music. "In this Neighborhood, all types of music are included, so it's every child's music," Ma says. "So these children [will grow up to] say, 'Wait a minute! I heard those things when I was three on Mister Rogers. You can't tell me 'It's not my music'!"

It's exactly this openness and vulnerability that allows artists — whether world-class cellists or children's television hosts — to access something transcendent. "I think the moments that I treasure in music and performing are the ones when I feel I'm participating in something much larger than what I'm doing at the moment," Ma muses. "The idea of service is probably not too removed from what a musician tries to deal with. Service to the composer's idea, service to just give, to celebrate, to share. . . . That's what Fred Rogers tries to do."

Zukerman is the author of Deceptive Cadence, Taking the Heat, *and numerous screenplays. She is also an internationally known flutist as well as arts commentator of CBS News'* Sunday Morning. *She has published in the* New York Times, Vogue, *and other publications and is currently working on her third novel. Yo-Yo Ma received an A.B. degree from Harvard and studied with Leonard Rose at the Julliard School of Music. He has appeared with Pablo Casals, Isaac Stern, and Leonard Bernstein among others and has performed throughout the world with major orchestras. He made his debut at age nine at New York's Carnegie Hall. Ma won the Avery Fisher prize in 1978 and has won several Grammy Awards as well.*

Musical Notes:

An Interview with Yo-Yo Ma

Zukerman: Yo-Yo, do you remember the first time you met Fred Rogers?

Ma: The first time I met him I was totally surprised. I wasn't comfortable when he sat next to me — about three inches away from my face — and smiled and said, "I'm so happy you're here." I started sweating. Then I realized that that's what our kids do to us. You know — "Daddy I love you so much," or "I'm so glad you're my daddy." Kids of a certain age really have no barriers and are not socialized to have certain . . . they don't have to be "cool," they don't have to be "with it," or whatever. I think Fred Rogers deliberately opens himself to such an extent that to a socialized person it seems somewhat ridiculous to act that way. But actually that's what three-year-olds are used to and that's what they want; they want to believe in somebody. I think Mister Rogers feeds on that trust, that pact that he has with his television viewers.

Zukerman: And it's this pact, this tremendous trust that he creates, that allows him to use music in a special way? So that he doesn't have to pander to kids but actually uses music in a way that other programs don't?

Ma: Absolutely. He is not there to entertain kids, and the parents don't have to entertain their kids, either. But I think kids also pick up on their parents' passions if the parents care to share them. If you are genuinely interested in something then you'll say something about it. It's not pandering and it's not saying "this is something you have to know." Instead, it's saying "this is something that is important to me and I want to share it with you." In Fred's case, I know he loves music. His wife is a pianist, and I think he studied composition in college.

Zukerman: He did, in Florida. Rollins College.

Ma: So he has a long history of playing music, writing music, and that's why the music is there. Of course, there are educational reasons, but I think one of the main reasons it's there is because Fred Rogers really loves it.

Zukerman: One thing that comes to mind is the function of music in our society. As civilization developed, so much of oral history was taught through music and chants—the important things of life were taught that way. I've always wondered, what is it that we've lost in today's culture? Have we lost our ability to impart emotion in story? In other cultures, they sit around and sing about the past and we get a sense of the emotion of it. Do you think that Mister Rogers' music imparts emotion in and of itself?

Ma: Music enters into the show in wonderful ways. Sometimes as a simple song that he reads at the beginning, or the little operas in the Neighborhood of Make-Believe, or with the tapes that Mr. McFeely brings in to show on Picture-Picture . . . it comes in at so many levels. There's the story level, the primal level, and the transitional levels that take us out of our present context into another context, into the lands of kings and queens and powerful figures. Yet somehow it is safe to deal with those figures. Then we come back to the present world and time frame with a different perspective. It's so good for a child, or even an adult, to be able to exercise that change in perspective because that develops our imagination.

Zukerman: As well as our sense of individuality. I think that's one thing Mister Rogers seems to talk about a lot, how "you make every day special just by being you." Stories about a cow who wanted to be a potato bug, for example—that theme of someone wanting to be someone else and then realizing who they are is just fine. Always the songs are about being who you are.

Ma: Right. I remember one song that [my son] Nicholas used to love: "You are special on the outside / you are special on the inside." So I know it affected at least one child to think about an inner life, their soul. I think it's really important that kids know that they own their souls and their bodies, their feelings.

The other thing I think Fred Rogers does is to make himself vulnerable. In some ways that's a precondition to listening to music—open to fear, sorrow, anger . . . to enjoy all those wonderful feelings, *and it's all allowed*. There's no taboo in his musical language. Anything you want to talk about — that's part of the unconditional thing that he has with the viewer — "I will discuss anything and then you can feel anything; you are allowed to feel anything." So often a part of socialization is that boys shouldn't cry, or we should be this way or that. It's part of growing up. But during that period when children are extremely open, Mister Rogers gives them as much as possible.

Zukerman: In a couple of segments that you did with him, Fred said to the viewer, "Yo-Yo's music touches something that is so deep inside." Do you think that kids could understand what he meant? Does saying that help kids to understand what the meaning of music is?

Ma: I am sure you have played in front of little kids in classrooms where they write something about what you did. Isn't it great that you don't know what they are going to say? Sometimes they feel sad; sometimes they feel like something is so beautiful they feel like crying. You get a real variety of reactions. They'll draw pictures or write poems. There are so many ways to react and the amazing thing is that every class that you play for will have a different set of reactions. That is what Fred Rogers tries to do on television.

Zukerman: I noticed in a segment you did with Nicholas, your son seemed to be so completely at ease and Mister Rogers seemed to be enjoying it so much. I thought that was one of the most extraordinary things I've seen you do. It's one thing to be comfortable in front of the camera, but with your child you must have been so aware of what his needs were and of Mister Rogers being there. Was it as relaxed as it seemed and did Nicholas feel particularly open because it was Mister Rogers?

Ma: I think Nicholas was at first frightened to see Mister Rogers with makeup — you know, the whole thing, the television crew, lighting, different house pretending that this was his house. We had to film it several times and still not get stilted, but it was a wonderful experience after those initial shocks.

Zukerman: It was lovely to watch. You were invited to play some Bach, and not a sound-byte length for little kids. That speaks a great deal about who Fred Rogers is and his feeling about music, doesn't it?

Ma: He doesn't just film for kids, he sets the mood: "We really love this music, we respect it, and this is a special person coming to play something—let's really enjoy it." I think that's all it takes. It's the same with adult audiences. If you tell them you really love this particular piece, they'll go along with you. I think Mister Rogers does the same thing.

Zukerman: Do you think Fred Rogers uses music to impart words that teach, or is he teaching music?

Ma: Both. Music deals with feelings or memory of feelings or abstract things or spatial feelings—you know, feelings of space, feelings of something grand. Fred Rogers uses it in all kinds of ways, as well as to make a point with a story. He uses music to show all these things are possible within you. It creates the space of *possible* knowledge, of feeling with words, stories, fears, all those things. Kids can go on to do whatever they wish to do with it.

Zukerman: Fostering individuality with the music.

Ma: I think so. And not just individuality but community—there's always the Neighborhood, there's some structure there. He is, after all, *Mister* Rogers, not "Fred." He's not, "Hey, I'm your buddy"; he's an authority figure but a very gentle one. The fact that he's a minister and that this is his ministry means something. I think the moments that I treasure in music and performing are the ones when I feel I'm participating in something much larger than what I'm doing at the moment. The idea of service is probably not too removed from what a musician tries to deal with. Service to the composer's idea, service to just give, to celebrate, to *share*, as opposed to the feelings of dominating, impressing, proving something. That's what Fred Rogers tries to do as a minister, dealing with children as his ministry. That's his audience. He just shares what he knows and cares about and that's again a feeling—probably the underpinning of the whole philosophy behind *Mister Rogers' Neighborhood*.

Zukerman: You know what comes to mind? I think it was Plato who said, "Music is a path between ourselves and the infinite." Do you think possibly that because Fred Rogers is a minister that he has a sense of music opening a spiritual door for children?

Ma: Absolutely. I think children are so open to all kinds of levels of thinking, yet sometimes it passes by. I think we all are kind of tuned into it. Some people more so than others. But I don't think he's proselytizing. I don't think he's saying, "This is the only way to go." He's saying that it's a possibility. Music is a possibility to a different way of thinking.

Zukerman: What about gentleness and music? His show is gentle and the music generally is gentle. Have you ever heard him use music to bring out dark feelings, fears, a child's sense of demons?

Ma: In the segment that I did with him I played a little snippet of [Dimitri] Shostakovich material — a very angry piece, so we did talk about feelings. I don't think he is adverse to including these darker feelings.

Zukerman: I did a piece for *Vogue* about Zara Nelsova, the cellist. She prepared for concerts by taking a nap in the afternoon, and when she lies down she likes to watch *Mister Rogers*.

Ma: Well that's very interesting . . . taking a nap, watching *Mister Rogers* to calm down — it makes sense. I think it takes you to a place that is just between consciousness and unconsciousness — freedom to associate, freedom to be very free while you are about to do something very structured. The thing I think about most before a concert — other than "Am I really going to mess this up? Please, just let me get through this!" — is the sense that I really love this, I really want to do it. So I let that be the dominant thought, rather than the fear. The program really could calm me down so that can happen; maybe that's why Zara likes it. Boy, that's wild. She loves it, eh?

Zukerman: Yes, it is wonderful. Here's a mature woman saying this very openly, but also like, "Don't write this — people would think I am silly."

Ma: I think it is very, very touching.

Zukerman: I want to talk a little bit more about the technique of the music on the program. Are you aware that Johnny Costa took the opening chords, I think sort of a four-note chord, from Beethoven's Sonata in C Major? Just look at how he mixes things! There are other things he took from Art Tatum. The keyboard sounds are very open texturally — they're never heavy. Yet the music is always improvised.

Ma: I love the fact that it's improvised. Johnny Costa talks about how the music is always different, but that somehow he has to make it end exactly at the right moment. The timing has to be exact, depending on the way Mister Rogers sings it. Each day is different, so why shouldn't the theme song be different? It's wonderful that they can do that.

Zukerman: The show has a trio now, with a bass and drums.

Ma: They have elements of jazz, classical, folk, dance; it's all inclusive, it's all there. Elements of everything [children] will hear as they grow up. That's so important in our sometimes divisive society where you have this kind of separation of art: "This is my music, not yours. I don't like your music." In *this* Neighborhood, all types of music are included, so it's every child's music. So those children will say, "Wait a minute! I heard those things when I was three on *Mister Rogers*. You can't tell me 'It's not my music'!"

Zukerman: Fred Rogers and Johnny Costa have worked together to almost make music the most important thing in the program. But because it's a kids' program, Fred's choice of lyrics are just as important as his choice of notes.

Ma: The things that kids learn before the age of three — it's like a scent; it's part of their permanent knowledge. Music can be like that. You say, "I remember that smell or that sound from when I was very young." It has a direct link to certain emotions or events. And so if you link an important word concept with music for a child when they're most impressionable, whatever they receive can go into their permanent memory banks. That's an incredible thing to do.

Zukerman: About his singing. . . . When you think about Mister Rogers' voice, you think of . . .

Ma: Luciano Pavarotti.

Zukerman: Okay, let's face it. This is *not* Pavarotti's voice, and yet, it is very effective in portraying whatever message it is that he wants to say. Maybe the fact that he is not Pavarotti makes the kids more comfortable to think, "I can sing like that."

Ma: It's interesting that he's not trying to be a performer, but yet he is "performing" on television by being himself. I think he is very much like that in real life. Like his make-believe, he's trying to be as natural as possible. . . . I know that he actually gets very nervous doing the shows — imagine! After twenty-five years doing the show . . .

Zukerman: Well over one thousand shows, I think.

Ma: Something like that. I guess he'll want to give it up soon. It must take too much out of him to do it. But when performers tell me they're quitting — I hate to hear that, whatever the reason. Yet I know it must be wearing. It's a lot of training, of doing things over and over again, so that it's absolutely natural.

Zukerman: The different musical textures that are in different parts of the show — you were saying these are things that we will remember subliminally. When it's time for Make-Believe, the trolley shows up, and there's a bell sound. Do you think that kids are aware that the music has changed and that the texture is different?

Ma: It's not, "Let's now make a leap of imagination and pretend," but "Let's get on the train and physically go someplace else." And you have the music going *dadadada dededede, ding, ding, ding!* There's always that piece of transitional music.

Zukerman: For instance, when he comes in the door and puts on his sweater? The music that's used for that is kind of a metamorphosis; we don't really have a sense of time, but instead the theme creates a mood.

Ma: It's just not a theme song that says, "I present to you Mister Rogers!" Mister Rogers just kind of slips into your consciousness. It's not wildly exciting; you're right. It's not unbelievably calm, either. It's a gentle song that creates a transition from whatever the kid is doing — or maybe whatever the parent is doing. Rogers does something physical: he takes his sweater off, and we shed our layers, too, to get into the show. And the music accentuates the physical change. He's taking off the jacket, the tie, the shoes, putting on the sneakers and the famous cardigan, one of which is now in the Smithsonian, right next to the Elvis memorabilia. So it's another kind of transition that is both gentle and physical.

Zukerman: In one of the segments where you played, you said that sometimes when you are on the road, you wish you were somewhere else; a sense of longing, I think you said. Wishes play a large part on *Mister Rogers* — you know, where kids want to be someone else. Mister Rogers acknowledges the wish, but drives home the point that who you are is just great. Do you think music in some way reflects that idea? Do you think that kids just intuitively pick up on the emotions that music imparts?

Ma: I think so. Child development studies show that all kids respond to music, and dance to music, when they are about two years old. It's programmed, so there are no unmusical people — there's no one who doesn't respond at all to music, unless they can't hear.

Zukerman: I think the music is in some way mood-altering for children. That may explain the tempo of the music that Fred Rogers and Johnny Costa choose.

Ma: Well, it seems that one of the absolute priorities of *Mister Rogers' Neighborhood* is that it be a safe program. The kids feel safe. So all the music, the imaginative loops, the transitions, have to be safe. You can deal with unsafe feelings, but the program itself has got to be safe. That's part of the trust.

Zukerman: And I guess it's something that works both ways. There is something that is so different about *Mister Rogers*—it's interactive, in a sense. Somehow the music interacts with the viewer.

Ma: It's interactive in that he accepts the unseen viewer, he allows the viewer time to respond to what he says to them in those long, uncomfortable silences. We're used to a faster-paced program where we're bombarded by stimuli; it's reflective of the real world outside. But in the safe environment he creates, Mister Rogers really allows the length of time you need to accept an idea or to feel something and to respond.

Zukerman: There is a real inner-logic to his music-making. It's almost as if the thoughts just come out musically, so it's part of our everyday life instead of something extraneous to it.

Ma: The music is part of your imagination, your journey from one place to another; it's part of being in that next place; it's part of his gentle arrival at the beginning of the show, and leaving at the end. It's totally integrated. I think that's sort of why you cannot think of a specific Mister Rogers' song, why it's hard to just sing one out of context.

Zukerman: Do you think of Mister Rogers as an arbitrator of musical taste to our children?

Ma: Maybe as an arbitrator of taste for two- to five-year-olds . . . well, I think he opens the path. Rather than say, "this is better," or "you're good, but this is better." Taste ends up essentially the choice of the individual but Fred Rogers provides a lot of possibilities on the Neighborhood. I think he creates possibilities, not taste. In the show's own musical compositions, a lot of improvisation goes on, so there are always lots of possibilities.

Zukerman: Right. He invites the kids into his Neighborhood and he invites them into the music as well.

Ma: When he stops doing his show, I think it will be a very severe loss. He helps form values, not taste, but values.

Zukerman: Plato said—I'm not quoting—that music is a moral law, it gives wings to the imagination, makes our spirit soar. Is there a sense in which Mister Rogers imparts that?

Ma: Music is so much a part of Fred Rogers' life, it's an extension of himself, an expression of his values. I don't know whether music is moral law. I think music — like anything, like a language — can be used for many purposes, so it's also how we use it. Is it moral to play Wagner's music at certain times for certain people? Because you associate certain things with it, it can take on other values. I think it is very difficult to discuss that.

Zukerman: What you are saying is that music is so powerful, that . . . well, look at some countries. Some governments are frightened of musicians and of music makers. They're frightened of poets and they're frightened of composers. Look at what the Soviet Union did to some of its musicians, forcing them to not write music that they feared would be revolutionary. It's ironic that Vaclav Havel is waiting to talk with you after this interview is over. . . .

Ma: Jazz musicians were arrested in Czechoslovakia; Beethoven was banned in China for a while. Yes, music can be a seditious force. . . . Having been on the show and knowing Fred Rogers, having my children watch *Mister Rogers' Neighborhood* has opened my life, *our* lives, to things that sometimes we don't think about. This conversation makes me realize how much thought went into this program that we take for granted. What a poorer place our culture would be if that program did not exist.

Susan Linn's appreciative essay on Mister Rogers' puppets begins with a bemused assessment of the puppets themselves: "Their mouths do not move. Their eyes do not track. They have no feet," Linn notes. "To the annoyance of my puppeteer friends, we do not watch the Neighborhood of Make-Believe to marvel at flawless manipulation." Instead, she says, her friends — and her children — are drawn to the puppets by something far more elemental: "We watch because we have come to care about the essence of these characters. . . . We recognize ourselves in their complexity."

As a puppeteer and a psychologist, Linn explores both the character and the role played by the four major (and longest-lived) puppets: King Friday, "X" the Owl, Lady Elaine, and Daniel Striped Tiger. Because these characters first came into being on live television (on The Children's Corner, *with host Josie Carey), Fred Rogers never knew what Josie Carey would say next. "Since dead air — unintentional silence — is anathema on live television, [he] had to respond, in character, and he had to respond quickly," Linn says. "In that kind of improvisational dialogue, a puppeteer has no time to censor or to formulate a careful response."*

As a result of such spontaneity, the puppets are deeply rooted in Fred Rogers' creative psyche. "They each began as an undefended projection of Fred Rogers' inner world," Linn says. "Just as a sculptor might perceive a figure as inherent in stone or wood, these characters were inherent in Fred Rogers."

Linn is the associate director of programming at the Media Center for Children, Judge Baker Children's Center. She received her doctorate from Harvard University in counseling and consulting psychology. She has performed nationally as a puppeteer and ventriloquist on television and in live performances. Her work with puppets and therapy for hospitalized children has taken her around the country and the world for presentations and demonstrations.

Susan Linn

With an Open Hand

Puppetry on *Mister Rogers' Neighborhood*

At the hopeful and determined age of twenty, I took a plane from Boston to Pittsburgh to meet Fred Rogers. The year was 1968. *Mister Rogers' Neighborhood* had been on public television for nearly one year.

I was, then, a fledgling performer with a penchant for puppetry and a growing interest in child psychology. *Mister Rogers' Neighborhood* was truly a phenomenon: a television show that embodied the developmental and psychological theories that fascinated me. Played out before my eyes were issues of self-esteem, body integrity, autonomy, and a full range of childhood preoccupations. I knew I had to meet him.

Much of our first encounter is a blur, but one sentence has stayed with me all these years. After I introduced Fred to my puppets and we chatted for a while, he remarked, "I think that somehow you must remember what it was like to be a child." That was his sole suggestion for success.

Twenty-five years later, mulling over Fred's puppets as I write this chapter, this comment reverberates. Somehow, Fred Rogers must remember what it was like to be a child — and his puppets are the realization of that child's voice. Above all else, it is that authenticity and richness that sustain the Neighborhood of Make-Believe.

The physical puppets themselves are simple, primitive creatures by the Muppet-centric standards of today's television puppetry. Their mouths do not move. Their eyes do not track. They have no feet. To the annoyance of my puppeteer friends, we do not watch the Neighborhood of Make-Believe to marvel at flawless manipulation. Nor do we sit in awe of the puppets' design. We watch because we have come to care about the essence of these characters. We, and our children, watch because we know them. We recognize ourselves in their complexity.

Fred's puppets belie the myth that children today only pay attention to high-tech design and gaudy special effects. In the hands of a lesser artist (someone with a less sophisticated understanding of children and their needs) the puppets would not work. However, like basic toys with perennial appeal — crayons, balls, and dolls — their simplicity provides space for children's imagination and becomes building blocks for creativity.

Four puppets in particular emerge as the soul of Fred Rogers' puppet repertoire: Daniel Striped Tiger, "X" the Owl, Lady Elaine Fairchilde, and King Friday XIII. These four embody the most complex and compelling personalities in the Neighborhood of Make-Believe. They seem to be at the center of many of Fred's scripts and, even as supporting players, tend to steal any scene in which they appear.

To understand the basic appeal of these four deceptively simple creatures, it is necessary to look at the process of their creation. When I once suggested to Fred that these four represented the heart of his puppet creations, he looked startled and replied that they were his oldest puppets. Fred's initial selection of the physical puppets was mere happenstance. The tiger that became Daniel was given to him at a dinner party the night before *The Children's Corner* was first aired. The others were brought from home for the first broadcast: a king (who became King Friday), a witch (who became Lady Elaine), and an owl (who became "X"). How he decided to make use of them has much more significance. Fred brought these puppets to life daily for eight years of spontaneous dialogue with Josie Carey, with whom he created *The Children's Corner*.

This history of intense, repeated, and spontaneous creation explains the puppets' richness and consistency. Seeds of their characters were sown and nurtured for eight years as Fred talked through them without the benefit, or limitation, of a written script. Although the creators may have agreed on a general topic for each show, Fred never knew what Josie Carey would say to the puppets. Since dead air — unintentional silence — is anathema on live television, Fred had to respond, in character, and he had to respond quickly. In that kind of improvisational dialogue, a puppeteer has no time to censor or to formulate a careful response. Therefore the dialogue emerges with only minimal mental editing.

When used in psychotherapy, spontaneous puppet play functions as a projective device designed to access internal experiences and perceptions that might otherwise remain guarded. Because all the thoughts and feelings expressed through a puppet can be safely attributed to a creature other than ourselves, we bring forth our inner world more freely and less self-consciously.

Because they were born of such spontaneity (more so than other Neighborhood puppets, who came into existence to further a plot or fill a need), Daniel, "X," Lady Elaine, and King Friday are deeply rooted in Fred Rogers' creative psyche. They each began as an undefended projection of Fred Rogers' inner world. Just as a sculptor might perceive a figure as inherent in stone or wood, these characters were inherent in Fred Rogers.

The essential integrity and honesty of their origin combines with their longevity to give these puppets a credibility that has enormous appeal. Much as real people are shaped by ongoing interactions with their environment, each segment of *The Children's Corner* added a layer of experience for these puppets that eventually developed into a full-blown personality. In other words, Daniel, "X," Lady Elaine, and King Friday carry with them an actual and unique history of growth and development based on numerous, varied, and spontaneous interactions.

Though these puppets are rooted in Fred Rogers' intuition, they also reflect his grasp of child psychology and development. Behind the apparent simplicity of Fred's puppets lies a complex wealth of knowledge and experience.

As *The Children's Corner* evolved into *Mister Rogers' Neighborhood*, Fred took courses in child development. He worked at the Arsenal, a laboratory school connected with the University of Pittsburgh. There, he began a long and intense association with Margaret McFarland, a noted child analyst who served as a mentor and as a psychological consultant for his scripts.

To fully appreciate the extent to which psychodynamic and developmental theory and practice have shaped the use of puppets on *Mister Rogers' Neighborhood*, it is essential to recognize the properties of puppetry that make it a powerful tool for psychotherapy.

In play therapy, a child speaking through a puppet can say or do things he or she might be unable or unwilling to express directly. Once the child's internal experience is brought forth into the realm of play, that experience can be manipulated and reflected upon. Such external manipulation enables the child to gain some control over potentially overwhelming thoughts and feelings. At the same time a therapist speaking through puppets can serve as a model for discussing feelings and coping with stress.

There are clear distinctions between puppetry on *Mister Rogers' Neighborhood* and puppetry as a clinical tool. *Mister Rogers' Neighborhood* is first and foremost a television program. Unlike a therapy session, its primary purpose must be to entertain. Yet somehow Fred Rogers can fulfill this objective without diluting or cheapening his *other* primary goal: contributing to the social and emotional growth of his audience.

Another distinction involves the nature of children's engagement with Fred's puppets. In psychotherapy, puppet play is geared to an *individual* child, who is encouraged to bring forth his or her own unique story or experience of the world. Television, the "cool medium," prohibits that kind of active, immediate involvement. In no way is the television audience asked to become a participant in the drama and engage in the risk of expressing previously unexpressed thoughts and feelings. The child watching does not influence or alter the events on the screen.

Yet Fred Rogers' puppets *do* function therapeutically. Through modeling, they can be viewed as tools for encouraging emotional growth and development. For instance, the puppets consistently provide models for prosocial behavior. Prince Tuesday shares his bicycle with Ana Platypus, whose parents can't afford one. "X" the Owl makes an elaborate book in reparation for an unthinkingly unkind comment to another puppet. The audience is not admonished "It's good to share" or "It's important to make recompense to those you hurt." Instead — and much more effectively — these values are played out by the puppets through carefully crafted scripts that nurture a young child's burgeoning sense of self.

The program also relies on modeling to encourage self-expression and mastery. With affect ranging from eagerness to reluctance, the puppets consistently share their feelings with each other, and are rewarded for doing so. They are encouraged to overcome their fears and move from passivity to action — to practice riding a bicycle or to search for solutions to problems ranging from war to hunger to hurt feelings.

By addressing common childhood concerns, insecurities, fantasies, and frustrations, the puppets speak — not for a particular child, but for universal childhood. They give voice to a wide range of feelings, including uncomfortable ones. Anger, fear, envy, and grief, as well as more positive feelings like love and joy, are addressed daily in the Neighborhood of Make-Believe. Not only are powerful emotions expressed in this fantasy world, they are accepted by its inhabitants without harmful repercussions.

In Fred's hands, with love and gentleness, the puppets draw forth the underside of childhood. By "underside" I do not mean macabre, warped, or seamy; they tap into the vein of fear, anger, awkwardness, and unadulterated self-centeredness that lies beneath the sunny surface of childhood. In direct contrast to most of the other puppets and fantasy creatures seen on children's television, the inhabitants of the Neighborhood of Make-Believe are complex, complicated, and utterly honest beings housed in rather rudimentary bodies.

In one of my favorite segments, Daniel Striped Tiger confesses to Lady Aberlin that he is frightened at a prospective visit by Santa Claus.

> LADY ABERLIN: I've got some very special news for you. . . . Santa Claus is coming to the Neighborhood of Make-Believe.
> DANIEL: Santa Claus? What's he going to do to us?
> LADY ABERLIN: Oh, well, I imagine it will be something good.
> DANIEL: Oh. I try to be good. But I'm not always good. Oh. I think I'm afraid of Santa Claus. I wish he weren't coming here.
> LADY ABERLIN: Daniel, I thought you'd be interested in seeing him.
> DANIEL: He sees you when you're sleeping, he knows when you've been bad or good. Oh, dear.
> LADY ABERLIN: Daniel, since he's coming, maybe you'd want to talk to him about just that very thing.
> DANIEL: I don't think I could talk to him about that.
> LADY ABERLIN: Well, I think you could try. I'm going to tell the others, Daniel.

Daniel's revelation to a trusted adult about his fear of a traditionally beloved figure is met with support and encouragement. Lady Aberlin does not join him in his feelings, nor does she reinforce them. She is clear about her assumption that Santa's visit will be pleasant. Yet at no time does she dismiss or denigrate Daniel's feelings. Instead she encourages him to directly face Santa Claus, the source of his anxiety:

DANIEL: I'm Daniel Striped Tiger and I'm not always good.

SANTA: Well, I'm Santa Claus and I'm not always good either.

DANIEL: You're not?

SANTA: No. Good people aren't always good. They just try to be. . . .

DANIEL: Can you see people when they're sleeping and do you know when everybody's bad or good?

SANTA: Of course not. Someone made that up about me. I'm not a spy and I can't see people when they're sleeping.

DANIEL: You can't?

SANTA: No, and I know that everybody's good sometimes and everybody's bad sometimes.

DANIEL: Oh gee, Santa. I like you.

SANTA: I like you too, Daniel. And I'm glad you asked me that.

In a few simple lines, Fred Rogers simultaneously accomplishes a set of complex and important tasks. Daniel gives voice to fears that young viewers might be afraid or embarrassed to address directly. By confronting and discussing his fears, Daniel (and the viewer) is able to get support and reassurance as well as guidance for how to cope with those fears. The pleasurable excitement about Santa's visit expressed by Lady Aberlin is a nice counterbalance to Daniel's fear, so that there is no pressure to identify with those fears unless children choose to do so.

At the same time, the sequence models for children the value of bringing fears and concerns to a trusted adult. (It also provides a model for parents and caretakers to supportively address these concerns and help children actively cope.) Lady Aberlin does not offer to speak to Santa for Daniel; instead she encourages him to speak for himself. This encouragement for emotional honesty and bravery is reinforced by Santa's affirmation, "I'm glad you asked me that."

Although all four of the main puppet characters possess a set of predominate characteristics, each personality is multidimensional. They cannot be understood solely as the embodiment of categories like "shy," "mischievous," or "domineering." Separately they are complex individuals with a past, present, and future. Together they represent a spectrum of attributes found in the personalities of healthy, well-functioning children.

In Daniel, we find a voice for fears and uncertainty hand in hand with the passionate and steadfast love young children can feel, especially for their parents. Daniel's relationship with Lady Aberlin, a mother figure in the Neighborhood, reflects not only her tender love and care for Daniel but also his reciprocal adoration. Daniel reminds us that children are capable of deep and passionate feelings far beyond their apparent cognitive capacities.

By contrast, in Lady Elaine we recognize a characteristically amoral, limit-pushing, and curiosity-driven aspect of early childhood. We see in her those children whose pressing need to know, to find out, and to see "what happens" is simultaneously a joy and a trial for their caretakers. These are the children who may be labeled as "bad" kids or as "troublemakers" in schools or other environments that cannot accommodate their exploratory mode of being in the world. (*Mister Rogers' Neighborhood* makes use of what I call the "cubistic" nature of puppet play, that is, its capacity to show all sides of a situation simultaneously, to let children know that curiosity in itself is fine but that there must be limits to its expression.)

Consider the following interchange between Lady Elaine and Lady Aberlin over a strange machine accompanied by a sealed envelope, which Lady Aberlin is delivering to the inventor and rocking-chair manufacturer Cornflake S. Pecially:

LADY ELAINE: What is this you've got, dear?

LADY ABERLIN: It's a delivery to Corny.

LADY ELAINE: Hmm. It looks like a new machine.

LADY ABERLIN: I guess so.

LADY ELAINE: Do you suppose it's something for his rocking chairs?

LADY ABERLIN: I don't know.

LADY ELAINE: Why don't you open that envelope and see?

LADY ABERLIN: Well, because it's not mine.

LADY ELAINE: But it's right there in front of you.

LADY ABERLIN: I know, but Mr. McFeely asked me to deliver the
　　whole thing, the machine, and the envelope just to Corny.

LADY ELAINE: Just one look, dear.

LADY ABERLIN: Lady Elaine, it's not ours.

LADY ELAINE: Spoil sport.

Lady Elaine is relentlessly determined in the immediacy of her "need to know." Her focus is undeterred despite Lady Aberlin's stalwart example. Here, as is often true on *Mister Rogers' Neighborhood*, the puppets are used to speak for the internal struggle fomented by a child's inevitable march toward civilized society:

LADY ABERLIN *(delivering the package)*: Speedy delivery, Corny.

LADY ELAINE: And everybody's wondering what it is.

CORNY: Well, thank you very much. I've been waiting for this for quite a while now.

LADY ELAINE *(more intensely)*: And everybody's wondering what it is.

LADY ABERLIN: Mr. McFeely wanted you to sign this receipt, Corny.

CORNY *(signs)*: Cornelius S. Pecially.

LADY ELAINE *(more intensely still)*: And everybody's wondering what it is.

CORNY: Well, it's a new machine . . .

LADY ELAINE *(impatiently)*: Everybody's wondering what you're going to make with this thing. We could just look inside this envelope.

CORNY: I'm not ready to share that with you yet, Lady Elaine.

LADY ELAINE: How about a hint, dear?

CORNY: I'll tell you when I'm ready.

LADY ELAINE *(exits in a huff)*: Well I hope that's soon. Toot-Toot.

LADY ABERLIN *(to Corny)*: Some people find it hard to wait.

CORNY: That's right. But it's a mighty important thing to learn.

Once again the deceptively simple dialogue transmits a complex message. It is acceptable to be curious. It is even acceptable to be persistent in your curiosity. However, it is essential to respect the privacy of others, and the capacity to wait is behavior that can be learned. Like Daniel, Lady Elaine does not get punished for voicing unacceptable or unpopular thoughts. In fact the intensity of her curiosity and her impatience with its delayed gratification find validation in Lady Aberlin's last, absolutely non-judgmental, comment, "Some people find it hard to wait." But in the end, *Lady Elaine does not get what she wants*. The sanctity of privacy is accorded proper respect by Lady Aberlin and by Corny himself.

Like the children whose personalities she embodies, Lady Elaine actually does exhibit some control. She does not grab the note and read it without Corny's permission. Fred's decision to restrain her behavior even at the expense of a potentially dramatic moment is yet another reflection of the dual purpose of his puppets as a medium for entertainment and for facilitating growth and development.

In fact, the puppets never exhibit any severely antisocial behaviors, even in jest. If a puppet does act out, such behavior is circumscribed and carefully presented only as a prelude to a solution. Lady Elaine, clearly the feistiest of Fred's characters, might stir things up or play an occasional practical joke such as pretending that her boomerang can really control invisible beings. Yet despite her occasional outbursts, Lady Elaine accepts the prevailing Neighborhood code of respect for others, even as she often rails against its more inhibiting components.

In "X" the Owl we find the well-intentioned but sometimes painfully awkward side of childhood. We are reminded of the times our children inadvertently whap us in the eye, bump heads, or somehow just can't find where to put their bodies. Fred Rogers has identified "X" as an adolescent, and he does seem like a friendly, gawky teenager. He is obviously no longer a child—he does not attend school with the younger children in the Neighborhood—but he is not an adult either.

His interactions with females seem particularly adolescent. When complimenting Betty Aberlin and Henrietta Pussycat on their bridesmaid regalia for a Neighborhood wedding, "X" seems shy and awkwardly awe-struck by their beauty. He is good-hearted, and eager to please, but has a habit of saying absolutely the wrong thing and then going to extraordinary lengths to make amends. We recognize in "X" the painful, uncomfortable, and uneven facet of development in which rapidly evolving minds and bodies seem to grow at different rates.

Finally, in King Friday we find the self-absorbed, absolute monarch lurking in all children: the imperious two-year-old announcing "I want that!" Every event for King Friday (and the universal child he represents) is experienced as being all about him. Even a wedding proclamation becomes a self-centered sentiment:

> KING FRIDAY: And when the dew is on the rose and the fragrance of life comes wafting to your nose, think of this day, this glorious day, when *your king* graced you with his presence and declared that you, James, and you Betty, are now husband and wife, whom the king has joined together.

The king's egocentricity extends to his belief that everybody thinks and feels exactly as he does. He cannot grasp that his subjects, or even his son, may have different likes or interests:

> KING FRIDAY: Have you two been playing airplanes?
> LADY ABERLIN: No, we've been playing with paper cups and pretending they were puppets.
> KING FRIDAY: Of course you could pretend they were airplanes. You could put them end to end and fly them around.
> LADY ABERLIN: Like this? (*makes airplane noise*)
> KING FRIDAY: But be sure they sound like a jet. Jet planes go very fast, you know. . . . You can pretend they're jet planes too, Prince Tuesday.
> PRINCE TUESDAY: I don't want to.
> KING FRIDAY: Of course you do. Everyone wants to think about jets. *I* certainly do.

His beleaguered family and subjects tolerate the king's self-involved authoritarianism, but they all persist in feeling and thinking exactly as they please. In spite of these difficult tendencies, the king is at no time reviled. He is even capable of overcoming his flaws enough to change his mind or listen to reason. In response to his wife's urging, for instance, he is able to replace his yearnings for a gasoline-guzzling jet plane, to an electric plane-car that will be less toxic to the Neighborhood. Like Lady Elaine, and all the residents of *Mister Rogers' Neighborhood*, King Friday is loved and accepted with all of his faults, just the way he is.

One of the major values of puppetry as a tool for psychotherapy is its capacity to bring into external focus our internal world. Puppet play allows us to express thoughts, feelings, and perceptions to which we may not otherwise give expression. Puppets provide a kind of psychological screen behind which we are free to give voice to aspects of ourselves that may normally be hidden from view.

In the hands of an artist who has engaged in this process of spontaneous play we find universal truths. The genius of Fred's artistry is that it is combined with an ethical and intellectual overlay devoted to helping children grow.

Through these puppets — the creative articulation of Fred Rogers' own memories and perceptions of the childhood experience — we recognize our children and ourselves. Fortunately for all of us, he has chosen to use that recognition to foster self-esteem, encourage discussion of feelings, and explore the ever-changing challenges of becoming human.

Fred Rogers' mission spans three disciplines: music, child development, and theology. William Guy focuses on the last and most problematic of these: the role of religion in Mister Rogers' Neighborhood.

To Guy, Fred Rogers' theology is the subversion of the mystification of possessions. "Commercial shamans" (as Guy calls them) would like us to believe in the power of possession; Rogers, on the other hand, demonstrates how things are made and how they work, thus shifting the emphasis from one of ownership to appreciation of the creation itself.

Likewise, Mister Rogers underscores how each of us is a capable creator — not only to make or fix things, but to make or fix relationships. "Far from serving solely as some kind of glorified Dr. Feelgood, bathing viewers in a vague glow of affirmation, Mister Rogers . . . [proclaims] an ethic of challenge and responsibility," Guy writes. "[Mister Rogers'] theology, like that of the Bible, is grounded in realistic psychology, a determination to deal with the human creature as he or she really is, not to issue dicta about the way said creature ought to be."

Poet and novelist William Guy received a Ph.D. in English literature from Princeton University. He is coauthor with William F. Orr of Living Hope and has developed a lecture series for the Pittsburgh Theological Seminary.

William Guy

The Theology of *Mister Rogers' Neighborhood*

In referring to the theology of *Mister Rogers' Neighborhood*, I do not mean theology as some system where assertions or categories about reality (whatever reality is) are amassed. However impressive such systems may be as intellectual exercises, too many of them seem to me to suffer from a defect of their "projections." They locate the divine dimension above or apart from the dimension of created things — "out there" somewhere in a great beyond. I tend to agree with theologian John A. T. Robinson that the divine dimension "may have to be witnessed to much more indirectly, obliquely, parabolically, brokenly — in action, in suffering, rather than in words [or in abstract ideas]."

Theology, then, needs to begin and end with "something given in our relationships in this world." The divine dimension needs relationships in which to manifest itself; a manifestation that will not be susceptible to skewering by the human desire to systematize. To quote Robinson: "It is impossible . . . to say what the word 'God' connotes. . . . It is possible only to say when one recognizes it, Yes, this is it again [or maybe for the first time]." It may be that we can experience the divine dimension only intermittently. Our theological formulations would therefore have to reflect this fact, resembling the story of the disciples on the road to Emmaus (Luke 24.13, 15–16). The divine is there and then not there, always elusive and mercurial. According to the Gospel of John, which first states that "no one has ever seen God at any time," the activity and the intention of God have been revealed in a human life, the life of Jesus of Nazareth (John 1.18). It embodies one of the strongest statements of the idea that the divine dimension needs to reveal itself in something "given in our relationships in this world."

It is with theology thus focused on human relationships that one can talk about *Mister Rogers' Neighborhood* as a kind of theological enactment, a fulfillment of Robinson's call for a witness to a divine dimension that will be carried on "indirectly, obliquely, parabolically."

The situation is as follows: On an average day, the American citizen engages in a sort of theological cat-fight. One is assailed by the claims of conflicting quasi deities to his or her allegiance, just as a citizen of the ancient world was so assailed, as we discover when we read the account of Paul's visit to Athens in the New Testament. The road to Athens, as Paul evokes it in his Areopagus speech (Acts 17.22), was lined with the shrines or statues of various gods. One can assume that in ancient Athens such shrines remained decently silent when a person passed by. No such luck befalls a twentieth-century person. The noise level of our modern quasi deities, the blare of the publicity, is truly mind numbing: "Buy me and you will be happy" they say, or "Leave your tribute money here at my shrine and you will get results, a lift to your existence." It is to people (not just children) thus bombarded by advertising appeals that Mister Rogers appears with his quite different kind of proposal for a meaningful life.

It is important to picture how his message serves as an antidote to this mercantile backdrop. Without an appreciation of this context it might appear that Mister Rogers is simply dispensing bromides, when in fact his message does full justice to the difficult setting in which we attempt to build up meaningful lives. The problem is that he makes his points with such apparent casualness that one can go on watching him for months without realizing what fundamental truths he is treating, what fundamental distinctions he is making. For instance, advertisers cloud the difference between make-believe (or fantasy) and the real world for the sake of someone's profit. Each day Mister Rogers dispels the illusion that our lives, the "way-down-deep-inside-us," would be qualitatively improved if we succumbed to the blandishments offered by ads and commercials. To take one simple example: In a week devoted to the topic of games, Mister Rogers shows what poor stuff a video game is made of by having a technician take one apart. Most importantly, lest a viewer think that the video game or those controlling it dispense a kind of disinterested care, Mister Rogers calls attention to the coin box — the cash nexus between the video game and those who play it. He reminds his viewers that they have to put their money into the box in order to partake of the hit that the video game promises — there is no free grace, no unconditional love in video game land. Then, to further the debriefing, he asks the repair man to divulge the surprisingly simple working of the wires inside the box — thus divesting the game of any magical powers it might have been thought to possess.

In this way, week after week, Mister Rogers frees his audience from the power of false gods. He does this by focusing on process, the way things work in the world. At the end of a sequence about a factory or about a farm, Mister Rogers points out that there is nothing magical about what it produces. The product, he notes, resulted from an idea that arose in a human mind, an idea that human beings then carried out — something his *viewers* might do in the future, something of the kind *they* might want to imagine and implement. To believe in magic, to ascribe inexplicable powers to something or someone, implies an essentially passive or powerless role for the "believer": one awaits salvation from without; one is not responsible for one's own spiritual health. Contrary to this sort of outlook, Mister Rogers inculcates an ethic of responsibility for one's own edification or fulfillment. He progresses from showing how a *human being* has designed something (made candles, for instance, or knitted sweaters) to suggesting that since his viewers are human beings, they might accomplish similar things. He does not imply that such accomplishment will be easy or automatic; he addresses the need to learn and to grow. The whole process is summarized in one of those musically enchanting songs that carry so much of the burden of Mister Rogers' message:

> You can make believe it happens
> or pretend that something's true,
> You can wish or hope or contemplate
> a thing you'd like to do,
> But until you start to do it,
> You will never see it through,
> 'Cause the make-believe pretending
> Just won't do it for you,
> You've got to do it.

This assertion that one can do various things — that one can participate in various processes oneself, that one does not have to feel excluded from activities of interest or of worth — arms viewers against the "doctrine" that without things that can be bought one's life will be empty. Mister Rogers draws the fundamental Aristotelian contrast between accidents and substance when he sings:

> It's you I like,
> It's not the things you wear,
> It's not the way you do your hair,
> But it's you I like,
> The way you are right now,
> The way down deep inside you —
> Not the things that hide you,
> Not your toys, they're just beside you.

This is the message that we all want to hear. It is also, sadly, the message mimicked by those who wish us to accumulate material incidentals. It is a message that we are afraid we will *not* hear without the right kinds of clothes adorning our bodies or the right kind of furniture in our houses or the right cars in our garages. Mister Rogers begins and ends with this message — that we are accepted and acceptable in our own right — as part of his strategy of divesting incidentals (most particularly bought things) of their power over us.

It is interesting, in the light of the anti-body bias of so many theologies, how in Mister Rogers' worldview the body is so often celebrated as part of the real person. For instance, farther along in the song "It's You I Like," the "you" being accepted and appreciated includes "Your skin, your eyes, your feelings, whether old or new." This same point — that the body is inseparable from the real person — is made the subject of another whole song, "Your Body's Fancy and So Is Mine." And the body comprising the person belongs to a world which one can delight in. When one is trying to read Mister Rogers' theology, it is important to note the strain of what theologian Paul Tillich called "ecstatic naturalism." This theme manifests itself in many of the beautiful nature segments that Mister Rogers' show contains (wind blowing through marsh grass; dogs and horses running together, their muscles rippling), in a sustained celebration of the body electric of the whole world, which Mister Rogers sings as fervently as Walt Whitman ever did. He refutes what some theologies, using loaded terms, would call their necessarily antipagan bias. For Mister Rogers, as for Robert Penn Warren, "the world is real, it is there." One often feels resurfacing in many of the Neighborhood segments a welcome feeling for the divine in nature, which other more abstract theologies suppress at their peril. By airing a Wordsworthian element, by centering the self-consciousness of his viewers in the beauty of this world (including the beauty of those creatures who inhabit it), Mister Rogers is saying that there are magical resources (including oneself) that one has access to and for which one needs no intermediaries, especially paid intermediaries. This message constitutes one way of telling his viewers that they can "do it" themselves without having recourse to shamans.

Each day, in concert with his television friends, Mister Rogers embarks on a quest for the source of true *numinousness* in this world. Invented things, such as consumer products, are not numinous, however worthy of admiration they may be. Things created in nature are numinous — or at least they can be in the sacramental view that Mister Rogers encourages with such lyrics as "there are so many wonderful things to learn about in this world" or with the song "Did You Know That It's All Right to Wonder?" But the main numinous element in the world is the human creature, each one of whom is a sufficient miracle in all the uniqueness of his or her existence. This tenet is propounded almost every day at the end of the show in that most gracious of all benedictions: "You make each day a special day for me — you know how — by just your being you — there's only one person like you in the whole world, and that's you yourself, and people can like you just the way you are." This point is reinforced in many ways. Like members of other large groups (snowflakes, pieces of popcorn), each human creature is unique yet similar to other members of the group.

It is at this point, though, that the second half of Mister Rogers' two-part fundamental message about the peculiar *quidditas* of human existence is often introduced, lest viewers be left in a sort of self-sufficient solipsistic afterglow, a glory of the egocentric perspective at having had their own specialness proclaimed. The other part of the message is that although each person is unique, each person also shares certain kinds of feelings with every other person, the need for love being the one most often mentioned on the show. Thus Mister Rogers' affirmation has two components — one of *grace* (the gift, the confirmation of one's own unique importance) and one of *claim* (the need to become aware of other people's needs, which are like one's own).

Far from serving solely as some kind of glorified Dr. Feelgood, bathing viewers in a vague glow of affirmation, Mister Rogers should be understood as proclaiming an ethic of challenge and responsibility. It is an ethic, however, that understands that care of others is not likely to be tendered by those who have been battered into submission or who doubt their own worth. We are like the so-called sinful woman who washes Jesus' feet ("her many sins have been forgiven because she loved much" [Luke 7.36–50]); her acts of love are an indication that her many sins have been forgiven, that she has been *freed up* to love. So the love-ethic that Mister Rogers propounds relies on the edified psyches of his viewers, whose own worth he is constantly affirming. Love is seen by Mister Rogers as a system of circulation; it cannot be all outgo, but neither can the grace that he imparts be hoarded up as merely income. It is an ethical system that depends, in part, upon each person's letting go of some of his or her gains, spreading those gains around, showing love to other people so that those other people can eventually show love in return. Of course such letting go in the first place constitutes a supreme act of faith; our deeply ingrained tendency is to hold on to what we have in the belief that we alone know how to look out for our own interests.

The human need to look out for our own interests, to protect ourselves, and many other psychological reflexes are what Mister Rogers holds up for calm and lucid examination. His theology, like that of the Bible, is grounded in realistic psychology, a determination to deal with the human creature as he or she really is, not to issue dicta about the way said creature ought to be, in purposeful disregard of how our psyches really function. He often takes himself as an example: For instance, he admits to once having wanted to upstage his own sister before their parents with certain flour-and-paste designs. The competitiveness that results from feeling underappreciated — the naturalness, the understandability of this sort of impulse — seems to be one of the premises from which the show often moves on until it eventually arrives at glimpses of a less defensive, more trusting way of operating in the ethical realm. The point that the program makes, though, is that there are no shortcuts to openness; one has to be sure about one's real feelings before one can improve upon them. "Faking it" would seem to be the real sin in Mister Rogers' world, if one thinks of sin in the root sense of the Greek word *hamartia*, that is, missing the mark, the mark being freedom and love. If one loves grudgingly or with doubts, suppressing one's objections or dissatisfactions, then one has not achieved the mark. Hence the high premium placed throughout the sequences of the show on saying exactly what one feels. One show ends with the statement, "When we can understand and talk about our feelings, then we're free to be what we like being." We are not free until we can understand and talk about our feelings, as the great song "The Truth Will Make Me Free" explains:

> What if I were very very sad
> and all I did was smile,
> I wonder after a while
> what might become of my sadness?
> What if I were very very angry
> and all I did was sit
> and never think about it?
> What might become of my anger?
> Where would they go
> And what would they do,
> if I couldn't let them out?
> Maybe I'd fall, maybe get sick
> Or doubt.
> But what if I could know the truth
> And say just how I feel?
> I think I'd learn a lot that's real
> About freedom.
> I'm learning to sing a sad song when I'm sad.
> I'm learning to say I'm angry when I'm very mad.
> I'm learning to shout, I'm getting it out, I'm happy
> Learning exactly how I feel inside of me.
> I'm learning to know the truth,
> I'm learning to tell the truth.
> Discovering truth will make me free.

The stress here is on learning. Honesty is something that our conditioning does not always encourage, and having lost it at a certain stage of our lives, we may often need to relearn it. The song's definition of truth is based upon honesty. Truth, in the theological outlook that Mister Rogers adumbrates, is not something imposed upon unwilling people "from on high," or something they are made to swallow unwillingly "in a spirit of obedience"; truth is something that they themselves help to define, that they contribute to. One has only to compare this grant of honesty and freedom with the dictates of many repressive theologies to see how radical and how full of faith about the potentials of untrammeled (one might call it grown-up) existence Mister Rogers is. "What if I could know the truth and say just how I feel?" Such candor is a prospect that would terrify some "religious" groups with their goals of mind-domination and rigid regimentation of the faithful. Similarly terrifying to some repressive theologies would be Mister Rogers' statement: "No one has to tell you exactly what to think or what to do, what stories to make up."

It is in terms of the need for absolute honesty that one begins to appreciate the importance of certain characters in that reflection that the Neighborhood of Make-Believe casts back, by means of parables, upon our real lives. For instance, Lady Elaine Fairchilde exemplifies the importance of wit—at least in Alexander Pope's sense of that word ("what oft was thought but ne'er so well expressed"). Stunningly unmeek, ornery, and "disobedient," Lady Elaine expresses her disgust with King Friday's prohibition of play on one occasion by simply vacating the neighborhood. Likewise, when King Friday expects everyone in the neighborhood to contribute to the Royal Foundation for the Arts, Lady Elaine wants to know why she should contribute. She expresses honest self-interest, does not pretend that altruistic behavior is the first or most natural impulse that arises in the psyche. One also appreciates the honesty of that most intrepid self-confessor Daniel Striped Tiger, who does not hesitate to express his doubts and fears, who is never willing to be stampeded into something simply because the rest of the neighborhood is heading in that direction.

The behavior of these two puppets is one way of depicting the kind of honest behavior that Mister Rogers posits as essential to healthful existence. One might point out here that he is raising questions of what it might mean to have a full and abundant life more than he is providing ready answers. He never seems to impose his own solutions or to force his viewers to acknowledge them. He sometimes offers insights of his own, but then he usually leaves them for his viewers to accept or to reject, thus allowing those viewers that same freedom which he proclaims as so important — there is no contradiction between what he proclaims and how he proclaims it.

Of course some would charge the show with something worse than dishonesty: with unreality. Their charges often seem to take a form like the following: "Oh well, the Neighborhood is all very nice as some sort of fiction, but things aren't like that in the real world; for instance, it isn't always such a great feeling to know you're alive." The essence of this kind of criticism is that Mister Rogers has excluded all unhappiness, the entire dark side of life. The fact is that he often invites his viewers to meditate upon unhappiness and what the reasons for it might be; he tries to help his viewers understand and control some of the things that make for misery instead of just succumbing hopelessly to them. In assessing the theology of Mister Rogers one recognizes those episodes in which people who, on the face of it, would have real reason for complaint are allowed to offer testimony about their outlooks. The most moving of all such sequences involves the boy in the motorized wheelchair who ends up singing "It's You I Like" with Mister Rogers. The boy admits to times of depression, but in general his outlook is so affirmative as to shame those of us who are spared such difficulties as he faces and yet still complain. There is also another sequence in which the blind saxophonist Eric Kloss appears. With her usual outspokenness Lady Elaine objects to the idea of a blind man being able to make music in the way supposedly normal people do — it doesn't seem to make sense, it ought not to be possible — just as a boy in a wheelchair ought not to be cheerful about his existence.

That those with overwhelming afflictions might have access to a certain happiness that is denied to the average healthy person is as frustrating and as humbling as the fact that the poor might very well be happy in a way that most prosperous people cannot understand. In the case of the boy in the wheelchair, the theological message might be the rather bold one that God is in the spinal cord tumor just as he is in the rainbow. It might seem cheap or easy to make such a statement when one has not suffered oneself from such a tumor. On the other hand, the response of the boy in the wheelchair himself, who obviously has to be allowed to know more about a condition like his from the inside than most other people do, almost seems to demand such an interpretation. The point here is simply that the freedom to see life as providing good feelings, which Mister Rogers enacts and invites his viewers to share in, the zest for living that he advocates, is not bought cheaply or dishonestly, at the expense of sweeping certain harsh truths or certain obstacles under the rug. The vision of Mister Rogers has been honestly earned. It has been built up over the weeks, months, and years by giving a fair reflection of life, both its good and its bad. If after having confronted and weighed all such samples, Mister Rogers still wants to affirm that "we can trust the universe not only at the level of certain mathematical regularities but at the level of utterly personal reliability that Jesus indicated by the word *Abba*, Father!" as John A. T. Robinson summed up one possible position, then — though some might call it his delusion — it is nonetheless his privilege. He has not shuffled the data in order to come by his results.

But once one is alerted to this element of listening to, or reasoning with, "the worst that may befall," then one can positively have one's breath taken away by the metaphysical openness and daring of some of the show's episodes, by the willingness to face abysses that various shows embody. In the week that deals with mistakes — in one of those intense personal encounters that he has the courage often to insist on — Daniel Striped Tiger speculates on whether he himself might not be some kind of existential mistake since he is not quite right as a tiger (he is too tame, likes humans, comes out looking like a failure in terms of the truism that "the strong never break"). Who at some point has not asked, "What is the good of my existence?" Who has not said, "There's no reason for me to be here, I'm not needed, I don't fit in, I'm a joke, I should be canceled"? Lady Aberlin's answer to Daniel's self-doubt is the same sort of answer she gives in another episode when Lady Elaine has been feeling left out, worthless, devalued because of the arrival of Harriet Elizabeth Cow, the new person in the neighborhood who has been getting all the attention: "We need you to be who you are."

This is undoubtedly a human kind of affirmation. That it might also have a theological dimension has to do with the fact that if there is a divine personal force at the center of reality, that force has no instruments other than human beings by which or through whom to convey its feelings about those same human beings. If one accepts Robinson's interesting concept of prayer ("Prayer is opening oneself to the claim of the unconditional as it meets one in all the relationships of life. It is life at its most intimate, intense, and demanding, requiring the response of the whole person"), then the scene between Lady Aberlin and Daniel might be looked upon as an instance of prayer. It is the unconditional presentation to Lady Aberlin of another person's need to be affirmed, to be reclaimed from the abyss above which he hovers, through the words of someone saying she loves him and needs him to be her friend. The exchange between Daniel and Lady Aberlin is like the equally moving instance of "prayer" recorded tersely by Robert Penn Warren in the dedication to his volume of poems *Being Here:*

> OLD MAN: You get old and you can't do anybody any good any
> more.
> BOY: You do me some good, Grandpa. You tell me things.

If one wanted to give a theological reading of the scene between Lady Aberlin and Daniel, if one wanted to aver that it contained a theological point, then that point might be (to quote Robinson again) that God is the foundation of life, the ground of being, the undergirding reality that prevents everything falling through into meaninglessness and dread. An interesting corollary to such a theological reading would be that in the world of Mister Rogers, the true heroes are those who have the courage to express qualms and doubts about themselves. Thus Daniel becomes an exemplar: far from being too tame, he is almost too intrepid — though not in the sense of the roaring beasts who usually, and falsely, represent his breed when it gets anthropomorphized. He quietly stands his ground, he is not afraid to be vulnerable, to show weakness or to avow inadequacy. The blusterers of this world, the ones who have to make a lot of noise to slubber o'er their own doubts about themselves, the ones who would rather drag a whole society down than ever admit to their mistakes are far more cowardly than Daniel: in Gertrude Stein's telling phrase about men, "They are afraid to be afraid." In terms of the "real world," however, it is the cowardly blusterers who get called tough-minded.

In *Mister Rogers' Neighborhood,* by contrast, much of what in the "real world" might be branded as weakness may turn out to be divinest strength in that it affords an opportunity for the divine affirmation of individuals to shine through and for familial bonds to be forged between people, as when Daniel reveals his need to Lady Aberlin. But the openness that the divine light requires is of a kind to frighten people who are conditioned always to appear tough and in control. The television columnist of the *National Review* reflected perfectly this secret terror of the supposedly strong when he gave the title "Gone with the Wimp" to his article on Mister Rogers. One suspects that the attacks on Mister Rogers that center around his supposed wimpishness, his supposed womanliness, his less-than-rugged manliness, his soft-hearted sentimental irrelevance, arise mostly out of subconscious envy on the part of the attackers: they must reject the caring ethos of the Neighborhood because they would so much like to partake of it; yet they are afraid to let down their defenses and admit that they too are vulnerable human beings. Their plight is in fact portrayed in the character of Wicked Knife and Fork in the opera "Spoon Mountain": Wicked Knife and Fork is the tough guy, the self-reliant "meanie," the nonsentimentalist who in the end breaks down when he sees how much his supposed enemies love one another. In other words, the theology of *Mister Rogers' Neighborhood* includes a depiction of the reasons for the rejection and the reviling of it by some people; it evinces compassion for the rejecters and the revilers and entertains the perpetual possibility of welcoming them into the fellowship. All they would have to do to be welcomed is to admit that they "feel want, taste grief, / Need friends," as Shakespeare's Richard II does when his self-sufficient kingly persona and all his royal defenses start to break down.

Ultimately, what Mister Rogers talks about is the very big subject of the search for power by human beings, a search that has been defined or unmasked by Sabina Spielrein, the brilliant associate of Freud and Jung: "And the search for power? What else is it but the need to attract more attention and love to oneself?" The need to achieve power would in this sense be the most basic human drive: we all want attention and love. What human beings differ about is the means to obtain this power. The antisocial self-assertion practiced by some people grows out of a fear that they will not be given the kind of acceptance and love that we all desire. Mister Rogers' shows abound in examples of this syndrome. For instance, during the week on games, fearing that she will not or cannot be loved as a loser, Lady Elaine tries to guarantee what she thinks would be the condition of her acceptance, namely victory. She proposes extorting power from society by the enactment of a guaranteed scheme for success. What Mister Rogers' shows are often directed toward is the idea that there might be another way for Lady Elaine to receive the same benefit of attention, love, and acceptance, and for that benefit to be multiplied so that everyone receives it. If we can all talk about our needs, and if we can all open up and respond to each other, then everyone will get the attention and the love that power seekers try to arrogate exclusively unto themselves.

The multiplication as if by miracle of a benefit that someone or some restricted number of individuals has historically tried to monopolize is a New Testament topic, perhaps *the* New Testament topic. It is a concept reiterated in the story of the loaves and fishes, or in Jesus' rather bold (and some might say totally unrealistic) promise that all the benefits that people care and worry about will be added unto them if they seek first the kingdom of Heaven and God's righteousness (Matthew 6.33). To understand Jesus' statement it is important first to understand that the Hebrew concept of righteousness does not involve toeing some kind of established behavioral mark, measuring up to some supposed or proposed standard, or making sure that one does not fall short of self-advancing rectitude. Instead, righteousness involves identifying society's victims and restoring them to their rights. Hebrew justice is active and remedial; Jesus is suggesting that if we find those who are in need and take care of them, we in turn will be benefited. A cynical interpretation might stress the appeal by Jesus to some sort of psychological profit motive, but what Jesus is really addressing is the need to let go, to stop clinging to what we feel as our protection and strength, the need to gamble on the greater riches that a caring, sharing society would confer upon each person. Jesus' words are in response to his disciples, who, in an act of buck-passing, turn to Jesus to deal with the five thousand hungry people in the wilderness. "They don't have to go away," Jesus says, calling the disciples' bluff, "*you* feed them yourselves" (Matthew 14.16). Or as Mister Rogers is in the habit of saying, you — we, all of us — have got to "do it" ourselves, no one "out there" or "up above" is going to do it for us. But this is not the same as a system of rugged self-reliance. Quite the contrary: in Jesus' system what we are being asked to do is to look out for one another. Under such a dispensation we too, like everybody else, would be looked out for. Here is where the miracle of multiplication comes in: the benefit that once only the cleverest or the most aggressive were able to garner unto themselves will now accrue unto all.

It is against such a set of assumed values that one must gauge a statement like one that Mister Rogers makes at the end of the week on day- and night-care giving: "You'll know you're growing by how much care you're giving." Not that other kinds of growth aren't singled out for praise in the course of various shows, but ultimately real growth for a person and then for society has to come through this capacity to care, not through the accumulation of objects (including people used as objects) thought wrongly to convey power and worth. One can see why a magazine like the *National Review,* with its gung-ho endorsement of more and more brute measures to ensure American "sovereignty" (which might mean America's perceived right to go on reaping and raping whatever inordinate percentage of the world's material goods our so-called power can provide us with), might get exercised over the subversive spectacle of *Mister Rogers' Neighborhood:* the image of what might happen if, as individuals, we ever unhitched ourselves for a moment from "the metalled ways of appetence and desire" and so, as a society, were able to consult our true interests. The danger to the *National Review* is that the people engaged in the work of honest self-assessment that Mister Rogers encourages would cease consenting to be objects, grist for the massive mill of accumulation in which it is assumed some victims will have to be ground up for the greater good of a few.

With his ecstatic naturalism, his reverence for life in all its forms, his attention to the feelings of individuals and to the holiness of each heart's affections, Mister Rogers questions what Adrienne Rich has called the whole "death-culture of quantification, abstraction, and the will to power which has reached its most refined destructiveness in this century, a death-culture which, as many feminist writers have shown, is an outgrowth of patriarchal values." The questions that Mister Rogers raises about such patriarchal values constitute another aspect of the threat detected by the *National Review.* A quotation from Carol Gilligan may help clarify the exact nature of this threat:

Women not only define themselves in a context of human relationships but also judge themselves in terms of their ability to care. Woman's place in man's life cycle has been that of nurturer, caretaker, and helpmate, the weaver of those networks of relationships on which she in turn relies. But while women have thus taken care of men, men have in their theories of psychological development, as in their economic arrangements, tended to assume or devalue that care. When the focus on individuation and individual achievement extends into adulthood and maturity is equated with personal autonomy, concern with relationships appears as a weakness of women rather than as a human strength.

If Gilligan is right about the association of caring skills with women (and therefore the denigration of them as female), then it would seem that Mister Rogers is trying to make women out of us all. *(Oh, word of fear, oh word of panic!)* What American male has not been conditioned to take as the ultimate insult in any area (from throwing a baseball to filing a brief) the imputation that he does it "like a girl"? What might become of us in the "real world" if we let the desire to build and maintain relationships predominate? How much control might we lose? How much might our superior position crumble? One again finds New Testament precedent in the action of Jesus, who undertook to wash his followers' feet (John 13), a task reserved for women and slaves.

It is important to stress that what is being proposed by Mister Rogers is not some dire dreariness of perpetual soul-numbing servitude, some permanent state of deprivation and inferiority, but rather a system of "grace upon grace," a system in which what had once been the sole prerogative of a few will achieve an infinite multiplication that redounds and accrues unto all. It is not possible to dismiss this utopia as "unworkable"; it has never really been tried. Such a system would require the faith to let go, the willingness to gamble — but such faith is seldom forthcoming. And where it *has* appeared, as Gilligan notes, it has been belittled as the attitude of women, a sign of weakness. It is a great deal easier to fall back upon, as reliable, the clenched fist and the rigid posture of self-defense, or the squinting, self-reliant outlook by which one builds up one's own turf (even though such turf can never really be secure). As many of the characters on Mister Rogers' program have remarked, friendships and feelings are problematic and messy, whereas as Adrienne Rich says, "To hold power over others means that the powerful is permitted a kind of short-cut through the complexity of human personality. He does not have to enter intuitively into the souls of the powerless, or to hear what they are saying in their many languages, including the language of silence." In other words, the supposedly powerful are spared a lot of hard emotional work, although one may wonder whether the work of denying others and of self-denial — the work of suppressing the truth that is demanded of them — isn't a lot harder for the "powerful" than letting go and being open would be. The outlook of this repressive group is exemplified by Prince Tuesday who, when discussing the disadvantages of the war that seems to be brewing with the neighborhood of Southwood, says, "Yeah, but what if you win a war?" In other words, think of all the hard work of human negotiation and compromise we could save ourselves. How easy is it then.

It may be helpful to step back from this analysis and make sure that we understand the context in which Mister Rogers is proclaiming his message. The competing message, that is repeated about fifteen times during the evening news, is that "I as an individual can have it all." One hears a message about how one might, by coming into possession of the right things, set oneself up in solitary soul satisfaction. Nor is this the message heard solely in the secular sphere. There is an analogous kind of message in the so-called spiritual realm: "I as an individual can and must be saved by establishing a personal relationship with my savior Jesus Christ." What seems to be blotted out by both of these world-pictures is — other people. Any impulse toward the establishment of communal, caring relations is removed or overlooked. In these two views of the world, the only thing that matters is what happens to *me*.

What Mister Rogers is "preaching," by contrast, is cooperative, communal life — the covenant community if one prefers, or even the Kingdom of God. His parables suggest that the answer to our problems of personal dissatisfaction lies in the establishment of a community in which people look out for each other and are looked out for in return. The establishment of this kind of community would obviate the solution Prince Tuesday envisions in which one wins a war and gets to take everything. In a caring community one could not so conveniently deny others as centers of importance corresponding to oneself, nor could one easily assume that people's true wealth consists in the number of things they can possess in lordly isolation from (or in victory over) others. During the week on work, the connection between labor and the accumulation of capital is clearly set forth, as is the limited nature of anyone's spending power (no matter how "rich" he or she may be). Mister Rogers calls Prince Tuesday's solution ("Yeah, but what if you win a war?") into question by telling his viewers that things like friendship and love — which do involve the recognition of one person's value by another — don't cost any money at all and are very important.

Mister Rogers' message seems to revolve around the New Testament paradox that the way to gain one's life is to lose it. At one point during the week on work he takes his television friends to a supermarket — thus, in his usual subtle, almost casual way communicating the connection that exists between work and food. As a child, he says, he wanted everything in the store at which his parents shopped. His parents, of course, refused; the conclusion is that no one can have everything. This is a harsh message, perhaps, especially in the societal context that seems to propound it almost as some sort of categorical imperative that we must satisfy every material desire.

To caution that we cannot have everything is not, however, the whole of Mister Rogers' message. It takes the rest of the week on work to come to fruition. The story line is about the construction of a swimming pool in the Neighborhood of Make-Believe, thanks to a surplus in the neighborhood budget. But the project founders on the ignominy of burst underground pipes, which it takes the whole of the surplus to replace. Again we hear the message that you can't have everything — both the pipes and a pool. One has to make painful choices in life (which Mister Rogers underscores at the end of one of the programs when he explains to his television friends how hard it is for their parents to decide how to spend the money they have earned by their work).

The upshot of the week on work, however, is that the Neighborhood of Make-Believe gets its pool after all when its citizens join their needs and wishes with those of Southwood's citizens, who still have money for a pool but who lack sufficient water for such an amenity. This could be seen as a Panglossian ending, an example of the unreality of Mister Rogers' world, but such a dismissal would represent the mistake of reading literally something that is meant to figure forth a kind of spiritual truth: how things might be if we revised our outlook in a spirit of cooperation. Paradoxically one *can* have it all, it would seem, but only after one has recognized one's own limits, surrendered any claim to total self-sufficiency.

A similarly far-reaching statement arises out of the week on conflict, which furnishes a chillingly accurate commentary on our dealings with the former Soviet Union. The week begins innocently enough, both in the real world and in Make-Believe, with piggy banks: in the real world an interesting piggy bank collection is on display at Negri's Music Shop, while in the Neighborhood of Make-Believe King Friday is putting money into his piggy bank and figuring out how much he has saved. One does not realize until the whole five-day sequence has been completed that the subject of war is being grounded in economics — a parable of the connection between war and wealth. The resources of any one polis, the week suggests, or any one group of people, are finite; if one spends money on war preparations there will be nothing left over for something so important as education, nothing for (in the context of the story) the record player that the school in the Neighborhood of Make-Believe needs. How interesting that Mister Rogers — the so-called irrelevant dreamer, the purveyor of harmless fantasies — should have isolated the essential question that we are still not ready or maybe honest enough to answer: When does the process of protecting a society from outside threats, real or imagined, so drain the society that there is nothing left worth protecting?

The alternative to war is proposed at the end of the five-day sequence: the production of record players out of the now-unnecessary parts from which weapons were made. The turning point from war to peaceful abundance in the Neighborhood of Make-Believe comes in the middle of the week when Chef Brockett (now General Brockett in the bristling militarized state of preparedness that King Friday has decreed) reads in Braille (befitting the blindness that the neighborhood has fallen into) a message that states, "That which is essential is invisible to the eye," a line from Saint-Exupéry's *Little Prince*. Lady Elaine interprets this oracle to mean that there's a lot more to the people of Southwood than the stories of their making bombs. Mister Rogers himself further glosses this message at the end of the week by adding that the only way to find out about other people is *directly* — they are the only people who know how they're feeling. In other words, the real work facing us is to enter into the feelings of others, the sticky necessity of having to deal with others, only this time on a societal scale. But this work in turn depends upon self-examination: before talking about finding out what other people are feeling, Mister Rogers explores how it is possible to imagine either good things or bad things about others and how what we imagine depends on what *we* feel.

If we examine what *we* feel, we may discover that our motives are really not that much more noble than the motives of those so-called alien others whom we dismiss in the hopes of implementing our own perceived interests. This is why we fear self-examination — we fear what we may find out; we fear how unflattering the discoveries may be; we fight to preserve certain cherished notions about our own high-mindedness. In exhorting us to examine ourselves, Mister Rogers isn't looking to say, "Aha! You're caught, you phony! You weren't so admirable as you thought." Rather he wants to lead us into admitting that we all need to be loved, loved not for our accouterments or our appendages but for ourselves alone. Until we can make such an admission, we are fooling ourselves as we search for what we think will be our happiness. In our various stopgap stratagems, our attempts at satisfaction in the face of what we sense to be our terrible time limitations on this Earth, we end up simply swelling the ranks of those who "from fear of death are subject all their lives to slavery" (Hebrews 2.15), perhaps without knowing how enslaved we are. To us in this plight the words of the song are again relevant:

> But what if I could tell the truth
> And say just how I feel?
> I think I'd learn a lot that's real
> About freedom.

The message of Mister Rogers is that it's all right to tell the truth about wanting to be loved and that people can love us exactly as we are. One admires the scrupulous care to be precise in this oft-repeated statement: after all, people may very well *not* love us exactly the way we are, a fact that causes most of our problems. But this message is not meant to be an end in itself; it is meant to strike a blow for further liberation: remember "her many sins have been forgiven because she loved much" — the idea that if one can achieve a sense of acceptance oneself, then one will be free to tend to others in their need. It is a theology in accord with the New Testament: to achieve this kind of freedom is to connect with the divine dimension. One meets God in the form of needy people (Matthew 25.40). The pretended self-reliance, our prickly, self-doubting, self-defensive postures, have to be broken down if the heavenly kingdom is ever to have a chance of coming into effect. Each person's need for love from others, each person's need for interdependence, must be acknowledged. What both the New Testament and Mister Rogers suggest is that a torrent of benefits might follow from our confessions of need.

"When I am weak, then I am strong," St. Paul says (2 Corinthians 12.10). It is a paradox that Mister Rogers propounds boldly, in the face of so much worldly wisdom to the contrary. One sees this paradox in action during the week that culminates in the Bass Violin Festival. The week begins with an ego-assertion on the part of King Friday, who attempts to elevate himself at the expense of others because *he* is the only one who knows how to play the bass violin. For him to declare a bass violin festival is a little unkind to his subjects, who are made uncomfortable by their apparent incompetence. They wonder and worry about how they will be able to fulfill the royal decree to perform on an instrument for which they do not have the skills. It is Daniel, that exemplar of candor and honesty, who suggests that the solution for King Friday's subjects may be to admit the truth of their own inability to perform on such an instrument, to proclaim their own weakness. It is from this apparent nadir that the week rises to its triumphant culmination in the festival at which so many inventions spring up out of what was apparently barren ground. The paradox here is that the festival can only result from the admission on everyone's part that there cannot be a festival, *then* this pooling of weakness results in great strength: The characters find creative ways to "play" the bass violin — by dressing as a violin or dancing as a violin or some other innovative demonstration of their *own* skills and talents. Again one must insist that this week is not to be interpreted literally; it exists rather as an enactment or a sign of what might happen if the citizens of the world could manage to reorient their outlooks and let down their defenses, to actually admit weakness.

What one fears is that we would prefer to destroy ourselves through an insistence on our pseudostrength because the prospect, the uncertainty, of letting go is too fearful, even if we are holding on to nothing but the blasted fruit of a dying planet. One is grateful for the still, small voice of Mister Rogers, who goes on witnessing to a very different kind of relationship.

Thirty years ago John A. T. Robinson issued a call for a new type of theologian:

> It is a call in the first place not to relevance in any slick sense but to exposure, to compassion, sensitivity, awareness and integrity. It is the call to bear reality, more reality than it is easy or indeed possible for a human being to bear unaided. It is to be with God in his world. And in each epoch or culture the place of the theologian is to stand as near as he may to the "creative centre" of God's world in his day.

It is in these terms that Mister Rogers can be called a theologian. In letting the facts about the human situation surface, in honestly facing those facts — and the peril they depict — and in consulting with his viewers about the best way to move beyond and to improve upon those facts, he stands "near the 'creative centre' of God's world."

As an educator long involved in civil rights, Paula Lawrence Wehmiller mines the disturbing issue of intolerance — both from without and from within. "In the face of all that we face as we raise our children in this troubled country and in this troubled world," Wehmiller begins, "one question keeps rising up into my work and confronting my dreams: What story wants telling?" Few can deny the lasting effects of racism, sexism, and countless other injurious manifestations of what Wehmiller calls a "national habit of people abusing power over people." And, Wehmiller says, "as I travel the country visiting schools, I hear the cloaked denial in the old 1950s guise of 'some of my best friends. . . .' I hear it in the righteousness of those who have accomplished the beginning steps of going to workshops, setting up committees. . . . 'We did diversity last year,' some have the chutzpah to say to me, as if 'doing diversity' were something you got shots for like the measles or mumps."

Easy answers such as "doing diversity" might be the product of asking the wrong questions. Wehmiller wonders if Mister Rogers' Neighborhood might be the target of such questioning. "What [is] Fred Rogers, a white, American-born, Presbyterian minister . . . doing on the Neighborhood about preventing and dealing with racism?" This, Wehmiller contends, may be the wrong question to be asking.

The story of Fred Rogers and racism is told here as two stories — one of Fred Rogers, the other of Wehmiller herself. It is a story of revelation and acceptance, an age-old tale about learning to love oneself before learning to love others. "So often," Wehmiller writes, "the very thing that was a struggle for each of us — the thing that was injurious, the part of the story where we felt disconnected from ourselves, not understood, not accepted by others — is the thing that we turn into the strength of our life's work."

Wehmiller received her master's degree in early childhood development and elementary education from Bank Street College of Education. She has taught kindergarten and elementary grades, as well as undergraduate and graduate courses in education. She has been the director of a day care center and the principal of an elementary school. Currently a consultant and author, she has written and spoken widely on teaching and learning in schools, conducting numerous workshops on racism for teachers, parents, and students.

Paula Lawrence Wehmiller

Mister Rogers

Keeper of the Dream

It is August 28, 1963, a hot, humid summer day between high school graduation and my first year of college. I kneel on the grass in the shadow of the Lincoln Memorial in Washington, D.C., and move my hand through the dark, still water of the Reflecting Pool. I am at once alone and a part of something much bigger than this moment in time can gather. Two hundred fifty thousand people have journeyed here by train and bus, by plane, in cars, some on foot from the D.C. neighborhoods, none of us knowing — or even imagining, I suspect — what moment we will look back on thirty years later.

My seventeen-year-old heart is filled with fear as I climb the steps of the old, rickety school bus full of strangers in the cooler, early morning hours back in Nyack, New York. It is not unlike the cool mornings of my childhood, when I dutifully climbed the big yellow school bus steps be-cause I knew I must (even as I knew that this daily journey would separate me by more than long, winding country roads from the sanctuary of my home). I am thankful at this moment for the years of practice climbing those steps against my will, because I know I must take this trip now.

The press has magnified the nation's collective fear, filling the head-lines and airwaves with frightening rumors of possible rioting and mass arrests in Washington. *Stay home,* they warn us. But right now a more urgent voice is lifted up into my heart. It is the voice of a lifetime of stories told 'round the family table, on long car rides, and in the holy moments of my parents' sitting on the edge of my bed in the safe darkness of my room, having tucked me between the crisp, clean sheets for the night. I hear my parents' patient, careful answers to my frightened questions about lynchings and bus burnings and churches bombed while little Sunday school children changed into their choir robes.

Could they come here? I don't remember asking this question out loud, but my mother must have guessed when she found me weeping in my sleep. I'd been having nightmares of the tiny choir room of Saint Paul's Episcopal Church — the crowded room where we'd fussed with each other on ordinary Sunday mornings as we changed into our red robes and freshly ironed white cottas — all blown up in flames and splinters. And though I cannot remember my parents' words, I feel the comforting tones of their voices and the warmth of my mother's hand in my hand, my father's larger hand squeezing my shoulder as they bravely, simply, taught their children through and beyond the anger and pain of their own firsthand memories of countless indignities perpetrated on our people. And then, as if my feet have their own memory of what my parents taught us next, I am lifted up the steps of this bus bound for the March on Washington. Something in me and beyond me is carrying on.

Now as the driver pulls closed the large silver lever of the folding bus door, as the old bus coughs and sputters away from the curb, I find myself comforted by the press of my seat mate's large right arm against my left shoulder, my right shoulder against the now-foggy bus window also familiar from years of crowded school bus rides. We are not all the way down the block before the bus is filled with singing and the pounding of fear in my chest makes itself at one with the heartbeat of the song rising up to fill the air: "My father was a soldier / He put his hand on the Gospel plough / When he got old and couldn't fight anymore / he just stood up and fought on anyhow." My voice easily finds the harmony it has found all my life at the family table, on long car rides away, on shorter car rides back home, in church, and on the sidewalks outside the local Woolworth's. The familiar songs and my voice's place in them connect me now to my story, the family story, the story the family tells about my people. The singing itself transforms fear into courage and brings me home to myself.

Two hours later, as I step down off the bus in the hot, crowded city, my body is moved into the March with the others. It is a march I've been on as long as I can remember. I feel no crush in the crowd, only a oneness with a people who know how to bring strength out of struggle, people marching home to ourselves.

We are gathered now in that oneness, a carpet of colorful humanity, shoulder to shoulder, singing, listening to speeches, some shouting back, all of us joined by our common struggle to manage our hot, sweaty, thirsty selves. Thankfully many of us have been raised to experience humor as a form of grace, and the complaints about the heat and the lengthy speeches are laced with plentiful laughter.

Then in a moment I cannot recollect the beginning of but will never forget being in the midst of, Dr. Martin Luther King Jr. speaks these words into a thundering silence, "I have a dream that my four children will one day live in a nation where they will not be judged by the color of their skin but by the content of their character."

It will be many years before I will learn the words for what I am feeling or will fully know what is happening to me as I stand here by the still water. But as Dr. King speaks of his dream, a dream is awakened in me. And even as I am a witness to these words becoming forever the words to my story, our story, I am rehearsing for a lifetime of witnessing this dream: that every child will be free to come home to him- or herself. One day I will look back on this moment and know that the ground where dreams are born and witnessed in their becoming reality is hallowed ground.

It is almost thirty years later in Pittsburgh, Pennsylvania. I am sitting in a tiny conference room off the main offices of Family Communications, the parent company of *Mister Rogers' Neighborhood*. Bronze plaques on the walls are engraved with awards and commendations to Fred McFeely Rogers, and as I wait just a few moments for him to come in for our interview, it strikes me how unlike my experience of him these fancy awards are. I have spent some months puzzling over how to approach the task I have been given, to write a piece about racism. I have reflected on the fact of the Neighborhood's birth during the times that followed in the footsteps of the 1963 March on Washington. Freedom songs were on the lips of many; civil rights marches were in the streets; and peace marches were in the parks. Martin Luther King Jr.'s words and work were in the life we were living. For many of us who worked with children, the principles of truth and freedom were at the center of our teaching, and the children we worked with challenged us to keep them there. They demanded that we reinterpret our beliefs in their times, strengthen them, and keep them alive.

I have been thinking about how Fred Rogers' work has had everything to do with the work at the heart of the Civil Rights movement and how today that work continues with its original honesty, clarity, and spirit. And like all good work with children, it has been and continues to be reinterpreted in the light of what children are experiencing in their world.

But what are children experiencing in their world now, I am asking myself as I anticipate treasured time with a person I know holds this same difficult question in his heart. Thirty years after the March on Washington, stories from the Civil Rights movement continue to instill in me new hope and sustaining faith. But I am humbled as I approach the task of reflecting on our efforts to be keepers of the dream and Fred Rogers' participation in that effort. In the face of all that we face as we raise our children in this troubled country and in this troubled world, one question keeps rising up into my work and confronting my dreams: What story wants telling?

The events of these times have penetrated any denial of the broad, deep, mean, and ongoing racism, sexism, homophobia, and countless other horrible injuries done to people whose stories are invisible. And yet, as I travel the country visiting schools, I hear the cloaked denial in the old 1950s guise of "some of my best friends. . . ." I hear it in the righteousness of those who have accomplished the beginning steps of going to workshops, setting up committees, and taking surveys and audits at their schools of statistics of people who are designated as minorities only because they are minorities in the context of school. "We did diversity last year," some have the chutzpah to say to me, as if "doing diversity" were something you got shots for like the measles or mumps. I feel the hurt when my eyes meet the eyes of young African Americans in schools who remind me of what I felt too often going off to school in a very white world. "Please don't bring it up," we are saying to each other, without words. "It's too painful, and when you go, we'll be left here exposed and alone to deal with it." All of this in communities where serious and good efforts are being made in multiculturalism, diversity, and global education, yet the word "racism" is taboo. What story wants telling?

In the late spring following the 1992 Los Angeles riots, I visited a school where the children were playing an old recess game with a new name. "You be Rodney King," these five-year-old white boys declared to the only black child in their class, and they began to play something we used to call "King of the Mountain." I personally hated the game by its old name. What story wants telling? What story will come forth to comfort a man who stands up at a school P.T.A. meeting and, identifying himself as a Native American, tells me that his eight-year-old child was asked to play the part in the school play of the Indian standing on the shore welcoming Christopher Columbus? What story do I tell the mother of a beautiful, dark-skinned African American girl who comes to school on Halloween disguised as a blond-haired Barbie? Daily, teachers and parents face the fear and exhaustion of darkened hallways and stairwells and streets where around any corner may lurk a mine encasing the explosives of the deprivation and destruction in our children's young lives. Our children are exposed to endless hours of TV coverage of violence, betrayal, rage over ravaged lives, and laws being designed in some states that would actually make it illegal to protect the civil rights of certain people. In the face of a national habit of people abusing power over people, what story wants telling?

The door to the small office opens and Fred Rogers and I greet each other. Now we sit, talking as though we were picking up in the middle of a conversation we had left off yesterday. In spite of the bustle of busy office noises on the other side of the door, there is a stillness in this moment, a sense that we have paused in the present tense. I am safe here to be myself, to let the question ask itself: What story wants telling? What story wants telling in the Neighborhood? How does Fred Rogers choose the story to heal the wounds and respond to the confusions brought on by this confusing world? It feels both urgent and possible to me to come right to the heart of the matter. And not surprisingly, Fred Rogers is no less direct in his response:

> I wonder if there isn't just one story. The way I feel about the Neighborhood is that we just have to be . . . ourselves. And if in some existential way that is in any way helpful to the being of whoever is receiving it, then that's fine. The space between the television set and the viewer or the receiver is very hallowed ground. What we do and say and broadcast — I think it's the attitude of it and the hope of it that makes much more of a difference than actually what it is. That image and those words

can be translated within the space of that television set and the viewer in ways that we will never know.

Hallowed ground. The ground on which dreams — "hopes," Fred Rogers is calling them — are born. What is he hoping for? What is the nature of his dream? What stories are being told in the Neighborhood of Make-Believe? What stories does he tell through the songs and the plays, the fables? What story is being told through the daily rituals, the pacing, the transitions from arrival in the Neighborhood to his promise at the end of each show to "be back when the day is new"?

"I'll never forget going to a little chapel in Nantucket," Fred Rogers says. He is, I know, beginning a story. It is not unlike the beginnings of hundreds of stories I heard him tell at five o'clock in the evening from the room next to the kitchen where, a decade and a half ago, my own children listened as Mister Rogers spoke to them in just this tone of voice. "This was years ago when I was still taking courses at the seminary," he says.

> There was this very, very old minister who had come to preach for just one Sunday because the regular person was off the island. And I sat there — Joanne was on one side and our friend was on the other — the whole pew of us. And I sat there with thoughts of my homiletics class at the Pittsburgh Seminary. And every imaginable thing was wrong about this man's sermon. It just couldn't have been worse. I mean, if he'd been in seminary, he'd have been lucky to get a D. And after the whole thing was over, I was just about to turn to our friend and say, "Wasn't that the worst you've ever heard?" And just before I said anything, I noticed that she had tears in her eyes. She said to me, "He said exactly what I needed to hear." I thought, "OK, Fred, this is one of the biggest lessons of your life." She came in with the need. I came in ready to judge. And she was the one who really received the Word. I'll be ever grateful for that experience. "He said exactly what I needed to hear." Something happened between that man's mouth and that woman's ears. . . .

And so, a parable about hallowed ground. And when I ask him whether it worries him not to be able to see the tears in the eyes of the television viewers the way he saw them in his friend's eyes, he says, "It's a mystery, an uncomfortable mystery. I think if it has to be just one story then the story has to be something about acceptance. I think that we all want to be accepted as we are. And we've learned that if we really can be, we can grow in amazing ways."

It is helpful to me to hear Fred Rogers welcome the mystery, the uncomfortable unknown. It comes as good news to me, having heard and experienced a professional lifetime-full of buzzwords, glib answers, fickle programs, and faddish solutions to the injuries sustained by children. Fred Rogers recognizes his part in a work far greater than the eye can see or the mind can hold, and he says so as the story of acceptance begins to unfold: "There is something about the eternal acceptance that I think we will know about once this particular paragraph has been read. I just think that this life of ours is a paragraph in a great big book. And some of the chapters have been before we were born; some are after we're gone. And I think that we maybe don't ever know completely what it's like to feel accepted exactly as we are, during this particular paragraph."

The story Fred Rogers is beginning to tell me now is not a story told in half-hour shows nor in anything measurable in human time. Rather it is the story of the acceptance of the presence of God in oneself and the myriad, multicolored, multitextured, multitemperamented, multicultured presences of God in others. Indeed, he is invoking an ancient law: "Love your neighbor as yourself."

"I mean, something has to look *through* these eyes to you," he says.

And if what's behind them is filled with judgment. . . . Dr. Orr [his mentor from seminary days] said to me one time that he felt that one thing the New Testament was not was that it was not a collection of writings of fault finding. He feels that if he could describe evil or Satan, he would describe that as the accuser — the desire to make people feel so awful about who they are that they will instinctively hate their neighbor. And then on the flip side of that, he says, is the example of Jesus as the person who affirms or accepts. So that if you can be truly accepted and loved for who you are and you can find that eternally, then you will live in a way that allows others to do that. But if you are going to be an accuser, then what that does is to spread just the opposite.

As Fred Rogers recalls the seminarian's lessons of inclusiveness and acceptance, I hear the voice of Mister Rogers describing the community of acceptance he has created on the Neighborhood — a place where it is safe for every child to come home to her- or himself.

There is a long pause. The office noises and the noises of the Pittsburgh street below barely penetrate this powerfully full silence. But somewhere in the not too far distance, a freight train blows its whistle and rings its bell. It comes at this moment of remarkable synchronicity — as if we have just returned to the Neighborhood from the land of make-believe to the familiar tune of the trolley whistle. Fred Rogers says, "On the Neighborhood we always say, 'You've made this day a special day by just your being you. There's only one person in the whole world like you, and people really can like you exactly as you are' — which allows *you* to like others the way *they* are." He smiles and says, "Pretty lofty!"

But the train whistle that has brought us back home to the sanctuary of the Neighborhood, to this familiar, intimate present-tense moment with Mister Rogers in which he lifts up his familiar refrain of acceptance and celebration of being special, is stirring a story awake. It is a story whose power and purpose are about to be revealed to us as the story unfolds. The story that is about to be told by Fred Rogers is his story. And just as he said it would be, it is the story of acceptance.

I know that ultimately the only story I can tell authentically and with confidence is my own story, and so I take the intuitive leap from my story across this mysterious ground to his. "Do people ever accuse you of having such a good childhood that you wouldn't know what difficulties they are feeling or experiencing? Do they ever say, 'How would *you* know?'"

"They might," he says quietly. "I don't know that they ever have. But I felt that my childhood had just as many challenges as somebody's who may not have had as many material things. I grew up in a fairly Victorian household, and a good deal was expected. I think it's tough, for one thing, to be an only child, and I virtually was for the first eleven years."

Then there is a long pause, the kind I have come to recognize as a sign of the story collecting itself and coming forth to be told.

"I think I always wanted to . . . to stay *settled*," Fred Rogers begins, "but I hadn't realized that until my later years. Our family spent three months every year in the South. It was right in the middle of my nine months of schooling. I had three months in the North and three months in the South and then three months back in the North." This is not a gentle telling;

there are no pauses here. Fred Rogers is periodically pounding the table for emphasis underlining the words that recount his moving back and forth.

> I didn't realize how disruptive that was until I took some extra careful looks at it. I think that's pretty fragmenting. Although I looked forward to seeing those people down in Florida every year, I think I would really have liked to have had some continuity of friendships all along. And finally when I was fourteen, I said, "I can't do this any more." I think that was interesting that I could do that — that I could say that! "I can't get through high school by taking the middle three months out."
>
> So I really had a strange kind of feeling for migrant kids when we did our project on migrant workers. They're far, far worse off than I would have ever known. But at least I knew the wrenches during the year.

Fred Rogers' pounding on the table punctuates his story, and his pounding resonates as a pounding in my chest, a stirring in response to the urgency of his remembering. At the outset of my work on this essay, I had been asked what Fred Rogers, a white, American-born, Presbyterian minister is doing on the Neighborhood about preventing and dealing with racism. And the question itself had bothered me. At the very least, it seemed like the wrong question to be asking. In my professional travels, working in public and private schools across the United States, I am constantly called to confront the subtle but injurious infliction of indignities that others choose to ignore. But then, as a black person raised in this country, I know to keep every cell in my body awake to the persistent possibilities of racism at any turn. It is in the memory of the fabric of everything from an ordinary trip to the grocery store or rental-car counter to being the brown-skinned principal of a mostly white elementary school. So I am certain that the question of racism, isolated from everything else, is the wrong question. To understand the way racism and other forms and disguises of injury inflicted on the wholeness of human beings bleed deeply into every pore of our lives, we have to be still and listen for the stirrings, the poundings, the moments of pain that rise up in the story and want telling. As Fred Rogers recollects the moment when at fourteen he had had enough of the unsettling moves, when he remembers the connections he had made to friends, and the place he was carving out for himself as a leader in his school community, his story takes on an urgency, and he uses the words "fragmented" and "wrenched" — wrenched from home and friends and school. And, I am thinking, wrenched from himself. The momentary picture in my mind is of the injury, the wrenching, the fragmenting — the challenge, Fred Rogers had called it a little while earlier. But that image is quickly eclipsed by another. The new image is colorful and warm and familiar. This one is gentle and welcoming. Somebody is playing the piano. There is a village with some buildings, trees, grass, streets and sidewalks, a trolley, a house, a blinking traffic light, a door is opening. Now we are inside the house — a house we've been in many times before. Mister Rogers comes through the doorway and welcomes us in with him: "It's a beautiful day in the neighborhood, a beautiful day for a neighbor. Won't you be mine?" We are home to *Mister Rogers' Neighborhood*. But more than that, we are home to ourselves. The story that wants telling in the Neighborhood is the story of acceptance, and the Neighborhood itself is a metaphor for just that — a community of acceptance where you are special just by being you, where you are liked just the way you are. Fred Rogers recollects his own challenge — the challenge of discontinuity. Then he takes that same challenge and turns it into the strength of his work.

I wait and then I speak out loud about the new place the stirring of Fred Rogers' story has brought me to in my mind. "It's so beautiful to hear that," I say to him, respectful of the courage I know it takes to revisit the hard places in the story, the places of discontinuity. "You've created this kind of continuity for children where, no matter how much discontinuity there is in their lives, they can turn on the television and you're right there in the same place every day — all seasons — no three months off."

"Now I understand," says Fred Rogers, sitting in the light of the revelation he has just heard in his own story, "why those cards and letters mean so much to me — the ones that say, 'We just moved, and we found you here, too.'" Children who have moved, children whose lives have changed around them in fragmenting and unsettling ways both traumatic and subtle, as all children's lives do, children who have spent the first monumental five years of life at home and are now spending long days at school — all these children are able to turn on the television set and come home safe to the Neighborhood, home to themselves.

I am reminded at this moment of the thousands of parents and teachers I have met on my professional school journey and the stories they have had the courage and generosity to tell in my presence. I am thinking about the myriad ways in which the pieces of those stories reveal themselves in their daily work with children. So often, the very thing that was a struggle for each of us — the thing that was injurious, the part of the story where we felt disconnected from ourselves, not understood, not accepted by others — is the thing that we turn into the strength of our life's work. In the hard work of remembering, discovering, understanding, naming, and acting upon the old hurt, challenge is transformed into a strength. And in the process of righting for the children what was wrong for us, we are, over and over again, righting it for ourselves. In the story, we return to the site of the original injury, and create out of it an opportunity to heal.[1]

Fred Rogers had reached back into the landscape of his memory and had recovered a piece of the story in which he felt fragmented and uprooted, when he longed to "stay settled" in one place. But what he also recovered is the memory of standing up for himself and insisting upon what it would take to feel settled and whole. It is not only the memory of the challenge itself that fuels his story but also the memory of the strength to face that challenge, to face and accept himself. On the Neighborhood, Mister Rogers lends children, not the story's sadness or loneliness alone, but also this moment of self-acceptance when he is saying, "I'm not doing this any more. I'm connecting myself to the world." The stories told on the Neighborhood, the songs, the plays, the tender explanations say, "This is the way we all feel inside sometimes. But this is what you are able to do for yourself." By being himself, by accepting who he is, different from everyone else in the world, Fred Rogers is able to reach out to "love his neighbor," to cocreate for children a neighborhood of acceptance where "You've made this day a special day by just your being you, where people can like you exactly as you are."

When I began to think about this piece, there was a feeling that followed me around in my heart, making it only part way to my mind. And with the feeling came a picture of a corner of the basement of a house where my growing-up family lived in Queens when I was two and three years old. In this ancient but very present image, my mother is folding the laundry next to one of those funny old washing machines with the squeeze-roller tops. We are talking, or maybe just she is talking and I am watching. I feel sad, but in this little, dark, damp corner of the basement, it feels safe to be sad.

I have learned to attend to the images that follow me from my dreams into the light of day, the pieces of tunes that insist on being sung, the characters from stories who visit my thoughts — some of them comforting, some of them downright disquieting. So I knew that when I discovered the source of this recurrent image from my early childhood that it would be an important teaching for me. It came from an ancient file of articles written by my parents early on in their shared professional lifetimes of working for justice and peace, wholeness and healing. Like so many things we grow up taking for granted as part of our childhood landscapes, the wealth of scholarship and wisdom in my parents' writings was a gift to me anew as an adult with a developing store of personal and professional experience and wisdom of my own.

I had rediscovered an article written by my mother, Dr. Margaret Morgan Lawrence, entitled "How Prejudice Begins."[2] It was familiar reading both in content and in voice. After all, these were the teachings I had grown up with, the views of life that were woven into the songs we sang, the stories told, the explanations given to our wonderings.

Speaking of what she calls "a mingling of feelings," my mother uses a story to illustrate how "attitudes towards skin color became part of a little girl's feelings toward herself and others." Though she substitutes the name "Sue" for the real little girl in the story, I now know why a forty-five-year-old memory of a corner of the basement in a long-ago house had followed me around with such persistence. It was the story about racism that wanted telling.

> Two three-year-old girls, one Negro, one white, were close friends in a nursery school. The two children were inseparable during school hours. The white mother called for her child at the end of the school day and walked around the corner with her to their home. The Negro child waved good-by to her friend and her mother, was ushered into the school bus by a careful hand and delivered at the home of a relative, where her working mother met her. The Negro mother was a stranger to the three-year-old group until one day when she gave a birthday party in the classroom. Her daughter's friend approached her, frowning. "What are

you?" she asked. "Are you French? Why don't you pick Sue up after school? I don't like you." The Negro mother reported that the next day Sue appeared listless at home. When a family outing was suggested, she fretted and would not put on her outdoor clothing. When she and her mother were alone she confided, "I don't want to go out. The sun will make me brown. I don't want to be brown."

The story goes on. I know it does because it is my story. But for now, I pause on the image of being alone with my mother, standing by the laundry machine, not wanting to leave the house because the sun might make me browner, confiding in her my confusion, my fear and anger and feelings of separation from her and separation from myself.

Two days passed before Sue could ask the question that really distressed her. "Why don't you come for me at school, mommy? Kate's mother comes for her." Sue's thoughts had run somewhat this way: "My mommy is a bad mommy. She is brown too. Kate's mother is a good mommy. She is white. It is bad to be brown." Sue's problem was of short duration. It helped that her mother, daddy, and teacher said they knew how she felt as she stepped into the bus, watching Kate and her mother walk off, arms about one another. They told her, too, that they were proud that she could help do the job of getting herself to the place where she met her mother every day. And in the course of realizing that her mother was a "good mommy," she also came to sense that her mother liked being brown.

Had Sue's doubt concerning her mother's love for her been more serious and unresolved, she might well have been left for life with an attitude, "Because I am brown, I have little value. I cannot be liked for myself, or trust myself to perform well in school and later in a job."

The discovery of this story is a painful uncovering for me. And my wish to keep it from rising up any further than halfway to my brain has everything to do with why the initial questions raised about racism were at once the wrong questions and yet pointed uncomfortably to the very questions that needed to be asked. Alas, I have come to know that the moment of pain, the moment in which the story comes alive, is the teachable moment. When I return to that moment in my own story, I return to the moment when I knew I could board not just the daily school bus, but the rickety old church bus to the March on Washington. In the teachable moment, I remember not my parents' words but "the comforting tones of their voices and the warmth of my mother's hand in my hand, my father's larger hand squeezing my shoulder as they bravely, simply, taught their children through and beyond the anger and pain of their own first-hand memories of indignities inflicted on our people. And then, as if my feet have their own memory of what my parents taught us next, I am lifted up the steps of this bus bound for the March on Washington. Something in me and beyond me is carrying on" — carrying me on to a lifetime of commitment to a dream. Over and over as I return to the teachable moment (even and maybe especially in the presence of this great teacher, Fred Rogers), I know why I have such passion for the wholeness of children and such attentiveness to their healing.

When I became a teacher I had found a way to live my dream, to be myself. The children demanded to know the truth about who I was, and in doing so led me home to myself. They challenged me to tell my story and insisted that they be allowed to become part of that story, too. The dream was their dream — to be known by the content of their character, not to have to unforget who they really were inside. And so, year by year, season by season, moment by sometimes treacherous moment, we retold the stories of the movement — we brought it forward into the present tense where we could live it together on the bus rides, at morning circle, in the block corner, in the made-up-for-real plays, as we settled arguments over recess games, as we celebrated our lives together, and broke bread together at the school table. The words of comfort and explanation came when they needed to, not from me but through me — from the dinner table and car rides and especially the bedside of my childhood. And as my healing hands held their hands or squeezed their shoulders and spoke the familiar words, something in me was healed over and over again as the story and the singing and the dream got carried on.

"Maybe the word 'racism' is kind of superficial," Fred Rogers says to me now, taking the intuitive leap that is also his gift. "Each one of us has a kind of racism inside, an inner racism."

Racism — the inability to love another, the directing of one's own injured feelings toward hurting another, the judging of another based on one's unfavorable judgment of oneself — is the second part of the story. But the first part of the story is this: our inability to love ourselves — what Fred Rogers has aptly called inner racism. We are faced with a choice between paths: one leading to connection and self-acceptance, the other to loneliness, alienation, and unresolved anger directed against ourselves and eventually against the world. When the moment of choice is pushed down inside or pushed away, when we are not able to be ourselves in it, to stand up to the moment and confess our confusions on behalf of our own wholeness, when we are not helped in overcoming the challenge, we are stuck in a lifetime separated from our own goodness, unable to accept ourselves and unable to love another. "We have the eyes and ears of what's behind these eyes and ears," Fred Rogers continues. "And we can't see somebody else or hear somebody else unless behind those things there's a certain acceptance of what's behind them."

Racism and other forms of inflicting indignities on others cannot be addressed without attending over and over to the myriad moments of inner racism in all their mystery, complexity, associations, and disguises. Response to this reality is tenderly, thoughtfully, truthfully, and continually lived out on the Neighborhood. In a world that judges — particularly a world that judges young children, measuring them early and often by arbitrary yardsticks — the Neighborhood offers children the chance to know themselves as special because they are different from everyone else in the world.

So much of the racism alive in this world is the result of our inability to expose our ignorance about each other. It is in the context of a truthful relationship with children that Fred Rogers encourages children to ask questions, to be in the habit of unburdening themselves of hurtful ignorance. Fred Rogers' security about and awareness of his own values creates a safe context in which to explore this difficult territory with children. In a series of episodes about conflict, there has been great misunderstanding in the Neighborhood of Make-Believe because King Friday is imagining that people in a nearby kingdom are making bombs. "You see, people can imagine bad, angry, hurtful, warlike things," Fred Rogers says in summarizing the program. "But people can also imagine good things, helpful things, happy things." And then, speaking of inner racism projected onto someone else as racism, he continues, "What we imagine depends on what we are feeling. When we feel angry, we might imagine that someone is angry with us. . . . The only way to be sure what people are feeling is to find out from them."

But *how* do we "find out from them"? *By discovering their stories.* The ancient Hebrews taught their young to tell the age-old stories in the present tense. They knew that retelling the story did more than remind people of what happened long ago. The retelling had the effect of bringing the past up into the present and giving it life.[3] And so it is in the Neighborhood. The song, the fable, the play in the Neighborhood of Make-Believe invite the viewer to participate in the parable, told by Mister Rogers in the present tense. Whether song or play, field trip into the stores, homes, factories, and nature trails of the village and the surroundings, or into the Neighborhood of Make-Believe, the parable itself becomes an event, one that can be experienced with Fred Rogers as welcomer and guide. "I want you to meet my television neighbor," he says to the person we are visiting in the music store, and we are right there in the present tense together.

Fred Rogers uses his own interior landscape as a source of knowing and empathy. And then, acting on that empathy, he tells a story. Mister Rogers is the griot, the rememberer, the one who uses recovery of his own story to awaken the child's story. Through the rhythms and rituals, in the music and stories, in the thoughtful explanations and the transitions that carefully connect it all, he creates a community, a place where the listener's story and the story of the teller meet. Fred Rogers attends to and honors each participant in the Neighborhood community as different from everyone else in the world. In every decision he makes about what to include on the show, how to say it, who needs to say it, how to present it, he acknowledges the complexities and subtleties of the differences brought to the television experience by each child. Even as a particular show evolves, he seems to be anticipating the wonderings of children. "The child[ren] at the television set [bring to their] watching and listening their whole being — everything they've been through: all the joys, all the sadness, all the fears," Fred Rogers once wrote. "All of that comes with them as they watch our work on television, just as all of that comes with them as they go to day care or nursery school or first grade or law school! In other words, as you and I work with human beings, what we say and do is received by each person in the light of what that person's life circumstances (and his or her reaction to those life circumstances) are at any given time."[4] The Neighborhood becomes the place where the story told in the teachable moment awakens the story in each child and brings her or him through their challenges into self-acceptance and on to acceptance of others.

Neighborhood visits are filled with adventures that provide a broad, deep, colorful, complicated landscape into which each child is invited to enter with feelings and experiences unique to his or her own story. The parables and songs and visits introduce Mister Rogers' television neighbor characters who bring with them their gifts, their uniqueness, their music, their colors and temperaments and stories. But it is in *being himself*, it is in telling his own story with clarity and honesty, that Fred Rogers offers children a sense of their self-worth by offering them acceptance of themselves. He creates a sanctuary for children, a place where they feel safe to be themselves, to express their wonderings and fears or even to be allowed to be shy about them. In helping children respond to and cope with injury, anger, conflict, trauma, and damage to their self-esteem, Mister Rogers is giving them life skills with which to live in a world that will continue to be full of obvious and subtle indignities inflicted upon who they are inside. Mister Rogers, a trusted, important, and even central adult in the lives of his television "neighbors," invites children to be themselves with all of their differences, their uniqueness, the gift of who they are, different from everyone else. "You know what good friends Elsie Neal, Bob Trow, Chef Brockett and I are," says Mister Rogers after a visit to Elsie Neal's studio. "And you also know how different we all are. But I think that's what helps us to be friends — because we are so different. I can't be exactly like Elsie Neal or Chef Brockett or Bob Trow or any of my other friends. That's why I need them to be my friends — because we are different. It is the same way with you. I can't be you. That's why I need you for my friend." By his active and continuous presence in their lives, by his understanding of and acting in the teachable moments, Fred Rogers makes the connection for children between their own strengths and the world they live in. "I like to make these television programs for you," he says at the end of a week of programs about conflict and war. "We prove to each other and to other people that we can talk about all kinds of things, and that's because we care about one another. I hope you'll talk with the grown-ups you love about how they feel about war and peace, being angry and loving. That way you'll be able to find out what the history of your family is and all the many ways they've celebrated peace in their lives."

Toward the end of our conversation, I confess a worry to Fred Rogers, knowing somehow that it is very much connected to the story of acceptance. In my travels to schools, I frequently see an inclination on the part of teachers and even some parents that I find deeply troubling. Schools and churches and community groups have invited diversity of all kinds, I tell him, and claim to be celebrating diversity. "And yet," I say,

> many people in schools are afraid of children who are different. Many white teachers in particular are afraid of African American children. They are afraid they might say the wrong thing, or they are afraid that if they address a problem with an African American child, they'll get called a racist. Some people are afraid of children because they are smart or because they are very big for their age or because they have some physical feature that is different from other people. Some people are afraid of children because they are sick. So when these children look into the eyes of their teachers, what they see reflected there is fear. I think that it is very scary for a young child to feel that someone is afraid of them.

"So you don't feel that people are able to give them limits?" asks Fred Rogers, in whom the gift of being unafraid of children is essential and present in his work. And then, "If someone can't give a child limits, that child very quickly learns that that person doesn't love him. If you can't tell me not to run out in the street, I quickly learn that you don't care whether I do or not."

When it is projected onto the child, this unresolved fear that adults may have inside them—their own inner racism—becomes a systemic manifestation of racism. And so I wonder aloud to Fred Rogers whether there is a story that wants telling on the Neighborhood about what it feels like when people are not helping you with limits, whether it is something that needs naming and acting out in the stories and fables and plays and songs.

"There was a week when we did talk about limits and about when parents and teachers say 'no,' " he recalls. "It is so often because they really love you, and they want you to grow in healthy ways, and they don't want you to get hurt. It's a very difficult concept. It's difficult *cosmically*. We don't want to hear 'no' from God."

"Then the flip side of that is also a difficult concept," I continue. "What does it feel like to have somebody not care enough to stop me?" Fred Rogers replies with another connection: "And what does it feel like when ultimately you are able to incorporate that stopping for yourself? I think that in some ways we try to communicate that to the kids. There will be a day when you'll be able to do that." To be able to incorporate limits for yourself is to be able to incorporate eternal acceptance of yourself, to be able to love yourself. To be able to love yourself is to be well on your way to loving your neighbor.

Television is a powerful and magnetic teacher. If it is used to silence children's stories or fuel and fill them with images of rage and fear and estrangement so that they cannot hear the awakening of their own stories, the ever-repeating patterns of inner infliction of pain and outer infliction of injury will continue. But when the power of television is used while honoring the mysterious ground, the holy ground we stand on in the presence of growing children, when it is used as Fred Rogers uses it — humbly, gently, knowingly offering parable, ritual, and familiarity to awaken the children's own stories — there is the possibility of wholeness and healing. And the miracle is this: that when the children know their own stories, when they know the feeling of acceptance of who they are inside, the stories that rise up from that place where eternal acceptance resides in them will have the power to right what is wrong in this wounding world.

It is five o'clock of any afternoon of my early days as a parent. The tiny kitchen of our house is next to the room we call the playroom. The playroom is abuzz all day with good people noises: toy trucks, buses, cars, music-making, Lego constructions, books, adventure plays, and visits from friends. Some days, the whole kingdom of stuffed animals is invited down from the children's bedrooms to be "fans" for their table hockey games, though the real joy is in the effort of setting up the "fans" in the bleachers more than in playing the game itself. The animal friends are also invited to watch the children's favorite television shows. My own growing-up years were in the country, and I loved the hours on end my friends and siblings and I had in the safety of the woods and fields and down the road making up our own adventures away from adults. So I am grateful for the layout of this house, which allows me to be present and accessible as mother of these children, but not underfoot of their ongoing play. It is five o'clock and I am especially grateful now that I can be nearby, beginning to prepare supper, winding down toward the end of the day. With one ear toward the play-room, I hear somebody playing the piano. Without looking I can picture a village with some buildings, trees, grass, streets and sidewalks, a trolley, a house, a blinking traffic light, a door is opening. Now we are inside the house, a house we've been in many times before. We are home. We are home to ourselves.

I am feeling now what I first felt standing by the cool water of the Reflecting Pool, when I heard Dr. King's words split the thundering si-lence: "I have a dream that my four children will one day live in a nation where they will not be judged by the color of their skin but by the content of their character." I know at this everyday, ordinary five o'clock with my children that I am in the presence of someone who is a keeper of the dream.

Lynette Friedrich Cofer was the first researcher (circa 1972) to compare the effects of television violence and Mister Rogers' Neighborhood *on children in natural settings. Along with her colleague, Aletha Huston-Stein, Cofer extended laboratory findings about television to nursery school classes and day care centers to observe how children in the real world reacted.*

In this essay, Cofer places her own work in a broader social context and explores how we have moved from past to present in our experience with television. Why, she asks, when the relation between television violence and aggression has been demonstrated in a vast number of studies, has television in our country become so much worse? Why have we been unable to halt commercial expansion that has invaded the lives of children and families and now threatens our free press?

"I overestimated the power of empirical research to affect public policy where enormous financial interests are involved. I underestimated the extent to which false political chasms had withered our political discourse," she says now. "I view our contemporary dilemma as one of unconstrained commercial greed — pure and simple — that has been allowed to affect all our access to information and entertainment." However, she believes, there may be a chance to turn the tide. Fred Rogers' Neighborhood "is a small civil society in which people work to discover truths about themselves as individuals and truths about the ways in which they are interconnected and can realize shared ends or civic goods. It has much to offer us in the struggle to give shape to democratic ideals."

Cofer is professor of psychology at the University of New Mexico. She received her B.A. from Stanford University and her Ph.D. from Cornell University. Her work has appeared in numerous publications including Child Development, Developmental Psychology, Review of Child Development Research, *and the* Minnesota Symposium on Child Psychology. *She is editor of* Human Nature and Public Policy: Scientific Views of Women, Children, and Families *(New York: Praeger, 1986).*

Lynette Friedrich Cofer

Make-Believe, Truth, and Freedom

Television in the Public Interest

Children's television is no longer the "vast wasteland" of 1961, but a "waste site, strewn with war toys, insipid cartoons and oversweetened cereals."[1] We seem unable to halt a technological and commercial expansion that has invaded the lives of children and families and now threatens our free press. This essay explores how we have moved from past to present in our experience with television, the failure of social science research to influence rational social policy, the ascendance of market choices over the Madisonian view of free speech and of corporate privilege over responsibilities in media ownership, and the diminution of public influence. But reflection on the achievements of Fred Rogers modifies this bleak trajectory and helps us to see what the media could become and how we might affect its course in society. The Neighborhood of Make-Believe is a small civil society in which people work to discover truths about themselves as individuals and truths about the ways in which they are interconnected and can realize shared ends or civic goods. It has much to offer us in the struggle to give shape to democratic ideals.

In the late 1960s, following periodic rounds of congressional hearings on the growing crime rate and a possible link to the viewing of violent television, Sen. John Pastore directed the surgeon general to provide new research to answer the question — does violent television affect aggressive behavior in children and youth? There were many laboratory experiments showing that viewing violent films leads to aggressive behavior in young children. The specific charge given to my colleague, Aletha Huston, and me was to determine whether these findings could be replicated in a natural setting.

145

Why, then, did we include *Mister Rogers' Neighborhood?* The brief answer is belief in a child. My first-born son, Matthew, was a toddler when *Mister Rogers' Neighborhood* entered our home in 1968. Matthew loved and trusted Mister Rogers almost immediately. He soon found words and insights in the Neighborhood that became an important part of his everyday life. When he was excited about a new accomplishment or creation or frustrated by a difficult task, he used language from the program to express his feelings. The content informed his efforts to handle rules, learn new skills, and get along with playmates. He was able to tell himself—and me—that "I need to take my time to do this by myself" or that "sometimes it is hard to share." If my child found such meaning in the program, why not include it in our design to see if other young children would respond in similar ways?[2]

Our proposal to include aggressive cartoons and *Mister Rogers' Neighborhood* in our study was more unusual than it may now appear. The laboratory research on aggression was guided by the tenets of social learning theory, which directed the eyes of the researcher to the behaviors learned and imitated from the observation of filmed aggression. Fred Rogers and his adviser, Margaret McFarland, shared a very different perspective on children—an Eriksonian view that stressed the importance of feelings and understanding in the developing child, and the belief that while children share similar feelings and progress through similar developmental stages, no two children grow in quite the same way. But the funders agreed to the expansion in design, and Fred and Margaret, in a leap of faith, trusted us to include the program.

Our entry into the real world of children came through the organization of a nine-week summer session at the Pennsylvania State University nursery school.[3] The first three weeks constituted a base period of observation. During the next four weeks children were assigned to one of three television viewing conditions: violent cartoons (*Batman* and *Superman*), neutral films (for instance, a nature trip), or *Mister Rogers' Neighborhood.* We selected several sequences of Mister Rogers programs in which dilemmas arose and were resolved, focusing on themes such as the uniqueness and worth of each person, learning to talk about and cope with one's own feelings, understanding the feelings of others and caring about others, learning to wait, and persisting in order to gain competence. The final two weeks were a follow-up period in which television was not shown.

During the entire period, trained observers categorized the behavior of each child for approximately three five-minute periods each day. Behavior fell into three major categories: aggression, prosocial interpersonal behavior, and self-regulation.

What were we able to contribute from our findings to the policy debate over the effects of television violence? Our results indicated that aggressive cartoons did influence interpersonal aggression, but only for those children who were initially above the group average in aggression. In interpreting this finding, we emphasized that these children were not extreme or deviant; the "above average" children constituted half of a sample of normal boys and girls. Our findings were consistent with a mass of data indicating that violent television instigates aggressive behavior for children from preschool to adolescence. Our unique contribution was the observation of *natural* behavior. Violent television has an effect beyond the controlled laboratory and prearranged play session; aggressive behavior increases in everyday activities and settings that are quite different from those in which the aggression is portrayed.

Another finding about children who had seen aggressive cartoons, which was not limited to more aggressive children, was a sharp decline in patience, in tolerating ordinary delays, as well as a decline in acceptance of the ordinary rules of the nursery school. These results suggest that violent cartoons may generally arouse tension and speed up impatient reactions. The child who does not wait for feedback is likely to be unresponsive to others' needs: to grab, push, and become easily frustrated. The negative effect of violent television on the tenuous self-control that most young children have may be at least as important as its effects on aggression.

And what of the children who saw the quiet and complex *Mister Rogers' Neighborhood* programs? They showed significant changes in behaviors that require self-control: increased persistence or the amount of time they spent concentrating on projects, greater ability to carry out responsibility without adult intervention in tasks like helping with cleanup, and greater patience waiting to take their turn or to be served at juice time. We also found significant changes for children from lower social class homes in the quality of their play with other children — increased cooperation, ability to express feelings, and sympathy and help for others.

The findings were exciting: we were the first to demonstrate that well-designed, creative television in the context of a good nursery school could affect behaviors that were important to healthy social and intellectual development. We had tapped, it seemed, a resource that went beyond sheer imitation, enabling children to develop the approaches to learning and to interacting with others that lead to achievement and social sensitivity and competence.

Our research agenda was to build upon these positive findings through attempts to link the content of *Mister Rogers' Neighborhood* to the child's experience in schools. We next conducted research with kindergarten children with only four programs in a series that focused on Henrietta Pussycat, a shy, timid character in the Neighborhood, and her feelings of jealousy and abandonment upon the arrival of her glamorous cousin from Paris and the attempts of others to understand and to help her.[4] We elaborated upon the themes from the Neighborhood through an adult using books or puppets to retell the unfolding story and to extend it to a parallel story involving young children. Children either answered questions in story sessions, used puppets to reenact the plot in puppet sessions, or were in sessions involving both books and puppets. A control group saw the standard neutral films. We assessed learning and helping behavior using a variety of measures.

In brief, we found that children can learn complex content from viewing only a brief sequence of programs. To translate this content into actual helping behavior in tasks different from the programs, however, required additional rehearsal and elaboration. Role-playing with puppets was particularly effective for boys, while girls showed the most helpful behavior if they had been in the sessions that combined books and puppets. These findings underscored our concerns that boys had fewer opportunities than girls to engage in positive fantasy play. While girls' play with dolls leads to nurturing and loving interactions, the toys sanctioned for boys as masculine often stimulate aggressive play. The structured interactions with the adult and puppets led to new kinds of experiences and learning.

The findings I have described are statistically significant because enough children responded to the particular experimental conditions or experiences that the behavioral differences measured cannot be accounted for by chance. Those are the scientific, normative rules that govern researchers. But it is easy to miss the individual child in such reports. One boy in the kindergarten study still frequents my memory, and he is an equally significant part of the research story.

I had visited a few of the training sessions early in the study and was a bit worried about this child, who was highly active, attention-seeking, and aggressive in words and actions in the puppet training session. (One of the graduate students dubbed him a "mouse on a hot rock.") Even our skilled teacher, Ann Clewett, had her hands full helping this child to wait to take his turn and learn to use his puppet as something other than a battering ram. He was the very profile of a child who would respond to violent television with gusto.

In a later testing session I was hidden from the boy, conducting puppet interviews from behind a small theater, using Henrietta Pussycat for a prop. He raced into the room, wiggled on his chair, and pulled his hair — but just as suddenly became rapt with attention when Henrietta told of her distress over her Parisian cousin, Collette. He slid on his knees next to the stage when she spoke of her fears of being replaced and of her despair. When she angrily knocked down Collette's picture and her necklace, he scooped up all the beads with frantic haste, repeating, "Don't worry, we'll fix it." He then placed his hand gently on the puppet's face and stroked it slowly, saying, "There's only one kitty like you, Henrietta. Don't you know that nobody can ever take your place? We love you and we will always love you no matter who else comes." He went on, speaking reassuringly and stroking the puppet's face for what seemed like many minutes. It was hard to keep the puppet still and keep to the script because tears were coming down my cheeks. I knew that for one child the program and an enabling teacher had made a difference.

We then launched our most ambitious project, a large field experiment in five Head Start centers with thirteen classes in inner-city Philadelphia over a period of many months.[5] Both black and white children were included, but they attended different centers due to the residential segregation of the city. After extensive baseline observations, classrooms were assigned to view twenty films in eight weeks in experimental conditions that ranged from neutral films and cognitive enrichment materials in the classroom to *Mister Rogers' Neighborhood,* with materials from the programs and training of teachers to incorporate the themes into classroom activities.

The Mister Rogers programs introduced alone into existing classrooms did not appear to have the same saliency demonstrated at Penn State. The established group atmospheres and more aggressive behavior patterns of children living in urban poverty may have been sufficiently robust that viewing the program without further alterations in the classroom did not significantly affect interpersonal behavior. However, in those classrooms in which the teacher was a trained participant who elaborated upon the themes with children, positive changes in social behavior occurred. We speculated at the time that the enthusiasm expressed by teachers involved with *Mister Rogers' Neighborhood* and curricular materials was important as well. They, too, felt reassured and encouraged about themselves and their ability to understand and work effectively with children and to enjoy the enhanced positive climate of the classroom.

Our studies provide strong evidence that viewing *Mister Rogers' Neighborhood* in the preschool and kindergarten settings can greatly benefit children. There was approval from the scientific community and, it seemed to us, considerable political support for a transformation of offerings to children. Grassroots organizations including parents, educators, religious groups, and physicians were clamoring for change by the networks. We thought that the proposed alternatives to harmful violent fare might be welcomed by the commercial television industry. We were wrong.

My view of the role of science in society was remarkably naive at the time of our studies. I overestimated the power of empirical research to affect public policy where enormous financial interests are involved.[6] I underestimated the extent to which false political chasms had withered our political discourse. Policy makers often want "proof" from research, that is, flawless scientific data that establish direct one-way causality. Does a temperature of 327.5° C make lead melt? Remember our charge: Does television violence cause aggression? It is the same sort of question asked repeatedly of researchers; for example, does cigarette smoking cause cancer? Responsible researchers cannot deliver that sort of irrefutable causal proof. Humans are far too complex and our theories and methods far too limited. Scientists hired by the networks (or the cigarette industry) launch attacks on this sort of simple "proof," resulting in months or years of technical talk that obscures the real issues of concern. At best we can argue probabilities.

The weight of convergent evidence supports the likelihood that television contributes to aggression for many young people. Is it of less social concern that many researchers have found that more aggressive children and youth both tend to seek out and to respond to violent television? Some of our most needy children are most vulnerable. Does that weaken the argument? And what of our "lost" findings concerning adverse effects on self-control? What of our "lost" positive findings that speak to the real concerns of the development of civic virtue and creativity? I now believe that when we frame and discuss social problems primarily as scientific ones, the larger purpose may be defeated.[7] The guises of objective, value-free sciences are dangerous, for meaningful discussion is obscured, cut short, and divorced from real concerns and lives.

I view our contemporary dilemma as one of unconstrained commercial greed—pure and simple—that has been allowed to affect all our access to information and entertainment. From this perspective it is no surprise that the debates over television in the 1970s resulted in minimal new offerings for children and minimal regulation of advertising. Nor is it a surprise that the rush to deregulate television—to enhance economic competition—in the 1980s led to a triumph of commercial interests and new levels of sex, violence, and advertising and a rapid decrease in children's educational programming.[8] In a climate of political distrust and polarization, the public failed to come together to challenge the assumptions of narrow economic theory and the murky terms used to justify greed.

Television was just a "toaster with pictures," according to FCC chairman, Mark Fowler. The "public interest" was redefined to mean "what the public wants" like any other marketplace commodity. What the public wants, of course, is determined by the viewing habits of the four thousand families who agreed to let the Nielson industry wire their homes. Yet 45 percent of the families approached for Nielson metering refuse to cooperate, according to an article in *Connoisseur* (September 1989). Such sampling techniques appear to yield a dubious picture of what the real public wants. At best they tell us which buttons people pressed, given their limited choices.

Newton Minow, FCC chairman in 1961, hit the mark in his speech to the National Association of Broadcasters by noting that ratings never tell what the public acceptance would have been if programming were better — "if all the forces of art and creativity and daring and imagination had been unleashed." In this speech, Minow also decried the use of ratings for children: "If parents, teachers, and ministers conducted their responsibilities by following ratings, children would have a steady diet of ice cream, school holidays, and no Sunday school." But most important, ratings yield market information that is irrelevant to the contribution of television programming to the public interest or to the public good.[9]

Minow and Lamay note that moral questions are rarely asked in current discussions mired in economic theories of efficiency and equity

> as if the public interest were merely a matter of distributive justice. . . . The who-gets-what conceptualization of the public interest is anti-democratic at its core, since it assiduously avoids having to make moral decisions that democracies, by definition, are supposed to make. Children are the biggest losers of all in this calculus, because they lack economic and political power and are dependent on the moral discretion of adults for their safety and health, their civic and academic education — their future.[10]

These sorry developments in the state of the media and in the language of our public discourse coincide with difficult times for U.S. families. Unemployment has risen sharply, while those who do work must speed up the pace and work longer hours. According to a *New York Times* article on September 3, 1995, parents are spending 40 percent less time with their children than they did thirty years ago. Despite these changes in the workplace, sharp increases in the cost of living and drops in male wages have diminished earnings. In 1988 the average family income was only 6 percent higher than in 1973 even though almost twice as many married women were working. The number of single mothers holding two jobs quintupled between 1970 and 1989. Yet we have the highest poverty rate for children in any of the world's industrialized democracies — one in five live below the poverty line.[11]

From these grim statistics it would appear that parents are working more, simply to provide for their children and to meet bare necessities. But the amount of work is also due in part to the lifestyle we have come to expect and the pressures of consumerism. We have been the target of $21 billion per year in advertising fees. Parents are not at home to monitor television — they are working — so children watch more television and see more ads. (More than 2 million children under the age of thirteen have no supervision either before or after school.) When parents do come home, they are often so tired that they only engage in passive pursuits — and television is first on the list. In this country, watching more television means watching more ads that tell us "wants" are "needs," that we "are" what we can buy. So the cycle of consumerism grows.[12]

Advertisers now spend slightly more than $470 million a year on broadcast sponsorship aimed at children. The number of commercials aimed at children nearly doubled between the late 1970s and 1987. In 1985 toy manufacturers and broadcasters were allowed to turn toys into entire programs. In the next five years, the time given to war cartoons grew from about one and a half hours per week to twenty-seven. The sale of war-related toys surged with it. Because toy-based programs generated huge sales success, they were by definition in the "public interest."[13]

Congressional efforts to halt the exploitation, watered down by compromise, have been ineffective. The 1990 Children's Television Act is another piece of what William Greider calls "hollow legislation." Toy-based shows, for example, could only be considered program-length commercials if they include paid advertisements for the toy on which the programs are based. But those toys are already part of wide advertising efforts. Mighty Morphin Power Rangers toys, featured in the Power Rangers show, grossed almost $1 billion in 1994. A new TV series as well as a movie on Mortal Kombat are to arrive soon to capitalize on the bloodthirsty arcade and home video games, which have generated nearly $2 billion in revenues. There are already deals for T-shirts, lunch boxes, and toys.[14]

These developments remind me of our "lost" findings and what we observed in the social interactions of children who had seen aggressive cartoons in a good nursery school without aggressive toys in the classroom — decreased self-control, speeded-up reactions, impatience, rule breaking. Not only are the new programs more violent, the technology has become more sophisticated, ever more capable of arousing emotion. Involvement is further intensified as those same program characters are featured in video and computer games that pull the child into interaction with the violence. Winning depends on speed of reaction. Matching toys insinuate the same scripts into interactions with other children. Even conscientious parents have felt obliged to grant requests for the toys while they have forbidden the program. As one mother explained to me, "I held out for months, but those toys were all that he wanted for his birthday. He was the only kid in his class that didn't have them. But," she added, "maybe I was wrong. I hate the way he and his friends treat each other when they play with those toys; it takes me hours to calm him down."

More subtle and dangerous developments in advertising unfold daily. One major company after the next has taken the "contempt for rules as cool" theme, emphasizing the joys of impulsiveness, self-indulgence, and freedom from restraint and responsibilities. Calvin Klein has long been an innovator in pornographic renditions of this approach, which he dubs a message of "strength of character and independence," according to a *New York Times* article of August 30, 1995. Nike's "Just do it," Burger King's "Sometimes you just gotta break the rules," and Isuzu's ridicule of teachers and rules are but a few examples of imitators of the basic message.

It is a message that celebrates the arousal experienced with violent fare and the diminution of self-control. Self-control and rules are old-fashioned and interfere with wishes of the moment, "my freedom to do what I want to do." What advertisers are teaching our children about "authenticity" has grave social implications. We see triumphant individuals, each defined by a unique point of view. Values? "Whose values?" Rights? "My rights," construed in personal terms, torn from their civic dimensions and responsibilities.[15] In an article in the *Albuquerque Journal* (August 22, 1995), John Leo notes that such advertisements are not only at war with traditional values, but with the "possibility that new common values will emerge from the current social chaos." By pushing self-obsession, narcissism, and contempt for rules, "they strike at the sense of connectedness that any society needs to cohere and care about its common problems."

Parents have indicated in many surveys that they are seriously concerned about declining values, but the imagery of the marketplace has invaded family life on so many fronts that parents feel powerless to control what their children watch, hear, and buy. Years of protest have been in vain, and parents feel that they are losing rather than gaining control. It is hardly surprising that families see television as a "hostile force" in their lives.[16]

We have yet to find the political leadership and public cohesion to ban commercial advertising to children, although it is clearly antithetical to the First Amendment obligation to provide civic education for our children. Advertising to young children who do not understand its intent was hardly what Madison meant by a prohibition against interference with free political speech. There are already legal precedents that allow protection of children.[17] We have had twenty years of technological advances used to undermine families and harm children. At the same time, the positive potential of television has been ignored. Commercial and cable television have distorted the creative talents of writers and actors and wasted opportunities to expand the horizons of children like the little boy who haunts my memory.

Ironically, it was our financially insignificant Public Broadcasting System and the National Endowment for the Arts that came under attack recently in Congress, not the hawkers of democratic destruction. One interpretation of congressional action is that it is less risky to battle David than Goliath. Another, however, is that these actions represent the false polarization in American political life that has come to divide us. Liberals are seen as seeking to restrain the market while they condone laissez-faire in cultural and sexual life. Conservatives allow market freedom but become the defenders of traditional values and seek to restrain laissez-faire in the cultural and sexual spheres.[18] We have not been able to find the middle ground, the compromises needed by our children and by our democracy. We have yet to identify the common threat. In the impasse, parents have been left powerless in a commercial culture that neither liberal nor conservative wants.

How have market forces become so powerful? Monopolistic media mergers, cloaked in economic terms like "synergies," have grown at an alarming pace since the 1980s. The developments in children's television are but one symptom of the crisis. All of our information, including news — "the picture of reality," as Walter Lippmann expressed it, "on which the citizen can act" — has been affected. Ben Bagdikian has long called for the investigation of the way in which large corporations have taken control over the major media in the United States and advertisers have influenced news content.[19] Conglomerates own newspapers, book and magazine publishers, record and movie production companies, theaters, cable and television networks. With their enormous profits these corporations have extended empires, rather than enhancing and diversifying media offerings. There is new reason to fear that a few corporations will control *all* of the important mass media not just in the United States but globally.

Carl Bernstein has recently reissued Bagdikian's challenge, noting that the story of the contemporary media is the great uncovered story in our country today. Whom, Bernstein asks, is the media serving? And what about standards, self-interest, and "its eclipse of the public interest and the interest of truth"? For, he states, "The reality is that the media are probably the most powerful of all our institutions today." Similarly, Robert Bellah and colleagues ask that we reexamine the role of the corporation in society, and reassert the claim that "incorporation is a concession of public authority to a private group in return for service to the public good, with effective public accountability."[20]

But the voices of critics who draw attention to the structure and abuses of media monopolies have not been elevated by the media and the politicians whose images they control to a level that can be heard by those many citizens who complain about content and values. It is more expedient in entertainment to reinforce our political divisions with slick images. Any criticism is quickly dismissed as "censorship." In the political vacuum, the commercial spiral has accelerated.

Entertainment turned into the fastest-growing business in the United States in the 1990s, and dominance increasingly became a function of owning both programming content and the distribution assets needed to deliver it. The deregulatory tide of 1994 was seen as justification for what corporations wanted, and they shaped a sweeping communications bill in consultation with House GOP leaders. The bill attracted scant notice from citizens and was not discussed at political town meetings. The *Wall*

Street Journal (August 3, 1995) reports that Commerce Committee Chairman Thomas Bliley believes that "It's too complex for the average citizen. . . . The average citizen is concerned with the crab grass, and will it rain, and getting the kids to Little League." This comment does not sound like one that reflects the sentiments of voters who wanted more participation in decision making and less bureaucratic control over their lives. But it does reflect the contempt with which the public is regarded by many politicians, who seem to have forgotten James Madison and his emphasis on the political sovereignty of the people.

Passage of the bill was expected to enhance monopolistic mergers (synergies) by allowing networks to own more of their own programming and to own more stations. The media giants would be given a much freer hand to expand nationally and to export and control media internationally. They could produce their own shows and sell them to their networks and cables, use them as reruns and as merchandise in overseas products. Exports will spark even greater growth. It is a real "Masters of the Universe" scenario.

In anticipation of this new deregulation, Disney announced a $19 billion takeover of Capital Cities/ABC. (Not to be bested by a competitor, CBS has now agreed to be acquired by Westinghouse, and Time-Warner and Turner are negotiating a merger.) Disney would own not only the Disney Channel, its theme parks and merchandise, but ABC, ESPN, Lifetime, A&E, and many local stations and newspapers. The Disney deal makes all kinds of business sense as the possibilities for advertising assaults, as indicated by their language, are almost endless. Consolidation brings leverage, and the ESPN sports "beachhead" in 135 countries means that sports and family entertainment can be sold in a package and provide a "wedge" to promote the sale of other Disney products, according to *The New Yorker* (August 14, 1995). In *Inside the Mouse*, the editors argue that "the success of Disney World . . . has largely to do with the way its programming meshes with the economics of consumption as a value system." In discussing *Inside the Mouse*, the *New York Times* (August 6, 1995) summarizes the critique of Disney as "equal parts marketing strategy and repressive mechanism."

These obtuse, but chilling, words evoke the parallels drawn by Vaclav

Havel between enormous private multinational corporations and socialist states that reduce human life to stereotypes of "production" and "consumption": "It's important that people not be a herd, manipulated and standardized by the choice of consumer goods and consumer television culture, whether this culture is offered to him by three competing capitalist networks or a single giant noncompetitive socialist network. It is important, in short, that the superficial variety of one system, or the repulsive grayness of the other, not hide the same deep emptiness of life devoid of meaning."[21]

Perhaps Disney and the other monopolistic giants have gone too far this time. Havel reminds us of the chasm that has developed between the presumptions of the unfettered marketplace and the democratic ideals and traditions of a free press. James Madison, the principal thinker behind the First Amendment, wrote of the political sovereignty of the people, the right to elect members of a free and responsible government, and the importance of public examination and discussion of candidates for the public trust. The free press was to provide the public with information "indispensable to the just exercise of their electoral rights." And what of diversity in the press? "Could it be so arranged that every newspaper, when printed on one side, should be handed over to the press of an adversary, to be printed on the other, thus presenting to every reader both sides of every question, truth would always have a fair chance." The value of a free press, wrote Madison, was evident to anyone who reflected "that to the press alone, chequered as it is with abuses, the world is indebted for all the triumphs which have been gained by reason and humanity over error and oppression."[22]

Freedom of speech serves democratic and educational aspirations. Commercial competition could never be the only measure of free speech and civic health; indeed Madison argued that partisan interests are adverse to the public interest. Through much of its history, the FCC endorsed these Madisonian tenets, as reflected in its recognition of the needs of children and in the "fairness doctrine," which required attention to public issues and diversity of points of view. Until the 1980s, the National Association of Broadcasters explicitly acknowledged or at least gave lip service to those responsibilities, noting their accountability to the public and "respect for the special needs of children, for community responsibility, for the advancement of education and culture, for the acceptability of the program materials chosen, and for propriety in advertising."[23]

But in 1995 media monopolies regard themselves as sovereign and the people as abject "units of consumption," who should know their place in the grand economic scheme. The people have not been well informed about the steady erosion of control over our information by market forces, but the threatened reversal of power should be clear now.

Is there hope to reverse the tide? I am cautiously optimistic. Quite recently, concerns over media mergers have been voiced by representatives of diverse ideological perspectives, from President Clinton, Bill Bradley, Paul Simon, and Jesse Jackson to Bob Dole and William Bennett. We can hope that the protest has just begun. These proposed mergers will have to be considered by federal antitrust officials and the FCC, which should lead to a public awareness of antitrust and public interest issues. The telecommunications bill has not yet become law.

We need discussion in many open, participatory forums — town halls, libraries, churches. But can we still talk with one another? Political writers have noted the diminution of the deliberative process from the pushing of yes or no buttons, to opinion polls, to judicial politics that freeze debate and deepen resentments. Neil Postman has vividly described the gradual erosion of public language and the framing of ideas as news coverage became entertainment, reliant upon pictures, photo opportunities, and sound bytes. However, we continue to resonate to the language of Mark Twain and Will Rogers. A new folk hero, historian Shelby Foote, emerged in Ken Burn's Civil War series on PBS. His balanced and sensitive commentary on an event that "defined us as a nation" struck a common chord. We recognize clear democratic speech when we hear it, and I don't think we've forgotten how to talk and listen to one another. We can use this crisis to renew our vision of ourselves as citizens, capable of acting for our children, the common good, and our collective future. There is an opportunity for the people to "challenge the concentrated ownership of communications on behalf of democracy."[24]

This essay began with Fred Rogers' Neighborhood of Make-Believe, a small civil society in which people work to discover truths about them-

selves as individuals and truths about the ways in which they are interconnected and can realize shared ends or civic goods. That imaginary world
offers another kind of hope.

For Fred Rogers, the medium is an *instrument* to be used for creative
expression, not the technical determiner of the message. In the tradition
of the storyteller, it is language which shapes the programs, gives them
meaning, and engenders understanding beyond the immediate particulari-
ties of pictures. In the Neighborhood, feelings, beliefs, and opinions are
listened to with respect. Often neighbors are puzzled or don't understand
views that are different from their own. In some instances this calls for
reassurance; in others it means a series of questions or challenges. But what
is common to each situation is the careful progression and clarification of
ideas and feelings that includes all participants.

Consensus is crafted over issues of importance. The process isn't easy,
but it happens. There are always surprises about which member of the
community will come up with the insight that moves others to find middle
ground. It is often the overarching, grand plans that are most difficult to
diffuse and reconcile. Clichés and pronouncements do not last long. Un-
considered ramifications of change emerge from the hearing given to different perspectives. But this description does not do justice to the richness
of the process in the Neighborhood. Rogers writes: "To me that's what
communication is all about . . . communing in a community where people
listen to themselves and others, where they try to understand what they've
heard and then respond with all the creativity and care that their life has
allowed them to develop."[25]

Each neighbor is a distinct individual with different strengths and
weaknesses, preferences, limits, and possibilities. Each has dignity and
worth and something unique to contribute. Characters in the Neighborhood come to understand that untrammeled egoism has harmful effects on
others, rights derive from responsibleness, and real freedom comes with
acceptance of limits and restrictions on their acts. Each person is in some
way different from everybody else, but similarities bind all human beings
together. In make-believe for very young children, Fred Rogers suggests to
us the relatedness among the spheres of identity, responsibility, creativity,
and human freedom. His creativity bridges the gap between society as we
know it, and what might be. But he never presumes to give us answers:

One of the mysteries is that as unlike as we are, one human being from another, we also share much in common. Our lives begin the same way, by birth. The love and interdependence of parents and children is universal, and so are the many difficulties parents and children have in becoming separate from one another. As we grow, we laugh and cry at many of the same things, and fear many of the same things. At the end, we all leave the same way — by death. Yet no two threads — no two lives — in that vast tapestry of existence have ever been, or ever will be, the same.[26]

During the course of Fred Rogers' career, we have seen the collapse of Marxism, one attempt to reduce humanity to predictable economic units. We have seen the loss of influence of positivistic science that sought to explain life in terms of discrete variables. Postmodern science is more humble and has more in common with enduring poetry, literature, and religious thought. *Being* itself is acknowledged as a deeply mysterious phenomenon. Barbara McClintock, the Nobel Prize–winning geneticist, spoke of the need to attribute to scientific description the life one shares with it. All of nature is complexly interconnected in ways that we cannot yet appreciate.[27] This is one of the truths we discover in Fred Rogers' Neighborhood.

It's not only children who are influenced by television; viewing affects the whole family system, writes Ellen Galinsky, co-president of the Families and Work Institute. In reflecting on her own guest appearances in the Mister Rogers Talks to Parents series, she notes that, unlike the unchanging nature of the Neighborhood, Fred Rogers experimented with formats and media to find the best way to talk with families: "In an age of bookstores crammed with 'one-minute manager' parenthood books, Fred Rogers' experimental approach seems both novel and old-fashioned." The evolution of the Mister Rogers Talks to Parents series, Galinsky says, "reflects the very message that it broadcasts — a 'playing around' with format until the substance and the style of the shows become one, until Fred Rogers becomes fully comfortable with what he is creating, until the right 'voice' is found."

In addition to serving as co-president of the Families and Work Institute, Galinsky is past-president of the National Association for the Education of Young Children. She holds a master's degree from the Bank Street College of Education. She has authored or coauthored eighteen books and reports, including (with Judy David) The Preschool Years (New York: Ballantine, 1991).

Ellen Galinsky

Mister Rogers Speaks to Parents

On Tuesday, June 4, 1968, following his victory speech in the California Democratic primary for president, Robert Kennedy was mortally wounded by a dissident Jordanian named Sirhan Sirhan. For the next twenty-five hours, the nation — already reeling from the assassination of Martin Luther King Jr. just two months before — kept a vigil by their television sets. Early on Thursday morning, June 6, Robert Kennedy died.

Hedda Sharapan, one of the creative team that puts together *Mister Rogers' Neighborhood,* recalls the day. "Fred came into the studio on Thursday morning. He'd been up all night. He remembered a conversation he had with Margaret McFarland about a child whose father had died. The child had not gone to the funeral and had never had the chance to grieve for her father. But when President Kennedy died, the child sat with his mother and watched the funeral and talked about death. Fred said that something had to be done this time around."

The answer would be a hastily organized, prime-time message from Mister Rogers to parents. The message was typically Fred Rogers — simple and profound: the need to discuss difficult ideas such as death, assassination, and grief.

Fred Rogers' concern was very real: the confusion young children might feel between fantasy and reality. For days, television was nothing more than Kennedy footage — clips of Robert Kennedy during his career, then videotape of his death, then more episodes where he appeared to be alive and another repetition of the assassination. Such contrasting images are bound to be perplexing — after all, cartoon characters are bashed about and even killed, yet come back again. For children, it is difficult to believe that death of a major figure, especially one known only through the television, is ever final.

163

Rogers worked all night on Wednesday. The program was taped on Thursday to be shown on Friday, the night before the funeral. There was no time for live shots, so they had to work with studio shots.

Sitting alone on his empty set, he talked to parents. If one didn't know the horrific event precipitating this special program, one might have initially concluded that this was a show on the importance of children's play. The pace was leisurely and reassuring. Mister Rogers told parents that on that week's shows, there would be a dancer working with children. After showing the segment of the dancer, Mister Rogers talked about how children learn by playing and by doing.

Then the action switched to the Neighborhood of Make-Believe and the subject matter of the show became evident: Lady Elaine wanted to play shoot-out but neither she nor Daniel Striped Tiger wanted to be the aggressor; both preferred to be the victim. By choosing this make-believe world, the program gave important access to a painful and confusing episode in our public lives. Rogers wanted to help adults hear children's concerns at a comfortable distance. Letting Daniel and Lady Elaine tell the story helped the adults to hear the children better. Near the close of the segment, Daniel asked Lady Aberlin what the word "assassination" meant.

Fred Rogers then spoke directly to parents about how their young children might respond to the frightening image of the Kennedy shooting, appearing over and over and over on television. He told parents that there was no *one* way to handle this tragedy with children:

> No one of us has all the answers. There's no prescription for every child. That's why listening is so important. Most of us talk a lot and that doesn't leave a lot of time for listening. I know that when I first started to work with children, I was so involved in trying to be somebody with them that I could hardly allow them to be themselves with me. And little by little, as I became more comfortable with myself, I think the children were able to be more comfortable with me.

The way most children communicate with parents, Rogers said, is through their play: "Play is the way that children talk to us best." Thus listening involves watching and understanding, for example, that a child knocking down a block building may be acting out the assassination as a way of trying to fathom this frightening and confusing event. The message of this show was that by listening, by watching children's play, parents could become aware of children's perceptions and misperceptions and then determine how to respond.

Fred Rogers closed the show with the statement that he was concerned about the graphic portrayals of the Kennedy murder being shown in the media. "I plead for your protection and support of your child. There is just so much that children can take without it being overwhelming." He concluded with some concrete suggestions about how families might grieve together, including whether to watch the funeral on television. He stressed his commitment to and alliance with his parent viewers, in working together "caring for the children."

Eleven years later, Mister Rogers embarked upon a project to create a series of eight programs for parents.[1] Although this series spanned several years, his purpose remained the same: to help parents understand their children, especially the role that make-believe plays in their lives. Understanding children involves slowing down, listening, observing, and finally understanding ourselves as parents. Although there is no single "prescription" solution for every child, parents who are in tune and in touch with what is going on with their own children can figure out what to do. They must, however, allow themselves to make mistakes, to continue to grow and learn.

Although the message of the programs in the series bore Fred Rogers' unmistakable imprint, the *format* of each program varied tremendously. What's important here is Fred Rogers' willingness to experiment with formats, searching for the best vehicle to carry his message.

In an age of bookstores crammed with "one-minute manager" parenthood books, Fred Rogers' experimental approach seems both novel and old-fashioned. In an interesting way, the evolution of the Mister Rogers Talks to Parents series reflects the very message that it broadcasts—a "playing around" with format until the substance and the style of the shows become one, until Fred Rogers becomes fully comfortable with what he is creating, until the right "voice" is found. It's a fitting metaphor for parenthood itself: trying new ideas while always presenting a loving, consistent message.

What's also interesting is to watch Fred Rogers, known as the *children's best friend*, speak with people his own age. One of the strengths of Fred Rogers' voice is that it is never condescending. He is always respectful of children, and he has that same respect for adult viewers. If we accept that as adults we are always reworking themes begun in childhood — autonomy, self-respect, self-worth — then the voice Rogers uses with adults also treats the same themes.[2]

Hedda Sharapan recalls another time Fred Rogers was in a group of adults, this time on the *Tonight Show* with Joan Rivers. Rogers began the conversation by complimenting Rivers on her concern for the family of one of the crew. He said, "It's great to know people can love each other — the ones they work with."

The audience laughed. Rogers turned to the audience and said, "I don't think that's funny."

"No, but it's funny because they expect you to be talking to a little person," Rivers replied. "If I sat at your knees and you told me that. . . ."

"But why can't big people talk with big people that way?" Rogers asked. The audience quieted.

"Because you get embarrassed," Rivers said. "Doesn't that make sense?"

"It does," Rogers replied, "but I think the more comfortable we are with each other, the better we can help this world be comfortable with others."

"You know, you're really good," Rivers said, but the rest of her response was lost in the audience's sustained applause.

Watching the Mister Rogers Talks with Parents series again is something of a personal odyssey. I served as the on-camera expert for the shows on starting school and on superheroes, so I knew them very well. Although I had seen the subsequent programs, watching them back-to-back was a different experience from seeing them, one by one, over a decade. This marathon viewing gave me a sense of both the continuity and discontinuity in the way Fred Rogers uses television to communicate with parents instead of children.

The major continuity is the subject matter, although this may seem surprising from the list of the show's topics. What do "pets" have to do with "school" and "superheroes"? All of the shows revolve around helping parents face difficult moments with their children. In some, the difficulty occurs within the everyday context of family life: how to discipline children and how to assist children in dealing with competition. The show on pets focuses on the birth and death of pets. In other shows, the difficulty involves a normal transition: beginning school or child care. The subject of divorce also involves a transition, not built into the life cycle the way that entering school is, but an experience with which half of American children must cope. Although the topics were chosen to coincide with programming for children, they have an amazing coherence.

The *discontinuity* is in the format. The shows filmed between 1979 and 1981 — on school, superheroes, competition, and divorce — are fast-paced, moving from video inserts of children, parents, and teachers to scenes from that week's Mister Rogers' programs for children, to audience questions from parents moderated by a media personality and answered by Mister Rogers and his guest expert. Although Fred Rogers remains calm and contemplative, the style of the shows themselves is quite the opposite. It is almost as if it is assumed that to appeal to adults, one must use a quick-take format, like the evening news shows.

The show on superheroes, a show on which I appear, serves as an example. Susan Stamberg, then host of National Public Radio's *All Things Considered*, is the moderator; she opens the program by asking Fred Rogers and me to comment on how to dissuade children from becoming violent when they play superhero. This is followed by Rogers' interviews with children, which help the viewer understand why children are so riveted by these larger-than-life figures. Next is a discussion between Mister Rogers and me about how children identify with superheroes as a form of protection against the vagaries of the world.

Following our discussion is a filmed sequence of children playing superhero, recorded at Yale University as a part of a research project. The researcher, Robert Ambromovitz, comments on how hero role-playing is a normal part of growing up. Another segment features actor Lou Ferrigno getting made up as the Incredible Hulk, followed by a live conversation with Ferrigno, who talks about how he explains his scary television role to his own children. Next is a parent question-answer sequence and a segment from *Mister Rogers' Neighborhood*. The show continues switching back and forth from the studio to taped inserts and back again.

Watching this show a decade later was disconcerting. At times, I felt like saying "Slow down!" or "Answer the parent's question!" as the show veered from segment to segment. In the parents' question-answer segments, there is occasional tension between Fred Rogers' approach and parents' desire for an immediate answer. Rogers is at his best when he turns the question back to the parent, saying that he bets that she or he has figured out what to do. In all cases, the parent has strategies that work, enabling Fred Rogers to make the point that the parent is the best expert. So overall, despite the sometimes jarring edits, the integrity of the show's message came through: listen to children; understand their development.

The programs on pets and on discipline, made in 1982, adopt a new format. The expert is gone, as are the question-and-answer sequences, replaced by a living room–style conversation between Mister Rogers and a group of parents. There are still inserts that bring in children's and parents' insights. For example, the program on discipline begins with interviews Fred Rogers has conducted with children, as well as his interpretations of the children's comments. The show then shifts into the group discussion, punctuated with questions and analyses by Mister Rogers. Some inserts are very compelling, one in particular of a mother recalling a fight between herself and her child, while the child sits by her and listens intently to the retelling of this incident. The warm interchange between mother and child transforms this incident from an upsetting moment to the status of a funny family story. In another insert, Rogers asks children how they feel when they are disciplined; one boy ponders whether eating forbidden food is a "bad thing" or a "bad, bad thing."

This format eliminates the more disjointed tempo of the first four programs in the series. It is more intimate. Because the show is no longer taped before a live audience, the material can be controlled and the sequence of moving from one idea to the next is smoother. Furthermore, shortening the show from one hour to half an hour sharpens the message (for instance, that children need limits to feel safe; discipline means to *teach* as opposed to *punish*). It is through their parents' examples and words that children learn how to manage themselves, important skills especially when they grow up and have to make decisions on their own. Mister Rogers concludes the program by saying that "discipline is a gift of love."

This format, however, does have disadvantages. The power of the show depends heavily on the parents in the discussion group: some are articulate, some less so. Sometimes the conversation meanders, causing the viewer's interest to wane and important points to be lost. Furthermore, some issues are raised, such as whether to use a "heavy hand" (spanking, I would assume), yet these important topics are never fully confronted.

When the shows depend heavily on a group of parent participants, their characteristics come sharply into focus. These individuals all seem to have one thing in common——they care about and respect the world of the young child. They are articulate and warm, appealing to watch and listen to. Racially they are diverse, including African Americans, Latinos, and Asian Americans as well as whites. These shows are unusual for their era — they fully acknowledge men as parents. Fathers ask questions and provide answers.

The people in the shows, however, seem decidedly middle-class. Furthermore, the issues these parents face seem mild indeed. No one is *really* struggling with parenthood in these shows. Yes, there are difficult moments, but the parents have it under control. They seem to have access to services and be well able to afford the assistance that they need.

The final two shows — *Mister Rogers Talks to Parents About Day Care* and *Mister Rogers Talks to Parents About Make-Believe* — try out another format, closer in style to a documentary. Rogers returns to the stool on the empty set that he used in the Kennedy assassination program. He speaks directly to his viewers. In the show on make-believe, for example, Fred Rogers helps parents understand the power of pretend play by interviewing parents and teachers and by his own commentary.

The program on make-believe contains one segment that is a virtual tour de force. It is the story of Chris, an aggressive boy who has had to repeat kindergarten. Chris is shown in the classroom, bullying the other children. His parents are interviewed, discussing their child's behavior. It would have been very easy to present this child as difficult, disturbed, a behavior problem, or hyperactive — the list of typical labels could go on and on. But his parents and teacher speak of Chris in only the most positive terms, portraying him as a child who is struggling to find calm ways of expressing himself. He is shown painting and building with blocks. The segment concludes with a spectacularly filmed episode in which Chris, on the final day of school for the year, builds a jail of large blocks and invites the other children to enclose him within the block building. It is a metaphor for the kind of control he is seeking over his raging feelings and actions. In all my years in working with parents and children, I have never before seen this kind of sensitivity captured by the camera. Fred Rogers' concluding message — that there is good and bad in all of us, that "play is the most important work there is" — has incredible power, thanks, in part, to the story of Chris.

The shift in the format is toward an increasing sense of intimacy. Although television is a one-way medium, Rogers and his staff have deliberately found a form that makes the last two programs as much like a conversation as possible. The willingness of Fred Rogers and his creative team to test different models of programming to find the right one is admirable, especially in the face of commercial television's typically formulaic programming.

Although the format of the series changed, the major messages to parents stayed constant: Take the time to listen to and understand your children and yourself, and the appropriate solutions to problems will become evident; you are the expert, so have confidence in yourself.

The Mister Rogers series for parents is brilliant in its efforts to help parents understand their own children. To achieve this, sometimes Fred Rogers has adults talk about children. Teachers tell about children on their first day of school or a bus driver describes children's reactions to going on the school bus. One of the most compelling stories is that of a teacher telling about a boy who dresses up in a red dress. He is not, as it would seem, pretending to be his mother or some other female. He is pretending to be a firefighter and this is the only red outfit available. The message to parents is: Things are not necessarily as they seem. Before jumping to conclusions, listen, watch.

Another technique in the program that is used effectively to help adults enter into the world of young children is actual observations of children — as in the episode of the aggressive kindergartner, Chris. The most frequent technique is having Mister Rogers interview children themselves. Once seen, who could ever forget the plaintive look on the child's face telling Mister Rogers that he had asked his daddy why he was getting divorced: "He just says that it's a fight, but he didn't tell us the rest of it."

Suddenly the power of this medium is made manifest, propelling a parent back in time to an empathic connection to the child within us all. I think here of the somber-faced little girl who confides in Mister Rogers that "divorce is so hard. I can't see my father because he lives in Philadelphia and he doesn't call and I don't know his number." The powerlessness of a child in these circumstances is rendered vividly clear to adults who are often so consumed by their own grief and anger that it is hard to consider their child's perspective. This show also helps us understand the questions that children typically have: Is the divorce my fault? If my parents divorce each other, will they divorce me, too? Will I become an orphan? Why can't my remarried father bring his new wife and live with us? Why can't I reunite my parents?

In addition to helping parents understand their children, this series gives parents insight into their own behavior. To accomplish this goal Mister Rogers often describes his own feelings as a parent. My favorite is his story of walking with his son, gripping his hand very tightly. His son finally turned to him and asked if he was angry. Mister Rogers told his son that he was indeed angry, then confided in his viewers that sharing his feelings with his son helped him to feel better. Another means of increasing parents' self-awareness is Fred Rogers' commentary throughout the shows, such as when he explains that enrolling children in school or child care triggers adults' feelings about separation. He also provides guidance through his reactions to viewers' questions. I was struck, over and over again, by his insight, by his ability to cut to the essence of what is really being said. For example, a mother talks of a child in such a way that it becomes obvious to the viewer that this mother is afraid of making mistakes. Rather than answer her question, he acknowledges her struggle to be perfect and then shares his philosophy that parents grow by learning from their mistakes. Similarly, he responds to a mother's statement that her son hates to lose competitions by asking her if this child has lost important people. "Yes," she acknowledges. "His father moved out."

A final but less fundamental intent of Mister Rogers' series for parents is to provide how-to information. I say that this is a lesser purpose because, as Fred Rogers says throughout the programs, there are no cookie-cutter answers. His approach is to understand the child and then custom fit the solutions, in my view the most pedagogically sound stance.

Although he tends to shy away from specific how-to suggestions, Mister Rogers informs these shows with guiding principles. In doing so, he often overturns conventional wisdom, giving parents a new and memorable way to think about their parenting skills. He says that discipline is a gift of love in that it helps children feel safe. Most parents tend to think of discipline as the necessary but uncomfortable act of policing. Likewise, he tells parents that one way they show their love to children is by providing for them economically. Many guilty mothers see their work as a deprivation for their children rather than a demonstration of their love. He tells one parent that if we as adults don't nourish ourselves, we can't nourish others.

The experience of watching the entire Mister Rogers Talks to Parents series was, for me, a personal and professional journey. Most significant was watching Fred Rogers grow in the use of this medium, especially in communicating with adults. He was willing to take risks, to try out various formats, and to play with the pacing of the shows. In the end, he found his unique voice, a style that reflects what it is he wants to say. It is a style that takes the viewers into the hearts and minds of children. It is a style that helps the viewers understand themselves. The series is aptly named; despite the limits of the medium and the occasional false starts, these programs cross beyond the limitations of television to feel like Fred Rogers talking to *us*.

Unfortunately, the Mister Rogers Talks to Parents series ended after only eight programs. There were budget and scheduling difficulties. The specials were scheduled for six o'clock on Sunday evening—a difficult slot, especially in the summer and especially in that pre-VCR era. Alas, even PBS must be sensitive to market issues.

In the decade since this series was created, there has been little else on network television for parents. Given the large proportion of parents in the viewing audience, this is a surprising absence. The lingering feeling I had after turning off the last program in the series was sadness. These programs are strong; they are even more necessary today than they were a dozen years ago. Why is there no programming of this caliber occurring now? It is a void our society can ill afford.

In addition to its target audience, Mister Rogers' Neighborhood *also attracts a sizable chunk of nontraditional viewers, especially among older folks. But that older viewership shouldn't be surprising, writes Mary Rawson. Older people are often grouped with children — they "are stereotyped as slow-witted, limited in ability. . . . They are condescended to or patronized, very often treated like children — that is, without respect." Fred Rogers offers the message of self-worth, that they are unique and valuable and worthy of recognition — just the opposite of the message society usually sends to older people. "The respect that Mister Rogers offers is precisely what older adults often lack in their everyday lives, where people they've just met call them 'dearie,' or discuss them with others in the third-person, as if they weren't there," Rawson writes. "Fred Rogers shows unfailing respect and courtesy toward everyone. And in terms of real life as experienced by children and older adults, such courtesy and respect can be very unusual indeed."*

A writer-producer for WQED Pittsburgh, Mary Rawson is also an actor and performer with Pittsburgh Ensemble Theatre and a teacher at Pittsburgh Filmmakers. Some of her documentary productions include A Map of Memories, *documenting the personal stories of older citizens that became a mural of Pittsburgh's history, and* Agewise, *a six-part series on growing older, produced under a grant from the U.S. Administration on Aging. Her honors include the American Film and Video Festival Award, the Golden Quill Award, the National Educational Film Festival Award, and the Cine Award.*

Mary Rawson

Other Viewers, Other Rooms

Like most television programs, *Mister Rogers' Neighborhood* keeps track of its demographics to see who's watching every day. The program is intended for a preschool audience of three- to five-year olds, with some spillover into the two- to eight-year-old range. Approximately eight million households — mostly little kids, often watching with their parents — tune in every week.

One way to track viewership is by reading the mail — the hundreds of letters that come into the program every month. Most of it, of course, is from young viewers. But the show also has a large group of regular viewers who are anything but young and who sometimes are a little surprised themselves to be watching *Mister Rogers' Neighborhood:*

"Greetings from a 61-year-old fan."

"I am an 88-year-old great-grandmother who thoroughly enjoys your programs."

"I'm still alive at 93 and a half. With a great deal of gratitude, I feel you are my neighbor and a friend who makes my heart sing."

"I am a retired army officer in my mid-seventies. One day I was changing channels on the TV, searching for something — anything . . . on came Mister Rogers. I was bitten by the fan bug and now watch every day."

Some of these older Neighborhood viewers watch the program with their grandchildren, or watch it as a way to stay connected with their grandchildren: "What a joy you bring to this old grandmother of 77 years. Every morning I have my breakfast in your neighborhood. . . . My 11 grandchildren watch you every day. They all live in different towns, but we all have an interest together, in that we are part of your Neighborhood." And some people, even though they aren't grandparents themselves, care very much about children: "I am 89 years old, and I never miss one of your programs! I have no grandchildren, but on behalf of all children everywhere I thank you sincerely. Hope you can keep giving them your wonderful help for a hundred years more."

Older people have always been important to Fred McFeely Rogers. One of the most significant people in his life was his maternal grandfather, Fred McFeely, after whom he was named. This grandfather gave the gift of unconditional love, which his grandson has passed on to millions of others: "You know, you make this day a really special day just by being yourself. There's only one person in the world like you, and I like you just the way you are."

Perhaps it is this understanding and acceptance that attracts older viewers to the program. Rogers has a one-on-one style that hearkens back to the time before television, when today's older adults were young. He emphasizes that each of us, no matter our age, contributes something special to this world. And he's been doing this, with very few changes in format, for over twenty-five years, making the show a stable, enduring presence that young and old can count on in a constantly changing world.

Mister Rogers' Neighborhood places a unique emphasis on the needs of growing children — dealing with feelings of anger, grief, love, loss, disappointment, and self-esteem. Fred Rogers once described the Neighborhood as "a place where friends help children find within themselves the courage to grow."

From its earliest days the program has been infused by Fred Rogers' attention to the principles of child development, and those principles provide a clue to the phenomenon of older viewers. Pioneer child development specialist Erik Erikson described human development as a life cycle beginning in infancy and proceeding through stages. Each stage has a specific psychological task that contributes to a major aspect of personality. Preschoolers develop a sense of creativity and initiative, for instance, while the school-age child gains a sense of competency.

As he himself aged, Erikson reflected on how old age fit into that cycle. He described the final stage of life as a time of opportunity, a time in which the lessons of earlier stages could be reworked into the "wisdom of age." Thus the sense of trust that begins to develop in infancy can lead, in old age, to an appreciation of interdependence: a greater understanding of both giving and receiving. And the young child's playfulness can grow into a sense of humor about life, a recognition that life is far too important to be taken seriously. Erikson pointed out that this reworking can lead to greater personal growth.

If the early lessons of childhood resonate throughout life, then, by addressing the growing child, Mister Rogers also speaks to any growing person — perhaps particularly someone "coming into wisdom." In an address to a public television conference, Fred Rogers described his mission: "For twenty-five years public television has given us the opportunity to communicate with children and their families. Our 'Neighborhood' and our viewing 'neighbors' have grown in many different ways; nevertheless, our original purpose remains: to encourage human beings to be honest with themselves and with each other and to grow in the conviction that each one of us is a unique and precious part of our world." The Neighborhood's mission "to encourage human beings" does not exclude anybody, but rather acknowledges that every person, no matter what age, wants to feel valued and to be spoken to honestly.

Dr. Edward Ansello, director of the Virginia Center on Aging and past-president of the Association for Gerontology in Higher Education, agreed with this assessment in an interview with the author: "The important concerns of growing children — anger, grief, love — are the important concerns of growing *humans*," Ansello notes.

> In watching Fred Rogers, elders connect to their own humanity. Mister Rogers affirms that their experiences of grief, wonderment, and loss are central to the human condition, when it would be so easy for them to be overwhelmed by seeing these events as the concerns or burdens of aging.
>
> While Mister Rogers' messages affirm the common "humanness" of all of his viewers, whatever their age, he also asserts their individuality and uniqueness. This is an important message in an era that lumps older adults into the category "age sixty-five and over."

Ansello himself started watching the Neighborhood as a young father in the early 1970s. He noticed that the message of self-worth that Fred Rogers sends to little children — that they are unique and valuable and worthy of recognition — was just the opposite of the message society sends to older people. Ansello sees a common assumption that we become more alike as we age. Older people are stereotyped as slow-witted, limited in ability, more tuned into the past than the present. They are condescended to or patronized, very often treated *like* children — that is, without respect.

Children endure such disregard for their feelings all the time — "That doesn't hurt," or "Stop crying," or "What are you making such a big deal about, it's just a haircut!" But Fred Rogers fully accepts the reality of a child's experience and feelings. He deliberately identifies and confronts the difficulties in a child's life. For many kids, getting a haircut *is* difficult. Instead of denying the feelings, Mister Rogers validates them. He responds by going to the barbershop himself and getting a haircut. This may not sound revolutionary, but consider such a gesture within the framework of television, where feelings and fears are rarely, if ever, acknowledged.

The respect that Mister Rogers offers is precisely what older adults often lack in their everyday lives, where people they've just met call them "dearie," or discuss them with others in the third-person, as if they weren't there ("Your mother does so well!"). Fred Rogers shows unfailing respect and courtesy toward everyone. And in terms of real life as experienced by children and older adults, such courtesy and respect can be very unusual indeed.

Perhaps another reason older people respond to the program is that the style is simple and "old-fashioned" — a term that most cultures would deem a compliment. The set hasn't changed its basic looks in twenty-five years. Mister Rogers' house and neighborhood could be something right out of 1960s television. There's no glitz because the Neighborhood set is as honest as Mister Rogers' cardigan sweater — simple and classic. Like the sweater, the Neighborhood has a familiar feel to it, and this kind of external familiarity appeals to older viewers.

The opening and closing shots of *Mister Rogers' Neighborhood* pan across the rooftops of a tiny model town. The beginning and the finale are two of the program's constants. And there are many others: Fred Rogers always greets us, enters his house, and exchanges his jacket and shoes for his sweater and sneakers; he always starts the show alone and others join him; some device (the trolley or Picture-Picture or "pretending") takes us to the Neighborhood of Make-Believe; and we always come back from Make-Believe to his house, where we say good-bye as we retrace our steps. He leaves his house as we take leave of the model town.

The program has a predictable beginning, middle, and end — again, a reinforcement to both younger and older viewers of something familiar, something to count on. It will never be haphazard. Even when our daily life seems confused and disordered, the Neighborhood keeps to its familiar ritual.

However, the fact that the Neighborhood looks familiar doesn't mean it's always easy and comfortable. Conflicts and difficulties arise. The difference is that in *Mister Rogers' Neighborhood* everything can be talked about, and anything that can be talked about can be dealt with — even divorce, even alienation, even death. The haven of the Neighborhood is not a false world, but it is a safe world, where "dangerous" feelings can be confronted. Violence and war, hatred and intolerance are not painted out of the picture, but neither are they allowed to destroy the canvas.

Ansello argues that *Mister Rogers' Neighborhood* embodies values in line with the traditional values today's elders were socialized with — being truthful, having courage, working hard, respecting yourself and other people. While "real life" serves up ever-more disturbing stories of crime and violence, the Neighborhood becomes a reconnection to that set of values. This does not mean that older adults do not watch or believe the evening news; rather, they want a verification that such violence is *not* the accepted norm, no matter how pervasive such violence may seem. Like children, older adults seem ready to believe in and work toward a different world instead of passively accepting the mind-numbing savagery that dominates both the news and prime-time television.

It is in this world of violent television that Fred Rogers takes time to talk with his audience. By doing so, he reunites older adults with the less-frenetic days of early radio. After all, this is a generation to whom Franklin D. Roosevelt's fireside chats are part of memory, not a lesson from a history book. Perhaps as children in the 1920s and 1930s, today's older viewers of Mister Rogers listened to the Singing Song Lady, or to a show like that of "Uncle Don," who broadcast to the children of New York original stories and songs, advice, birthday announcements, and other features with direct personal appeal.

Mister Rogers' Neighborhood was far in the future when the older adults of today were children. But the style with which Mister Rogers addresses his audience is reminiscent of radio shows that may be ingrained in their memory. He speaks distinctly, focuses on a topic, and then explores it in depth.

He is not simply transmitting information, he is communicating. Ansello says, "This style is actually the simplest form of communication. It's like sitting down and talking to a friend. That's why when children watch Mister Rogers, they talk back to the television. It's riveting because it's so real."

Ansello suggests that this kind of trustworthy reality is very important to older people because it implies stability: "At a time of life when so many things are changing for the aging individual — grown children having children, old neighborhoods passing, friends moving away or dying — 'trustworthy' is an anchor."

To illustrate how "trustworthy" a program like *Mister Rogers' Neighborhood* is, consider the program within the continuum of television and its history. The older generation remembers the world before television and has watched television since its start. In that time, they have viewed many televised instances of sincerity as well as insincerity. Their judgment is well informed. In particular, newscasters have a unique opportunity to communicate, delivering information that keeps viewers up to date and in touch with the world. And over the years some newscasters have even become trusted friends on whom we rely to guide us through momentous or terrible events. Walter Cronkite is such a person. He told us when John Kennedy was shot, and watching him, we knew that underneath his professional demeanor, he was as shattered as we were. And in 1969 he was as excited as any viewer when Apollo 11 landed on the moon. Even if the President of the United States failed us, as in the Watergate scandal, we could believe Walter Cronkite.

Today, the standard that Walter Cronkite set for trustworthy journalism remains, but no matter how good a reporter or newscaster is, the most that he or she can give us is a clear window on the outside world. What Fred Rogers gives us is a window on the inside world.

Fred Rogers once said that "television may be the only electrical appliance that's more useful after it's turned off. What's on the screen is just the beginning." He tells the story about a two-year-old who, after watching the Neighborhood visit with Yo-Yo Ma, started using a Popsicle stick on an old guitar and begged to learn to play the cello. Fred tells this story to illustrate what television can offer. He says, "The question is not, 'What can we sell them?' . . . or even 'What can we give them?' . . . but rather, '*Who are they?* What do they bring to the television set?'"

It is this kind of respect for the individual that makes Fred Rogers' communication unique and is the controlling element of his style. Talking directly to someone and also recognizing the other person's contribution to the conversation is what communication is all about — even in the cool, one-way medium of television. When the commercial spokesperson or the newscaster addresses the viewer, there is no break in the communication, no conversation. On *Mister Rogers' Neighborhood,* Fred Rogers talks, but he also pauses, leaving space for a response — a quaint, archaic practice once known as "listening."

In the same spirit, Fred Rogers always talks to just one person. He learned this approach in the early days of television when he worked as a floor manager for the cowboy actor Gabby Hayes. He asked Hayes how he felt about talking to a huge audience of children. Hayes replied that he only ever thought "of one little buckaroo." This one-on-one philosophy is the key to the intimacy of television that Fred Rogers has developed to a high art. Parents report that the younger the child, the more interest they show in the parts of the program where he is on the screen, often in close-up. But the attraction doesn't seem to wane. People find someone who talks warmly and conversationally while making direct eye contact appealing and soothing at any age: "I am 81 years old. . . . I must tell you how much you have helped me. Every time I listen to your program, I pretend you are talking to me as you talk, and it gives me so much help from day to day, as though I had a good friend talking to me."

CBS News reporter Harry Smith once asked Rogers why he thought he had lasted in television so long. Rogers responded that people, no matter what their age, long for honesty, and that he tries to be honest with children in a quiet, unhurried way, that he works hard at understanding as well as he can what the joys and struggles of growing human beings are, and then responds with television programming in as helpful a way as he knows how.

Why do so many older people watch *Mister Rogers' Neighborhood?* Considering the momentous changes witnessed by older adults during the course of their lives, it's not surprising that "one honest adult" would be so appealing. So the final and simplest explanation might be that older people find in Fred Rogers just what children find — one honest adult who is also a friend.

Mark Shelton confronts a different kind of stereotype: that of Fred Rogers himself. The popular concept of Mister Rogers (all sweetness and light) blinds us to one of his essential (and unsweet) messages to children: The world is a strange place, so when adults try to tell you it isn't, don't believe them. And that, Shelton argues, is what makes Fred Rogers so . . . well, subversive. "Adults are adults precisely because they have learned, first by making a series of daring forays, and then, over time, by simply getting used to it, that the outside world is fraught with danger, with problems, with fearful and strange things. The world outside each individual is a place we seek refuge from. Children know this, too — easily as well as adults — but we have forgotten they know it. Fred Rogers hasn't."

And the "scary outside world" is no better evidenced than in our treatment of children in the hospital or children with disabilities. When children in wheelchairs and children who use crutches appear on the program, Shelton notes, "Rogers acts exactly as adults 'learn' not to act: He calls attention, he asks nosy questions, he requests demonstrations, he asks to try out the crutches himself. . . . He doesn't paper over difference the way adults learn to do when they're being social. . . . He makes what everyone notices as 'strange' (in the sense of different) become, or start to become, familiar."

Perhaps, Shelton concludes, Fred Rogers is so likable and trusted exactly because he tells the truth about the larger world, about, even, the adults who surround children and take so seriously the responsibility of protecting children from the outside world.

Shelton is the author of Working in a Very Small Place: The Making of a Neurosurgeon and The Next Great Thing: The Sun, the Stirling Engine, and the Drive to Change the World. He was associate editor at both Pittsburgh Magazine and Ohio Magazine and received his MFA in fiction writing from the University of Pittsburgh.

Mark Shelton

A Neighborhood with Forest *and* Trees

Allies, Coalitions, Kids, and Mister Rogers

In the vast sea of television broadcasting, out there among the horse latitudes of television research, *Mister Rogers' Neighborhood* is taken as a sort of fixed point, a North Star, from which more esoteric or subtle investigations begin. Fred Rogers is seen as an ally of children and his program a place of refuge.

This was not always the case, particularly in the terra incognita that existed before Huston-Stein, Friedrich-Cofer, and others did their seminal work in the 1970s. (These researchers and others made the audacious suggestion that, despite contrary claims of network executives, repeated viewing of violent television programs *did* have an effect on children — and they had the results to prove their point.) Even a cursory look through the literature establishes *Mister Rogers' Neighborhood* as the gold standard for "positive" children's programming, the anchor to which what little we know about the "relationship" (for lack of a better word) between viewer and program is attached. Although it's sometimes astonishing what we seem to know about television viewing (and, likewise, sometimes astonishing what we do *not* know, or can't find out), the best tools in the hands of the best researchers who have turned their attentions to children sitting in front of *Mister Rogers' Neighborhood* agree on this point: Fred Rogers makes his Neighborhood a place where nothing bad happens to the children who spend time with him there, and good things do.

It is in this sense, of course, that Fred Rogers and *Mister Rogers' Neighborhood* are, respectively, an ally and a refuge; "ally," in the sense of a union toward a common purpose (and modestly, but importantly, different from a "coalition," which we'll come to in a moment), and "refuge," in the sense of shelter and protection in a gentle and safe place.

This alliance seems at first glance somehow misplaced. "Allies" must *actively* enter into an alliance, must consciously choose such a partnership, and children of age three or so do no such thing, one might say.

Well, one would be wrong.

Anyone who reads words like "ally" and "refuge" and simply nods or mutters an impatient "Well, yes, of course, who *wouldn't* think of Fred Rogers as an ally and a refuge?" will be given a chance presently to think about those words again. Our muttering is motivated by our confusion between forests and trees. It's the oft-mistaken difference between what we see, as distinct from what is there before us — the crucial difference between allies and coalitions.

We want to say "of course," because we — the adult "we," those of us who observe and analyze and form webs of understanding in making our way in the world — are used to seeing the world, and making our way through it on our toes, as it were. If you're not on your toes, you're not getting anywhere. We take for granted that *Mister Rogers' Neighborhood* is a place we (adults) understand. In truth, the show is utterly and completely subversive — and all the more so for being invisible. Fred Rogers is subversive; and if he weren't, he wouldn't be nearly so good at what he does, and children would not be the better for it. It has to do with allies and coalitions and refuges, but also with what we adults see: the trees all around us. Because we are adults, we do not (or cannot) see the forest we live in, or the role of a refuge like *Mister Rogers' Neighborhood*.

Allies and coalitions, it turns out, aren't exactly benign. While both terms suggest joining forces, they also imply that forces need to be joined in the first place *against* something, just as a refuge is a safe place to escape *from* something, and not simply a safe place to be. It's important to note that the explicit term used by Fred Rogers, "neighbor," implies proximity rather than relationship: "neighbors" are those who live near us; "friends" are those we know well. And "allies" and "coalitions" are those we seek out for some purpose.

A "coalition" is usually seen as a union among individuals or groups for some specific reason. (Parents with more than one child are often exquisitely aware of "coalitions" in this sense, if only because they regularly face them.) "Allies" also combine for specific purposes, like fighting a war. Less extreme, perhaps, but surely as appropriate an example, are the alliances of families or friends sought or made for social or political purposes. College curricula are full of such classifications — literature classes commonly discuss coalitions such as the uniting of estates in eighteenth- and nineteenth-century British novels, or the arranged marriages in Shakespearean drama. On a practical level, coalitions can be as prosaic as the PTA. Society teaches us — as Fred Rogers teaches us — that we have friends, but that we also have, or *should* have, allies. We live near neighbors, we grow to know our friends, but we *need* allies.

The reason for this is apparent, although perhaps a bit unsettling, so intent are we on protecting children from the perils of the outside world. If no one is out to get you, or if you can do just marvelously on your own, of course, there is not really a need for an ally. On the other hand — and in reality — if you do need to protect yourself or your estate, your family or your name, or what's inside your head, or simply your own freedom, then you need not just a friend, but an ally; not just a compatriot, but a coalition; not just a nice place, but a refuge.

If this seems all too bellicose for *Mister Rogers' Neighborhood*, it's simply a sign that you're an adult — an adult, certainly, who "protects" one's children (in the particular, but also in the more general sense of supporting things like good schools, safe streets, proper nutrition, and quality children's television programming) from the very need to be bellicose. We, as adults, think *we* do the fighting — and thus the alliance-making and coalition-building and refuge-constructing — *for* children, so that they can *be* children. And Fred Rogers is perfectly happy for us to think this way, as a good subversive would be. Not just a Trojan Horse, *Mister Rogers' Neighborhood* is a Trojan environment, the whole damn Trojan world. We can admire him from the elevated point of view of adulthood, and we are glad of that, because it just seems right. But we're not quite on the same team as Fred Rogers and the children he engenders are. In fact, we're not on the team at all.

Those with a stout heart can now feel free to rise and quote Walt Kelly's *Pogo:* We have met the enemy, and he is us. The "real" or "outside" world that we indulgently think we are protecting children from is, in fact, the reason *for* the precious coalition that Fred Rogers has so carefully built with children over decades, and which he reinforces with them each day. We — the outside world "we" — are in fact what Mister Rogers helps children form a coalition against: the outside world is a bellicose place, and children need someone to help them face it.

This is no chimera. The notion of alliances and coalitions seeps through the professional literature as clearly as it seeps through *Mister Rogers' Neighborhood* itself. But because we agree with the motives, we don't often think much about the methods beyond trying to identify them or label them. As is so often the case in studying Fred Rogers, we marvel at him while taking his methods — and his message — as being absolutely straightforward.

For example, Palmer, Taylor Smith, and Strawser describe it (well, remember it) this way: "As child viewers, we relaxed with our soft-spoken friend as he shared a variety of guests and a 'Neighborhood of Make-Believe' designed to help us get in touch with our feelings and cope with our problems. Mister Rogers was safe. Mister Rogers was secure. He was our friend, no matter who we were. And research indicated that the prosocial messages of friendship, persistence, delay of gratification, etc., were behaviorally internalized."[1]

But safe from what? Secure from what? Fred Rogers knows, which is why the posture of the show is frankly and exquisitely subversive — which is as it must be, if it is to work at all. All of the world outside us, whether we are adults or children, is just that: *outside us*. Adults are adults precisely because they have learned, first by making a series of daring forays, and then, over time, by simply getting used to it, that the outside world is fraught with danger, with problems, with fearful and strange things. The world outside each individual is a place we seek refuge *from*. Children know this, too — easily as well as adults — but we have forgotten they know it. Fred Rogers hasn't. Many children (and some adults) find exactly that refuge in *Mister Rogers' Neighborhood*, a place with an ally who escorts children on expeditions to places (geographical and otherwise) that are by definition dangerous places, because they are outside the place where children spend their lives: inside themselves.

An evocative study by Suzanne McFarland and WGTE alludes to this phenomenon. McFarland evaluated the use of *Mister Rogers' Neighborhood* in child care environments to determine how the program effected changes in attitudes and behaviors of children, their parents, and their child care providers. For starters, McFarland asked child care providers why they chose to show *Mister Rogers' Neighborhood* in the first place. The expected answers — for educational purposes and for "quiet time" — are not surprising, and, indeed, match up with what seems to be known about children who watch *Mister Rogers' Neighborhood*. There was another answer given, though, that is intriguing. The term that McFarland uses is "transition," in which the program fills the interstices between one activity and another in the course of a busy day (for the child, of course, as well as the child care provider).[2]

"Transition" is a noteworthy word, because one key to understanding those who watch *Mister Rogers' Neighborhood* is understanding not just how they see the program, but how they see the world. To make the transition from one activity or task or experience to another via a television program is to provide time, certainly, but also a place for children to be inside themselves. In this sense, the program is a place for passage (without even considering the larger metaphorical implications of this, such as the transition from childhood to adolescence) from the external world to an internal one. And with the external world so full of strangeness and challenge and unfamiliarity, the internal world becomes a refuge, a place for respite. *Mister Rogers' Neighborhood* is thus a tangible "place" in a child's internal world.

The program itself is full of literal and metaphorical transitions, from the archetypal changing of jacket for sweater and dress shoes for sneakers as Mister Rogers comes inside, to the changes of scene from living room to the Neighborhood of Make-Believe and even the careful mise-en-scène of toy houses on make-believe streets each time Rogers leaves the set and visits a box factory or a doctor's office or a library. But all of this takes place inside the program, and thus serves as a nested series of transitions that blur the larger moves that Mister Rogers helps children make: if they are to survive happily in the outside world, children must move from the interior world they know best into the larger, scarier, and altogether intimidating world all around them. Refuge inside ourselves is something frankly prized by adults, but only after we have learned enough about the outside world to feel safe inside ourselves. By prizing the interior world as Rogers does with his repeated reinforcement of self-worth, children find an ally who seems to know exactly what they face when they do battle with strangeness and difference.

The irony is in the paradox. In order to engage with the outside world — a necessary step to adulthood — children must feel safe within themselves. That security, however, is formed through contact, by engaging others who are strange and different from ourself. We — the adult we — assume that this difficult nexus between the outside and the inside is purely a grown-up concern. We do not remember that children, con- consciously or not, are struggling with these same questions of boundaries and connectedness.

Establishing a safe place inside oneself comes at a price. Keeping one's place "safe," therefore, takes on both physical and metaphoric importance. For this reason, issues of medicine and health and abilities versus disabilities have always played an important role on *Mister Rogers' Neighborhood*.

A particularly startling example of this is often hidden — as so much seems to be in what Fred Rogers does — in indirection. In a special series of programs called Let's Talk About . . . , Fred Rogers deals with issues such as going to the hospital, going to the emergency room, and having an operation. In one episode, there is this exchange: "You use the X-ray machine to see inside someone," Rogers says to a radiologist. "Can you see someone's thoughts and feelings with this machine?"[3]

After the radiologist assures Rogers and the viewers that indeed, such a thing is not possible, Rogers himself makes the point again, turning to the camera and telling viewers that even though the radiologist may be looking "inside" your head, he can't see what you're thinking. The nominal frights of an X ray — large robotlike machines, strangers touching you and turning you this way and that, being left all alone in the room while the X ray is taken, being away from your parents, all the while hurting from some frightening mishap or accident — are all present and all dealt with in standard Mister Rogers style, and with standard Mister Rogers aplomb. But what gets the emphasis is the worry that someone is going to be looking at thoughts and feelings without your permission. It likely wouldn't occur to us (the adult us) that children would feel any need to hide their thoughts from adults; we cannot imagine their brainwaves to be full of anything but innocence and wonder. But Rogers knows differently and reassures his partners that their secrets will remain secret. Likewise, in another show,

Rogers goes on at some length about how the doctor can't see thoughts and feelings with an otoscope. The safe place, the refuge, is inside themselves, and because Rogers seems to know this, he is an ally. (After all, most adults do quite the opposite, asking children what they're thinking, engaging children in "adult" conversation, trying to enter a world that Rogers suggests belongs to the child alone.)

As adults who fully believe that we're on the side of children, that we're part of the coalition, this can be puzzling. We take for granted that because we care so much for children, because we have the interests of children (especially our own children) so clearly at heart, children would not worry that "someone" — parents, doctors, friends — might see inside their heads. We "know" there is nothing a child could be thinking that we wouldn't want her to feel she could share with us; we are in fact always trying to find out. And we think we're being benign when we do so, but of course we're not. We're the ones, after all, who take children to doctors' offices and hospitals and the like in the first place, the ones who leave children in frightening rooms with total strangers who use large machines to "see" things that eyes cannot.

So it's not the large machines and the strangers that are frightening. It's the startling differences between the outside world and the child's interior existence that make things scary and make children seek a bond, and thus a coalition. The famous "I like you just the way you are" mantra is demonstrably valid as a method of engendering self-esteem;[4] it is also, however, the principal way that Rogers reminds children that he knows what they know: that everything is different for each individual child.

The episodes of *Mister Rogers' Neighborhood* that demonstrate this diversity are particularly telling in what they emphasize, and what they don't. The introduction of a different species of fish into the aquarium is for Rogers typically metaphorical, and — considering the sledgehammerish approach generally given in mass media to the notion of cultural, social, or ethnic diversity — typically subtle: the point is not so much tolerance or accommodation of diversity, but rather the fact of diversity itself, which has to be acknowledged before anything else can happen. People, in fact, have to be exceptionally different on *Mister Rogers' Neighborhood* for their differences to be commented on, because the most important differences to Rogers are the differences of which his audience is most acutely aware.

It takes all types is something we might say; *everyone is different from me* is closer to how we really think. What makes *Mister Rogers' Neighborhood* unique is that he *says* this, aloud, all the time.

African American visitors or guests on the show, to take another example, are rarely explicitly described or referred to as different, even as they sometimes occupy all manner of roles and professions that are traditionally or stereotypically not held by African Americans — physicians, classical musicians, and so on. We adults on the outside think (a bit smugly, perhaps) that what Rogers is doing is what we do, try to do, think is the "right" thing to do, and that is not to call particular attention to difference, as though we don't notice difference. But this effort of assimilation is what *adults* do; children — and Rogers — approach it much differently. The act of not commenting is exemplary, in a sense. Rather than "celebrate" difference, he confronts children with difference, and then — paradoxically — doesn't make more of it than he makes of difference in most other circumstances, a sort of inoculation of difference. (It's notable that *Mister Rogers' Neighborhood* is quite out of step with mass media in this regard, in that race and ethnicity are not presented as a sort of *tableau vivant,* but rather as part of Rogers' world, and by extension, part of the viewers' worlds as well.)

Further, when difference *is* commented upon, Rogers does so in a way that might make the diversity police frankly uncomfortable, something that again reminds us how we're on the outside looking in — and the children in the audience are notably inside. Think, for example, about when children in wheelchairs and children who use crutches appear on the show. In these circumstances, Rogers acts exactly as adults "learn" not to act: he calls attention, he asks nosy questions, he requests demonstrations, he asks to try out the crutches himself. By doing so, he does two things, simultaneously. First, he brings these nominal "outsiders" into the coalition he works to establish with the children who watch, making, in a sense, a part of the "we" that is not at all the adult "us."

But what he doesn't do is equally important. He doesn't paper over difference the way adults learn to do when they're being social. Not at all. Rather than doing what we comfortably assume he's doing — assimilating children into our world — he's actually doing the opposite: he makes what everyone notices as "strange" (in the sense of different) become, or start to become, familiar. This is as true of the differences he points out among people as it is true of the differences he points out among places and things: These are the sorts of things you'll encounter — that you already know you encounter — outside the Neighborhood, he implies, so let's grow familiar with them. Now.

In other words, they are allies together against all manner of things that we like to think Fred Rogers is helping children learn to accommodate, a distinction with a difference. After all, the places and devices that are frightful (operating rooms, toilets, trips away from home), the people who are unsettling because they're different, don't grow less different or less frightful once we've seen them. (Is anyone, really, comfortable in the doctor's office, even after repeated visits? We may ask our children why they are frightened, but usually we'll end up telling them the same thing our parents told us: "Don't worry." And our children, just like we did at their age, will take this as a sure signal to start worrying in earnest.) What these strange things *do* become is something children can learn to face, in coalition with someone. By establishing an alliance and a refuge, *Mister Rogers' Neighborhood* prepares children not to live in a world of gentleness and comfort, but in the world that we all live in, where things are not always gentle, comfortable, or familiar.

While this is certainly subversive, it is certainly not destructive, although it's easy to see how it could be. It works because all the things that children quite early on recognize as false are represented as false by *Mister Rogers' Neighborhood*, something that we adults tend to forget to do in constructing worlds for children. We give them the real world, and pretend it's not frightening; Rogers gives children a clearly false world, and uses it to teach them how to deal with the real one.

For example, it has been commented upon quite often that the entire weird setup of *Mister Rogers' Neighborhood* — the faux stage set, the cheesy props, the almost tuneless songs, the startlingly concrete Neighborhood of Make-Believe, which is about as fanciful as a file cabinet — is so literal and fake as to make us wonder how such patently artificial devices can "fool" anyone, can suspend any viewer's disbelief. Well, they don't do any such thing in the conventional "imaginative" sense that adults could understand. And it doesn't have anything to do with the notion of small children being limited by nascent minds, either, but in fact has to do with quite the opposite. It's *not* that the minds of children are less "developed" than the minds of adults, and thus somehow satisfied by obviously fake shrubbery, but that children recognize — almost before they recognize anything else — the difference between real and false, and it's the real world that is frightening, while the demonstrably false one is secure. (Fitch, Huston, and Wright's survey of children's perceptions of reality captures this quite succinctly: by age four, the perception of reality and falsity is acute.)[5] The conjuring up of Mr. McFeely, the on-cue phone calls, coincidences such as both Mister Rogers and Chef Brockett having crutches on the same day — these are magical (perhaps) for the youngest or newest viewers, but don't remain so. Instead, they become icons of honest falsity against a world that is too often hurtfully false. "That's going to hurt, isn't it?" Rogers asks the emergency room doctor when she begins to describe stitching up a cut, in stark contrast to — and shame on them for saying it — well-meaning adults who tell children that it won't hurt a bit. Rogers is the one who tells the truth, the one who points out what is obvious to viewers (that some of the things doctors do are going to hurt), and instead of glossing over this truth, turns it into a little (and tuneless) song, "I want to know when something is going to hurt."

The world, in other words, is going to hurt, and children old enough to hold their heads up learn this every day. The blatant falsity of pretending that things don't hurt is what we as adults do out of a wish to protect; *Mister Rogers' Neighborhood* tells the truth, and strikes a blow for autonomy — we know it's going to hurt, so why not tell us so?

This particular episode can stand, then, as a metaphor for how the program works so well. Rogers is likable and trusted because he tells the truth about the larger world, about, even, the adults who surround children and take so seriously the responsibility for insulating children from the outside world.

He is able to do so because he allies himself with children against the things that they know are going to hurt, and we on the outside abet this by being blind to it. It is our world, of course, that children are brought into, and no one confirms the suspicions that children have about it more straightforwardly than Fred Rogers.

The secret of understanding this coalition requires us to find the forest among the trees. Perhaps it's best that the well-meaning souls among us pretend we don't understand that *Mister Rogers' Neighborhood* is a place where children retreat to learn the truths we often try to keep from them and that we don't know that Fred Rogers is someone on whom they can depend to tell the truth about the rest of us. As adults schooled in the pop-psychoanalytic art of self-examination, we should be grateful that Fred Rogers is not on our side, but on our children's side against us.

Lynn Johnson

A Very Special Neighborhood

A Photo Essay

The last essay in this collection belongs to Fred Rogers himself. In these photos you see the life of a person committed to children and families, both ours and his. Between the first shot of the young Rogers, gesturing with open arms to welcome an unseen audience, to the last, a solitary thoughtful, mature Rogers, comes forty years of experience and caring.

Many of the writers in this volume have commented on the consistency of Rogers' work, his reliance on unity of theme. Such constancy may have been drawn from his earliest experiences with his family, especially his maternal grandfather, Fred McFeely, for whom he is named. Six decades later, Grandfather Fred plays with young Alexander, and the viewer cannot escape the sense of continuity, a circle complete.

The photos of Rogers at work on *Mister Rogers' Neighborhood* demonstrate other facets identified by the essayists: Rogers as clown, as puppeteer, as colleague, as guiding force; able to change with technology but true to the original gentle civility that has marked his television persona since *The Children's Corner*. The pictures of Fred as listener, with staff, with children, even with a cow, bring an awareness of this man's indelible signature on his life's work.

In these photographs one sees moments of tranquility, a sense of comfort, a life dedicated to us and our children, capturing the very special Neighborhood created by Rogers, and his colleagues and friends. We close this volume with these images of Fred Rogers in our mind, and hear the echo of the careful, redemptive words that end each Neighborhood day for more than 10 million children around the world:

You know you make each day special.
And you know how, too:
By just your being you.
There's no one else like you.
I like you just the way you are.

Mark Collins and Margaret Mary Kimmel

This essay was shot primarily by photographer Lynn Johnson, known for her sensitive documentary work in both color and black-and-white. Since 1984 she has been a contract photographer for New York's Black Star photo agency, producing photo essays for such magazines as National Geographic, Life, Sports Illustrated, Fortune, Forbes, Newsweek, New York Times Magazine, German Geo, Stern, *and* Smithsonian. *She has received five World Press Awards, the Robert F. Kennedy Journalism Award for coverage of the disadvantaged, and the 1994 University of Missouri Picture of the Year Award—first place for photo essay.*

Mister Rogers on the set in the early 1970s. (Photo courtesy of Family Communications, Inc.)

A young Fred and his mother at the beach. (Family photo)

Mister Rogers at Cape Cod, one of his favorite places.

Fred with his parents, James H. and Nancy McFeely Rogers. (Family photo)

Fred in a stroller; he was an only child until age eleven. (Family photo)

(*Left*) Fred celebrates his tenth birthday with his maternal grandfather, Fred McFeely. (Family photo)

(*Opposite, top*) Nine-year-old Fred with Grandfather McFeely at the organ; Fred was interested in music from an early age. (Family photo)

(*Below*) Fred Rogers enjoys a special moment with his grandson, Alexander Rogers.

(*Opposite, bottom*) Grandfather and grandson play hide-and-seek.

Fred Rogers and his wife, Joanne, at their Cape Cod home, "Crooked House."

Rogers and Margaret McFarland, long-time friend and adviser.
(Photo by Jim Judkis)

On the set of
*Mister Rogers'
Neighborhood*,
late 1960s.
(Photo courtesy of
Family
Communications,
Inc.)

In the living
room of *Mister
Rogers'
Neighborhood.*

(*Left*) On *The Children's Corner,* the predecessor to *Mister Rogers' Neighborhood,* Fred Rogers was the behind-the-scenes puppeteer.
(Photo courtesy of Family Communications, Inc.)

(*Below*) Mister Rogers, Lady Elaine, and neighbors Chuck Aber and Robert Trow/Troll.

(*Opposite, top*) Mister Rogers on the set with Chelle Robinson, assistant director; Jim Seech, floor manager; Bob Walsh, director; and Margy Whitmer, producer.

(*Opposite, bottom*) Puppeteers Fred Rogers, Carol Switala, Lenny Meledandri at work on *Mister Rogers' Neighborhood.*

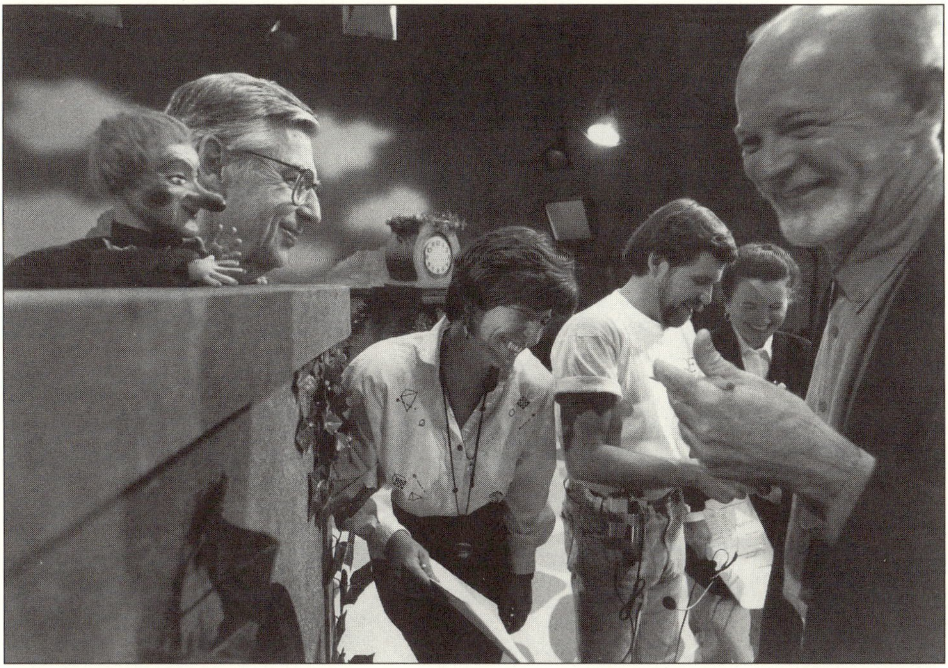

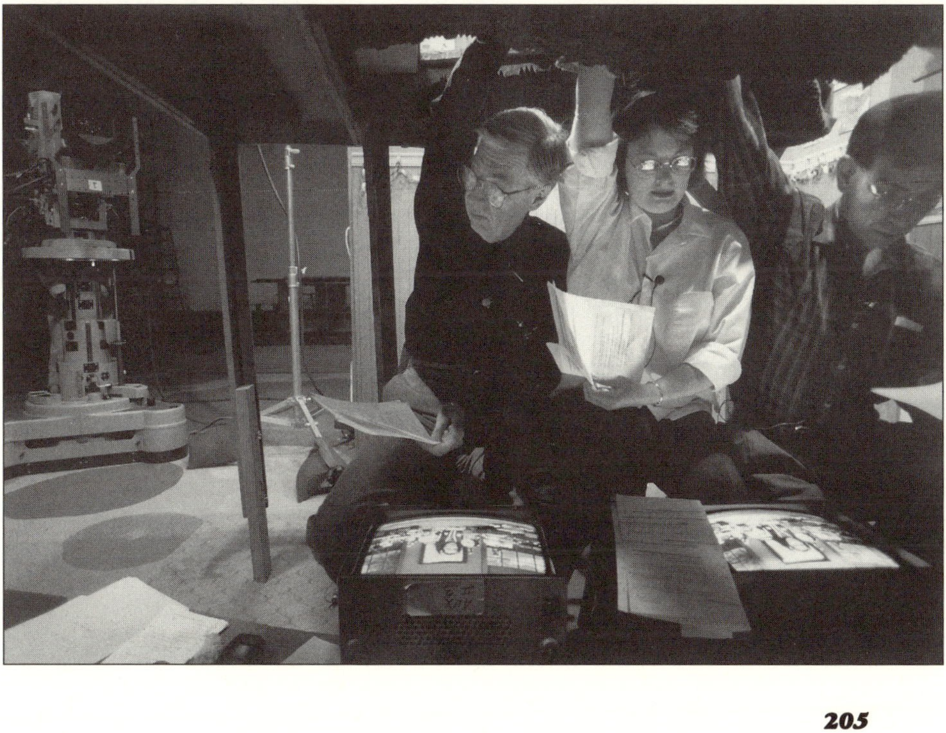

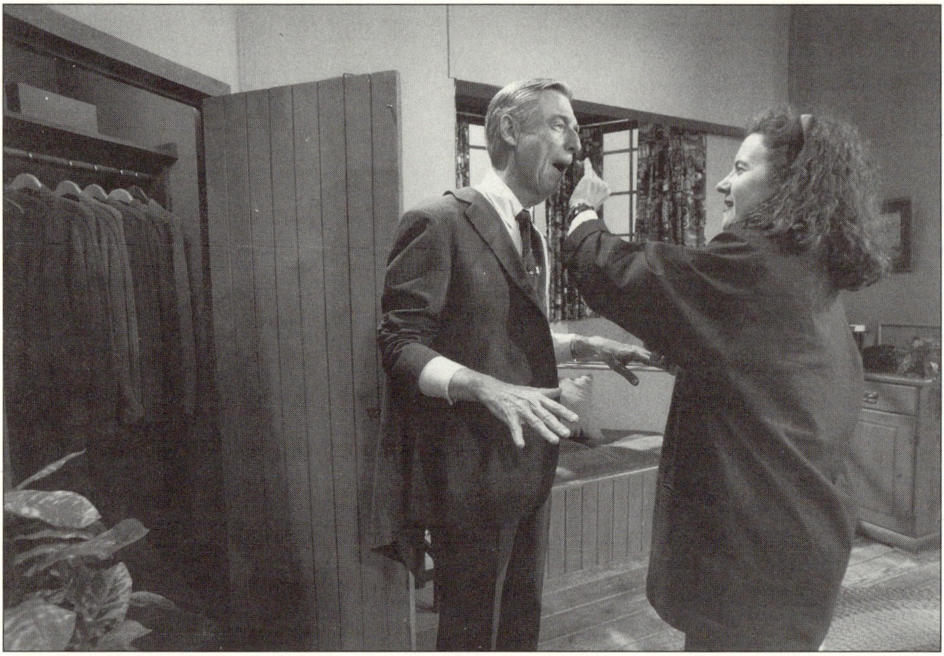

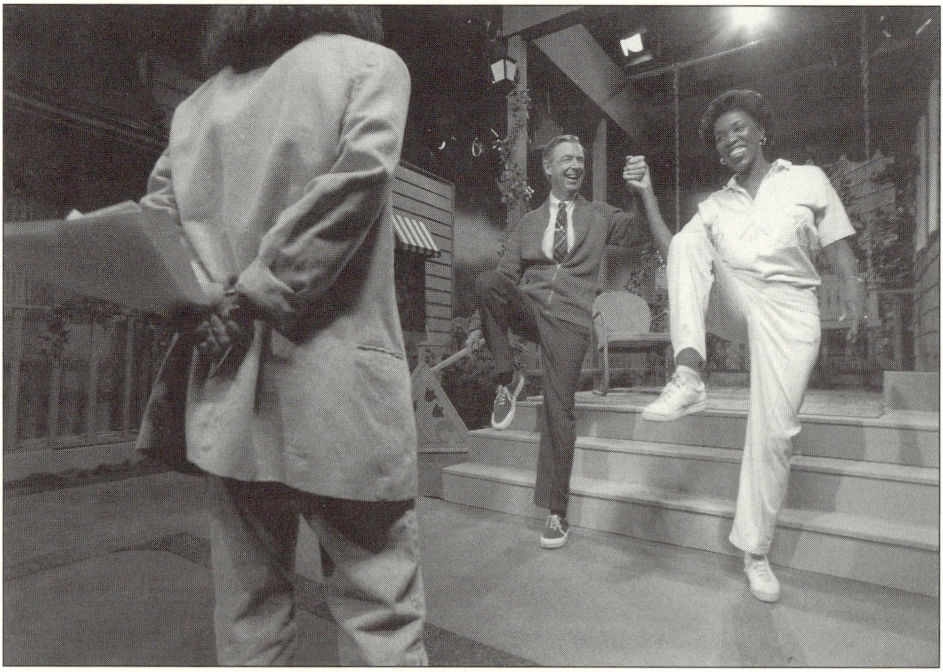

(*Opposite, top*) Producer Margy Whitmer applies make-up to Mister Rogers.

(*Opposite, bottom*) Mister Rogers and neighbor Marilyn Barnett dance as the program's producer, Margy Whitmer, watches.

(*Above*) Mister Rogers and Chuck Aber sing a song in the Neighborhood of Make-Believe.

(*Right*) Mister Rogers clowns around by balancing a box on his head.

Mister Rogers gestures expansively on the set of the Negri Music Shop; music is an integral part of the program.

"X" the Owl peeks out of the carry-all as Mister Rogers carries the famous sneakers in his other hand.

The sneakers may be a more visible symbol of *Mister Rogers' Neighborhood*, but Fred Rogers' ability to listen is a critical part of his success — and of his appeal to audiences of all ages.

He listens to guest Krissy Thompson . . . (Photo courtesy of Family Communications, Inc.)

. . . colleague Johnny Costa . . .

. . . and a child in the midst of a busy airport.

Fred Rogers and Sam Newbury, director of productions, share a laugh during filming at a dairy farm.

On the way to Boston University commencement, Mister Rogers takes time to greet fans.

From preschool to college commencement, Mister Rogers' appeal endures.

Mister Rogers has been a good neighbor for more than thirty years.

A Nation of Neighborhoods

The United States has changed enormously since that day in the late 1960s when Fred Rogers first walked into his television "living room," exchanged his jacket and street shoes for a sweater and tennis shoes, and invited America's children to be his neighbors. In the past three decades, economic and social tidal waves have battered our families, our neighborhoods, and our schools, and have altered our demographics and our workplaces. Now, as Fred Rogers' first young neighbors become parents themselves, the stresses and challenges of child-rearing have never been greater. They are daunting enough for well-educated and economically comfortable families. For moderate- and low-income families the stresses can be virtually overwhelming. The consequences for American children are profound.

Since the late 1960s there has been a steady march of mothers into the paid workforce — out of choice and out of necessity. In addition, parents are spending more time on the job than they did thirty years ago, leaving them less time and emotional energy to meet their children's needs for guidance and attention. Many more children now live only with their mothers, and many of these children receive little regular economic or emotional support from their fathers.

A higher proportion of children, especially preschoolers, are living in poverty today. Over the past two decades, America has allowed children as a group to become its poorest citizens. And our children are exposed to violence as never before — on television, in their homes, in their neighborhoods, and in their schools.

The cumulative effect of these and other changes is that many American children are growing up fearful and insecure, without adequate attention and guidance, without hope for the future, and without a steady internal compass to help them navigate the perilous journey to adulthood. And these are not just poor and minority children. Countless affluent and middle-income white children, like their less-advantaged peers, are growing up so adrift that by early adolescence they turn to alcohol and drugs, sex, or mindless materialism to fill the space once occupied by self-respect, empathy, and hope.

The impact of these changes is more than economic. What we've lost is more profound and intangible. We've lost our sense of community.

I grew up in South Carolina during the days of segregation, but its ugly, negative effects were mitigated by our strong black community that made me and my peers feel valued and important. The watchful adults in our church and community paid attention to us, found ways to keep us busy, reported to our parents and chided us when we strayed from the straight and narrow of community expectations, and praised and supported our achievements when we did well. While life was often hard and resources scarce, we always knew who we were and that the measure of our worth was inside our heads and hearts.

Today, fewer children of any race receive such nurturing and guidance from nearby extended family and longtime neighbors, which means that Mister Rogers and his Neighborhood are more important than ever. Fred Rogers provides some of the same antidotes that "real" neighbors were likely to furnish in earlier times to help children overcome negativity, neglect, or indifference. He offers every child — whatever her color, family background, or economic class — a priceless extra dose of emotional support, affirmation, and sound moral guidance. He offers basic information to help young children make sense of the adult world. And by example he shows parents how they can better help their children love themselves and cope effectively with life's challenges.

The authors of the essays in this volume are far more qualified than I am to explore Fred Rogers' genius for evoking feelings of comfort, security, and self-affirmation in his young television neighbors. What I want to do is highlight briefly some of the most significant aspects of the changing context in which Fred Rogers has been enriching children's lives over the past quarter century.

This context is critical because our families do not exist in — and our children do not grow up in — isolation. Children grow up happy, healthy, and productive when their families are able to nurture and provide for them. When the economic and social environment does not support families' efforts to meet their children's needs, it is children who suffer.

The increasingly stressful forces of the past several decades are expected to continue into the next century. Yet America is just now considering how to respond. Until recently our society has given little thought to helping families cope with problems created by the decline in well-paying blue collar jobs; the shortage of good, affordable child care for working families; shrinking health care coverage for dependents; the increase in single-parent families; the withering of community supports; and the shortage of affordable housing. In fact, instead of looking for ways to strengthen families, we've tended collectively to blame parents for faltering in their ability to overcome such obstacles.

Today's parents did not cause the changes in the national economy, the health care crisis, the deteriorating condition of our inner cities, or the myriad other changes that have so altered America in the past quarter century. While individual families must contribute to America's efforts to reorder our public and private priorities, restore the strong American family, and reclaim our democratic and family values, individual families cannot do it alone.

Child development specialist David Hamburg, president of the Carnegie Corporation of New York, has written:

> The nature of this new generation of problems was poorly understood; emerging trends were insufficiently recognized; and authority tended to substitute for evidence, and ideology for analysis. Until the past few years, political, business, and professional leaders had very little to say about the problems of children and youth. . . . [The nation must] face the nature and scope of the problems and their growing severity, and to take responsibility in a shared, cooperative way throughout the society.[1]

A sense of shared responsibility for America's children is exactly what I am urging. The risks America's families and children face today are so significant and pervasive they must be tackled not only by extraordinarily gifted and dedicated individuals like Fred Rogers, but by all of us.

First, however, I want to review some of the ways in which life has become harder for young families in the past several decades.

Today there are more poor children in America than in any year since 1965, despite the net 88 percent growth in our gross national product. Contrary to popular myths, a majority of these poor children are *not* black and are *not* on welfare. Most poor children live outside our inner cities in small-town, rural, and suburban America. Among all American children, one in five is poor; among preschoolers, one in four.

Cathy, a fifth-grader who lives in New Mexico, is one of America's 14.3 million poor children and one of the estimated 5 million American children who go hungry each day. In the mornings, she told a reporter, her family walks around town "looking for food in garbage cans. We find cereal boxes with a little cereal left in it and a rotten apple," she said. Often, there's nothing for lunch, said Cathy. "At six o'clock we start walking to the church for our dinner. That's the way my day crawls by."

The shift in the economy from manufacturing to service has seen the decline in real income for blue collar families. One consequence of this trend for young families with children (those headed by a parent younger than thirty) was devastating. Between 1973 and 1990, these families saw their median income plunge 32 percent, after adjusting for inflation. While older families lost some ground, many young families fell into poverty. As a result, a staggering 40 percent of the children in young families lived in poverty in 1990, double that of 1973.

To make matters worse, government programs such as unemployment insurance, Aid to Families with Dependent Children, and food stamps — programs created precisely to shield families from the worst consequences of economic instability — were themselves weakened. In 1979 nearly one in five otherwise poor families with children was lifted from poverty through government assistance; by 1991 only one in eight was.

All of these trends mean that many families are living in decrepit, unsafe, or unsanitary housing that nonetheless eats up huge proportions of their income. Some families resort to doubling up with friends or relatives, but these arrangements are unstable and stressful for children and adults alike. Eventually, many doubled-up families find themselves on the streets, with nowhere to go but to shelters. At the end of the 1970s, there were virtually no homeless families in America. Today, families with children make up more than one-third of all homeless people. Unstable housing takes a tremendous toll on children; poorly housed or homeless children fare poorly on all key measures of health, nutrition, emotional well-being, and educational progress.

Health care costs bring additional worries to unemployed or under-employed people. Although health care for pregnant women and children generally improved during the 1970s, progress stopped in the 1980s as the cost of health care began to skyrocket and employer-based health insurance for dependents became harder to find. Nearly 1 million infants each year start life at risk of serious disadvantage because their mothers did not receive early prenatal care. More than 250,000 babies annually are born at low birthweight, many of whom face a lifetime with disabilities as a result.

Cost is only one of the difficulties many families face in getting health care for their children. Tens of millions of families live in communities where doctors, hospitals, and health clinics are scarce. For these families, getting a routine prenatal checkup, their children vaccinated, or a sick child to a doctor may be next to impossible because there are simply too few doctors and clinics to serve them; those that do exist are far away. And the structure of health services in our country creates barriers even for families that are insured and have access to a doctor or clinic. Health care and related social services often are so overburdened, fragmented, and intimidating that many families just give up in discouragement. The rates at which children are vaccinated against preventable childhood diseases are considered good indicators of how well a primary health care system is working. Today, less than 60 percent of two-year-olds in most states are fully immunized, a sobering indication of how seriously the present system is failing our children.

With mounting evidence of the toll that poverty and related problems such as poor housing and inadequate nutrition levy on children, it becomes clearer every day that America's future depends on its response to the economic plight of young families. Sustained economic growth is necessary, but it's not sufficient. Other promising strategies for placing a basic economic floor under children are a refundable children's tax credit, an improved minimum wage, and when necessary, supplementation of the earnings of low-wage parents to help them pay for basic necessities such as food, child care, and housing.

Changing family composition accounts for some of the decline in the economic health of young families over the past twenty years. The high divorce rate and the increase in the proportion of births to unmarried mothers, especially among teenagers, have increased the proportion of children living in one-parent families. While about 12 percent of children lived in one-parent families in 1970, by 1990 the proportion had increased to 25 percent.

Many children in mother-only families also miss out on sustained male nurturing. A survey by the National Commission on Children revealed that just one-third of children living apart from their fathers report seeing them at least once a week, and nearly one in five has not seen his or her father for five years. Recently a Head Start teacher in York, Pennsylvania, reported that the three- and four-year-olds in her classroom are so starved for contact with males that when a male social worker comes into her classroom "it's like Santa Claus has arrived." For children whose lives don't include daily interaction with a nurturing, adult male, regular visits with Mister Rogers via television may be especially important, suggesting at least some aspects of a relationship with a caring father figure.

The trend toward out-of-wedlock childbearing is partly the result of changing sexual and social mores and partly the result of other developments: the increase in child poverty, the general failure of our schools to foster achievement among poor and minority students, and the lack of positive youth development activities in low-income communities.

To stop children from having children, our communities must offer children the types of early experiences that, over the long term, engender the motivation and hope to plan for a productive future and avoid the trap of too-early pregnancy. These opportunities include good health care and child care, schooling that fosters academic success and healthy self-esteem, a vastly improved system for assuring that absent parents pay child support, a chance to contribute positively to the community, and sustained interaction with concerned adults.

The steady increase in working mothers may be the most profound change families in general have experienced in the past quarter century. Since the 1960s, mothers have streamed into the paid workforce as a result of the increase in mother-only families, worsening economic fortunes for young families generally, and changing attitudes about women's roles. Between 1970 and 1990 the proportion of women with children younger than six who were in the paid workforce rose from 29 percent to 60 percent. In 1987, for the first time, more than half of all mothers with babies one year or younger were working or looking for work. At least two-thirds of working mothers work full time, and about one-quarter are the primary wage earners for their children.

With more and more mothers joining the labor force, the need for child care has become acute. In 1990 about 10 million children younger than five were cared for by someone other than a parent. Twenty-five years ago, most employed parents preferred having relatives care for their children, but that option has become far less available as more grandparents and other relatives are either in the workforce themselves or live far away.

I recently watched a videotape of children being cared for in a child care center where infants were left for hours in infant seats, and many toddlers and preschoolers wandered aimlessly, their fussing largely ignored because the caregivers had too many children to care for. This was not an inexpensive child care program, yet the staff was not providing the attention, interaction, and activities children need in order to thrive. All children need and deserve good quality child care, and it's especially critical for children whose home situations are stressful or unstable. Yet many states do not have child care licensing standards that ensure good quality care.

The national child care legislation finally enacted in 1990 has provided desperately needed federal funds to help low-income families find and pay for decent child care. States now are able to offer many more parents the assistance they need in order to keep working to support their children. Alabama, for example, now provides child care assistance to twice as many low-income children as before the act was passed. But the available funding still doesn't come close to meeting the need.

With more mothers working outside the home and both parents spending more hours on the job to support their families and advance their careers, families spend less and less time together. One in two fathers, one in eight mothers, and one in three single parents regularly work more than forty hours a week, according to the National Commission on Children. Parents have difficulty finding time to participate in their children's school and extracurricular activities, and the stabilizing family routines of sharing meals, talking, taking family outings, and worshiping together play a diminished role in family life. Fully 59 percent of parents say they would like more time with their children and cite work outside the home as the major limitation.

Urie Bronfenbrenner, professor of human development and family studies at Cornell University, has captured the essence of family life for many middle-class families:

> In a world in which both parents usually have to work, often at a considerable distance from home, every family member, through the waking hours from morning till night, is "on the run." The need to coordinate conflicting demands of job and child care, often involving varied arrangements that shift from day to day, can produce a situation in which everyone has to be transported several times a day in different directions, . . . a state of affairs that prompted a foreign colleague to comment: "It seems to me that in your country, most children are being brought up in moving vehicles."[2]

The family and medical leave bill passed by Congress and signed by the president at the beginning of 1993 is a significant step toward helping parents fulfill their obligations as parents without jeopardizing their jobs. One regional bank now gives parents two hours of paid time off each week to take part in children's school activities. Some forward-thinking employers also give their employees paid time off to volunteer at their children's schools and participate in their children's school activities, but our children need all American employers to become much more sympathetic and active partners with parents as they struggle to harmonize family and work life.

When parents' desperation, isolation, or addiction lead to child abuse or neglect, our child protection agencies generally remove the children from their families and place them in foster care, group homes, or institutions. Wherever they are placed, these children face grim futures. All of them suffer from the trauma of being separated from their parents, siblings, and schools, and thousands of them may never again have a permanent home during childhood. Shuffled from one temporary foster setting to another by our overloaded and understaffed child protection agencies, these children often are neglected or jeopardized by the very agencies that took them from their families to protect them from such treatment.

An estimated 429,000 children lived apart from their families in 1991, and experts believe that close to 900,000 children soon will be in out-of-home care unless we begin doing more to strengthen families before children are endangered.

Child welfare experts are urging state and national legislators and social service agencies to develop a new approach to helping vulnerable families. Thankfully, some states and communities are making some progress in that direction by beginning to develop networks of community-based services that include voluntary preventive help such as parent education, prenatal classes, parent support groups, and early help for children whose development is delayed.

The downward spiral of economic and social stress fuels the increase in violence. The prevalence of crime corrupts a child's basic need for security, yet violence and the fear of violence have become a part of daily life for tens of thousands of American children. A recent poll of children between the ages of ten and seventeen commissioned by the Children's Defense Fund and *Newsweek* magazine revealed a generation of children growing up in fear. Asked what concerns them and their families most, 56 percent of the children said they worried about violent crime against a family member. One in five children polled said they don't feel safe walking in their neighborhoods after dark. And the fear reaches children in small-town and rural America, as well as those in big cities. Only 31 percent of children in small cities and towns and 47 percent of those in rural areas sense they are very safe in their own neighborhoods at night.

And, of course, violence reaches into the homes of virtually all American children through television. Preschoolers watch an astonishing thirteen hundred hours of television each year — one-quarter of their waking hours. Hopefully, some of those hours are filled with *Mister Rogers' Neighborhood, Sesame Street,* and other worthwhile children's programming. But most young children also watch programs that expose them to an outrageous amount of gratuitous violence. Prime time television typically depicts five acts of violence every hour; children's Saturday morning programming includes even higher rates of violence, although it is packaged differently.

What effect do violence and the threat of violence have on children? James Garbarino, president of the Erikson Institute for Advanced Study in Child Development, and others tell us that children who regularly watch violence in the media are likely to become more aggressive in their behavior. Children who actually live with violence may become hypervigilant, so intent on avoiding risks that they have little energy or motivation to explore or master their environment. These children, says Garbarino, are likely to show a diminished sense of achievement and self-confidence and have greater difficulty trusting others and forming attachments. Some children become depressed, and some seem to develop what might be called an "addiction" to violence. The *Washington Post* recently reported that young children in some neighborhoods now spend time talking with friends about the kind of funeral they want.

What happens to a nation that allows a significant portion of its children to grow up in conditions that resemble a war zone? America will have the answer to that question all too soon unless we shake off our inertia and begin taking action to reduce the violence in our country. Each of us can and must do something. As individuals we can speak out against violence as well as encourage and help implement antiviolence and conflict resolution courses in our schools, communities, and congregations. We can support responsible gun control legislation and make it clear to our elected representatives that we expect them to support it too. We also can protest excessive violence in our popular culture by turning off the TV, writing letters to the media and to advertisers about their programming, and refusing to patronize excessively or gratuitously violent movies.

Despite the enormity of the challenges, our nation *can* change course if we are all willing to take inspiration from Fred Rogers and work together to rebuild communities that support parents' efforts to nurture and protect their children. Creating family-friendly neighborhoods requires efforts from every one of us, working from the bottom up in every community in America. Let us assess the extent to which the community groups, religious organizations, and business organizations to which we belong support families in their child-rearing role, then work with those organizations to help them do more. We can find out which family needs aren't being met in our community and encourage local groups to take the initiative to meet them. Parent education programs, for example, are wonderful projects for religious organizations to organize and sponsor.

All of us who care about children must work harder to make sure our cities and communities and neighborhoods embody the basic values we want to teach our children. If, for example, we want our children to understand and value the importance of individual effort and hard work — as Fred Rogers teaches children to do — we must have public and workplace policies that make it possible for parents to find jobs that pay wages families can live on, and we must have employers willing to adopt workplace policies that allow parents to fulfill their role as parents without jeopardizing their jobs.

If we want our children to grow up eager to learn and confident in their abilities — attitudes that Fred Rogers consistently fosters — our employers, churches, community organizations, public agencies, state governments, and private child care providers must all work together to develop child care policies and services that make it possible for all young children, regardless of family income, to be cared for in safe, stimulating, and nurturing environments while their parents work. Head Start, the comprehensive preschool program for poor children, must receive enough funding to allow all eligible children to participate.

And if we want our children to respect and cherish human life — as Fred Rogers always teaches — our public policies must ensure that all American children grow up in safe, healthy surroundings where *every* life is valued and protected. This means we will have to do more than tell our legislators to beef up police forces and build prisons. As a nation we will have to address the poverty and lack of opportunity that breed hopelessness, rage, and violence in so many neighborhoods. And we will have to take steps to get guns out of our homes and schools, and off our streets.

In a recent pastoral letter titled "Children and Families," the National Conference of Catholic Bishops commented eloquently and wisely on the critical interplay between private and public values. "No government can love a child and no policy can substitute for a family's care," the bishops wrote, "but government can either support or undermine families as they cope with the moral, social, and economic stresses of caring for children. . . . The undeniable fact is that our children's future is shaped both by the values of their parents and the policies of our nation."

It's up to us to work in our own communities, to communicate with our local, state, and federal representatives, and to use our vote to create a nation of neighborhoods that put children and families at the top of our agenda.

On behalf of children and families all over America, I thank Fred Rogers from my heart for using his enormous talent to support and supplement our public and private efforts to foster children's emotional, social, and spiritual development. I hope that the deepened appreciation of Fred Rogers' contributions we have all gained from reading this volume will inspire each of us to do more, both personally and professionally, to make America a more family-friendly nation. If we are not able to bring about this change in America, I am afraid that even Fred Rogers will not be able to save this nation's children.

But I am hopeful. Historically America has responded with energy, creativity, and determination to challenges that have threatened our deepest values and way of life. Now that Americans finally have begun to understand the peril we invite by ignoring our children's needs, I believe we will do what is necessary to make sure no child is left behind.

Marian Wright Edelman

With a law degree from Yale University, Marian Wright Edelman began her career with the NAACP Legal Defense and Educational Fund as a staff attorney and later became director of the field office in Jackson, Mississippi. She was the first black woman admitted to the Mississippi Bar. In 1968 she founded the Washington Research Project, a public interest law firm and the parent body of the Children's Defense Fund, of which she is currently president. Mrs. Edelman has received many awards and honors, including the Albert Schweitzer Humanitarian Prize, and was a MacArthur Foundation Prize Fellow. She has participated on many boards and commissions as a spokesperson for children and their families. Her writing includes Families in Peril: An Agenda for Social Change, The Measure of Our Success: A Letter to My Children and Yours, *and* Guide My Feet: Prayers and Meditations on Loving and Working for Children.

NOTES

The Reality of Make-Believe

1. As an aside, I also knew Fred and Joanne Rogers as parents. Not only did I have the boys in preschool, but I visited the Rogerses when they were in Canada for that "development" year for the television program. They met my friend and me at the airport, and as we drew up to their Toronto home, we were aghast to see fire trucks and cars surrounding the house. We were greeted by a tearful housekeeper who told us in tones of faltering horror that their toddler son had somehow gotten his leg stuck in a basement drain. We all rushed down the basement steps to comfort and help extricate the child, who was sitting, foot in drain, happily feeding cookies to his firemen rescuers. Fred's song "You Can Never Go Down the Drain" certainly must have had its roots in that fatherly experience, from which I am sure many of his other themes around children's fears, interests, and concerns emerged.

2. In *Revolution from Within*, Gloria Steinem notes that "so much has been blamed on parents, especially on mothers, that we need more realistic and compassionate ways to think about parenting." She defines Winnicott's term "good enough mother" as a "relief from the 'good mother' ideal that produced guilt in women who couldn't meet its impossible standard of self-sacrifice, and guilt in those children for whom those mothers sacrificed themselves." Of course, Steinem adds wryly, "Winnicott perpetuated a big part of the problem by leaving fathers out of the equation." The concept of the "good enough" parent, Steinem concludes, "helps us to realize that, if we love and respect our children as unique individuals, do not neglect them or use them to satisfy our personal hungers, and treat them at least as well as we treat ourselves (something that children, with their innate sense of fairness, are quick to recognize), then we will probably be 'good enough' parents." (*Editor's note*)

3. Winnicott, *Playing and Reality*, pp. 108–09.

4. Primary process thinking has all the characteristics of fantasy: condensation, displacement, and strong use of symbolism (for example, the two-year-old may refer to all furry animals as "fuzzies" and all large animals as "mooies"). We

adults are more familiar with this process through our dream life, while artists can express such images through music, art, or drama.

On "building internal working models," see Bowlby, *Attachment and Loss*.

Fred's Shoes: The Meaning of Transitions in *Mister Rogers' Neighborhood*

1. It didn't used to be that way, incidentally. Ms. Sharapan recalls that in the early days of the show, "Fred used to say, 'Oh, maybe it's time for the trolley.' Or the trolley would come out and sort of interrupt him. It was as if the trolley was coming on its own. As he grew in his work," she says, "Fred felt he wanted to be more honest with children, and he actually had a switch installed at the window seat. It was a way of saying, 'This is how I bring the trolley.' "

2. In the film, the orphic poet enters the underworld, not through a cave but through a mirror in his Paris apartment. Guided by a mundane, wingless angel named Heurtebise, Cocteau's Orpheus crosses a dim wasteland and is ushered into the presence of Death, represented as a beautiful woman.

Mister Rogers: Keeper of the Dream

1. Wehmiller, *Face to Face*, p. 6.
2. Lawrence, "How Prejudice Begins," 11.
3. Charles Winters and William Griffin, *Hebrew Scriptures*, (Sewanee, Tenn.: University of the South, 1990), p. 169.
4. Rogers, "The Past and Present Is Now," 13.

Make-Believe, Truth, and Freedom: Television in the Public Interest

1. Newton Minow's superb "wasteland" speech of 1961 is included in Minow and Lamay, *Abandoned in the Wasteland*; the "waste site" reference is from Rep. Edward Markey in the 1987 Telecommunications Subcommittee Hearings on Children's TV, cited in Minow and Lamay, p. 54.

2. During the years in which my career focused on the study of *Mister Rogers' Neighborhood*, the family grew to include Peter (1969) and Paula Lois (1970) as well as Matthew. Each has become a person of democratic disposition. I am grateful to Fred Rogers for the contributions he made to their lives.

3. See Stein and Friedrich, "Television Content"; Friedrich and Stein, "Aggressive and Prosocial Television Programs."

4. See Friedrich and Stein, "Prosocial Television and Young Children."

5. See Huston-Stein et al., "The Relation of Classroom Structure; Friedrich-Cofer et al., "Environmental Enhancement of Prosocial Television Content."

6. Minow and Lamay, *Abandoned in the Wasteland*, present a detailed analysis of the policy debates. Montgomery, *Target: Prime Time*, provides a thought-

provoking account of the failure of public interest groups, social scientists, and boycotts to affect commercial television.

7. Friedrich-Cofer, "Body, Mind, and Morals."

8. Cofer and Jacobvitz, "The Loss of Moral Turf."

9. Quotes cited in Minow and Lamay, *Abandoned in the Wasteland*, pp. 189, 190.

10. Ibid., p. 116.

11. On single mothers, see Hewlett, *When the Bough Breaks*, and J. B. Schor, *The Overworked American: The Unexpected Decline in Leisure* (New York: Basic Books, 1991). On poverty rate, see Minow and Lamay, *Abandoned in the Wasteland*.

12. On pressures of consumerism, see Bellah, "The Invasion of the Money World," and Schor, *The Overworked American*. On advertising fees, see *Connoisseur*, September 1989.

13. Minow and Lamay, *Abandoned in the Wasteland*.

14. W. Greider, *Who Will Tell the People: The Betrayal of American Democracy* (New York: Simon and Schuster, 1992); on the Mighty Morphin Power Rangers, see Minow and Lamay, *Abandoned in the Wasteland*; on Mortal Kombat, see *Business Week*, August 4, 1995.

15. On authenticity, see C. Taylor, *The Malaise of Modernity* (West Concord, Ontario: Anansi Press, 1991); on civic responsibilities, see J. B. Elshtain, *Democracy on Trial* (New York: Basic Books, 1995).

16. On imagery of the marketplace, see, for example, *New York Times*, August 20, 1995; on parents losing control, see Cofer and Jacobvitz, "The Loss of Moral Turf"; on "hostile force," see Whitehead, "The Family in an Unfriendly Culture."

17. Cofer and Jacobvitz, "The Loss of Moral Turf"; Minow and Lamay, *Abandoned in the Wasteland*.

18. Elshtain, *Democracy on Trial*.

19. Bagdikian, *The Media Monopoly*.

20. Carl Bernstein, "The Idiot Culture: Reflections on Post-Watergate Journalism," *New Republic*, June 8, 1992, 22–28; Bellah et al., *Habits of the Heart*, p. 260; J. B. White, "How Should We Talk About Corporations: The Languages of Economics and Citizenship," *Yale Law Journal* 94 (1985): 1,416–25.

21. Vaclav Havel, *Disturbing the Peace: A Conversation with Karel Hvizdala* (New York: Knopf, 1990), 15–16

22. "Indispensable to the just exercise" quote cited in R. Ketcham, *James Madison* (Charlottesville: University of Virginia Press, 1990), p. 402. "Truth would always have a fair chance" quote from S. Padover, *The Complete Madison: His Basic Writings* (New York: Harper and Brothers, 1953), p. 296. "Error and oppression" quote cited in Ketcham, p. 401.

23. Minow and Lamay, *Abandoned in the Wasteland*, p. 195.

24. On political writers, see Elshtain, *Democracy on Trial*; Neil Postman,

Amusing Ourselves to Death. "Challenge the concentrated ownership" quote from Greider, *Who Will Tell the People*, p. 328.

25. Rogers, *You Are Special: Words of Wisdom*, p. 122.

26. Ibid., p. 11.

27. E. Keller, *A Feeling for the Organism: The Life and Work of Barbara McClintock* (San Francisco: W. H. Freeman, 1983).

Mister Rogers Speaks to Parents

1. In 1979 Fred Rogers made an hour-long show entitled *Mister Rogers Talks to Parents About School*. This was followed in 1980 with a one-hour program called *Mister Rogers Talks to Parents About Superheroes*. Two hour-long programs were created in 1981: *Mister Rogers Talks to Parents About Competition* and *Mister Rogers Talks to Parents About Divorce*. In 1982 he switched to a half-hour format with *Mister Rogers Talks to Parents About Pets*, *Mister Rogers Talks to Parents About Discipline*, and *Mister Rogers Talks to Parents About Make-Believe*. The last program was broadcast in 1983: *Mister Rogers Talks to Parents About Day Care*.

2. According to Hedda Sharapan, Rogers once began to write a song with the line "The child is in me still, and sometimes not so still." It was never finished, but represents the issue that there are many things as important to young children as they are to us, no matter how old we are.

A Neighborhood with Forest *and* Trees: Allies, Coalitions, Kids, and Mister Rogers

1. Palmer et al., "Rubik's Tube," p. 151.

2. McFarland, *Extending the "Neighborhood,"* pp. 3, 7, 32. For a discussion of transitions within the program itself, see Roderick Townley's essay "Fred's Shoes."

3. As an example of how Fred Rogers speaks to children of a certain age and only of a certain age, this quotation is without peer. At some age, we come to understand that our thoughts and feelings are metaphorical, not concrete — a freedom that does, however, have to be learned.

4. Rubenstein, "Television and Behavior," 820.

5. Fitch et al., "From Television Forms to Genre Schemata," p. 42.

Afterword: A Nation of Neighborhoods

1. Hamburg, *Today's Children*, p. 13.

2. Brofenbrenner, "What Do Families Do?," p. 5.

BIBLIOGRAPHY

Alpert, Hollis. "A Nice Neighborhood for Kids." *Woman's Day*, April 1968.

Anderson, Jack E. "Talking to KidVid's One-Man Class Act." *Miami Herald*, May 7, 1978.

Bagdikian, B. *The Media Monopoly*. Boston: Beacon Press, 1987.

Bakshian, Aram, Jr. "Gone with the Wimp." *National Review*, September 26, 1985.

Banas, Casey. "Mr. Rogers of TV Works to Ease Fear in Children." *Chicago Tribune*, November 24, 1976.

Bandler, Michael J. "Mr. Rogers: Everybody's Neighbor." *Parents Magazine*, March 1989.

Bass, Sharon L. "A Lovely Day at Yale: Mr. Rogers to Lecture." *New York Times*, November 21, 1988.

Bellah, R. "The Invasion of the Money World." In *Rebuilding the Nest: A New Commitment to the American Family*, edited by D. Blankenhorn, S. Bayme, and J. Elshtain, 227–36. Milwaukee: Family Service America, 1990.

Bellah, R., Madsen, R., Sullivan, W., Swidler, A., and Tipton, S. *Habits of the Heart*. New York: Perennial Library, Harper & Row, 1986.

Bender, Bob. "Mr. Rogers Never Left the Child Behind." *USA Today*, April 15, 1984.

Benson, Betsy. "It's 20 Years in the Neighborhood for Mr. Rogers." *Pittsburgh Business Times and Journal*, September 7, 1987.

Berkvist, Robert. "Mr. Rogers Is a Caring Man." *New York Times*, November 19, 1969.

Bianco, Robert. "The Quiet Success of Fred Rogers." *Pittsburgh Press Sunday Magazine*, March 26, 1989.

——. "Weekend TV: Viewers Can Visit 'Children's Corner' One More Time." *Pittsburgh Press*, December 12, 1991.

Bianculli, David. "Mr. Rogers Looks at Divorce." *Akron Beacon Journal*, February 15, 1981.

Bierly, Kenneth. "Interview with Mr. Rogers." *Instructor*, February 1979.

Blank, Edward L. "Fred Rogers, a Teacher: I Like You as You Are." *Pittsburgh Press*, June 24, 1970.

Blau, Eleanor. "Rogers Has New TV Series on School." *New York Times*, July 20, 1979.

Blyskal, Jeff. "Can You Say 'Economics'?" *Forbes*, January 30, 1984.

Bowlby, J. *Attachment and Loss*. 3 vols. New York: Basic Books, 1969–73.

Boyum, Jon Gould. "The Tube as Childhood Friend." *Wall Street Journal*, April 7, 1972.

Brady, James. "In Step with Mr. Rogers." *Parade*, August 6, 1989.

Briggs, Kenneth A. "Mr. Rogers Decided It's Time to Head for New Neighborhoods." *New York Times*, May 8, 1975.

Brofenbrenner, Urie. "What Do Families Do?" *Family Affairs* 4 (1–2): 5 (1991).

Bunce, Alan. "Mr. Rogers Explores the Rhythms of Childhood — and Life." *Christian Science Monitor*, March 9, 1987.

Burch, C. A. "Puppet Play in a Thirteen-year-old Boy: Remembering, Repeating, and Working Through." *Clinical Social Work Journal* 8 (20): 79–89 (1980).

Cassell, S. "Effect of Brief Puppet Therapy Upon the Emotional Responses of Children Undergoing Cardiac Catheterization." *Journal of Counseling Psychology* 29 (1): 1–8 (1966).

Christy, Marian. "How Mr. Rogers Keeps His Neighborhood Ticking." *Boston Globe*, February 17, 1985.

Coates, Brian, and others. "The Influence of Sesame Street and Mr. Rogers' Neighborhood on Children's Social Behavior in Preschool." *Child Development* 47 (1) (1976).

Cobb, Nathan. "Can You Say Mr. Rogers?" *Boston Globe*, March 16, 1988.

Cofer, L. F. "A Modest Proposal: Everyone Wins — The Networks, Advertisers, and Young Viewers."

Cofer, L. F., and R. Jacobvitz. "The Loss of Moral Turf: Mass Media and Family Values." In *Rebuilding the Nest: A New Commitment to the American Family*, edited by D. Blankenhorn, S. Bayme, and J. Elshtain, 179–204. Milwaukee: Family Service America, 1990.

Collins, Glenn. "TV's Mr. Rogers — A Busy Surrogate Dad." *New York Times*, June 19, 1983.

Cross, Robert. "No Kid Stuff for Mr. Rogers When It Comes to Business." *Chicago Tribune*, March 17, 1983.

Cushman, Sandi. "Neighborhood Emphasizes Every Individual's Value." *New York Sunday News*, February 22, 1976.

———. "This 'Neighborhood' is Truly a Child's Delight." *New York Sunday News*, March 12, 1972.

Daley, Eliot A. "Is TV Brutalizing Your Child?" *Look*, December 2, 1969.

———. "Chewing Gum for the Eyes: Fred Rogers and the Forum on Child Development and the Mass Media." *QED Renaissance: Pittsburgh's New Public Television Magazine* 1 (11): 21–27 (Nov. 1970).

Darovich, Donna. "Award-Winning Rogers: Kid's Special-izer." *Fort Worth Star-Telegram*, February 13, 1981.

Davis, Flora. "Mr. Rogers Talks to Mothers." *Redbook*, January 1975.

de Courcy Hinds, Michael. "Paying Tribute to Television's Soft-Spoken Neighbor." *New York Times*, March 5, 1990.

DiFranco, JoAnn, and Anthony DiFranco. *Mister Rogers: Good Neighbor to America's Children*. Minneapolis: Dillon Press, 1983.

Dundon, Susan. "Pretend, Just Pretend, That Mr. Rogers Is an Adult's Friend." *Philadelphia Inquirer*, April 14, 1981.

Errigo-Stoup, Paula. "Mr. Rogers Comes to Migrant Children." *Migrant Education Messages and Outlook*, March 4, 1986.

Evans, Phyllis. "Meet Mr. Rogers." *American Baby*, August 1981.

Ferretti, Fred. "$500,000 Is Given to 'Mr. Rogers'." *New York Times*, January 17, 1970.

Fitch, M., A. Huston, and J. Wright. "From Television Forms to Genre Schemata." In *Children and Television*. Newbury Park, Calif.: Sage Publications, 1993.

Fonzi, Gaeton. "Friendly Fire." *Miami–South Florida Magazine*, September 1984.

Friedman, Max J. "Understanding Sibling Rivalry." *American Way*, July 1982.

Friedrich, L. K., and A. H. Stein. "Aggressive and Prosocial Television Programs and the Natural Behavior of Preschool Children." *Monographs of the Society for Research in Child Development* 38 (1973): 4, whole no. 151.

———. "Prosocial Television and Young Children." *Child Development* 46 (1975): 27–38.

Friedrich-Cofer, L. "Body, Mind, and Morals in the Framing of Social Policy." In *Human Nature and Public Policy: Scientific Views of Women, Children, and Families*, edited by L. Friedrich-Cofer, 97–174. New York: Praeger, 1986.

Friedrich-Cofer, L., A. Huston-Stein, D. Kipnis, E. Susman, and A. Clewett. "Environmental Enhancement of Prosocial Television Content: Effects on Interpersonal Behavior, Imaginative Play, and Self-Regulation in a Natural Setting." *Developmental Psychology* 15, no. 6 (1979): 637–46.

Fryxell, David A. "Mapping Mr. Rogers' Neighborhood." *Pitt Magazine*, May 1987.

Futterman, Ellen. "Mr. Rogers Still Special at 60." *St. Petersburg Times*, June 1988.

Gendler, M. "Group Puppetry with School-age Children: Rationale, Procedure, and Therapeutic Implication." *The Arts in Psychotherapy* 13 (1986): 45–52.

Grace, Bob. "Fred Rogers Is Worried About Children's TV Shows." *Houston Chronicle*, May 2, 1982.

Graves, Susan B. "Mr. Rogers: The Little Peoples' Spokesman." *Good Housekeeping*, February 1970.

Greenberg, Nancy. "A Beautiful Day." *Philadelphia Sunday Bulletin*, February 16, 1975.

Greenwald, Arthur, and Barry Head. *Going to the Hospital*. Pittsburgh: Family

Communications, 1977. Let's Talk About It series for parents; illustrated by William Panos.

——. *Having an Operation*. Pittsburgh: Family Communications, 1977. Let's Talk About It series for parents; illustrated by William Panos.

——. *Wearing a Cast*. Pittsburgh: Family Communications, 1977. Let's Talk About It series for parents; illustrated by William Panos.

Gregory, Jane. "Mr. Rogers: A Special Friend Takes on a Special Problem." *Chicago Sun-Times*, February 2, 1980.

Hamburg, David. *Today's Children: Creating a Future for a Generation in Crisis*. New York: Times Books, 1992.

Harabuda, Judy. "Six from the Neighborhood." *Carnegie Mellon Magazine*, March 1990.

Harrington, Richard. "Mr. Rogers Gives Sweater to Museum." *Baltimore News American*, November 23, 1984.

Head, Barry, and Jim Sequin. *Who Am I?* Austin, Tex.: Pro-Ed, 1975. I Am, I Can, I Will series; photographs by Walter Seng.

Henderson, Keith. "Mr. Rogers' Neighborhood Keeps on Growing." *Christian Science Monitor*, January 13, 1986.

Hendrick, Kimmis. "Mr. Rogers — He Talks with Children Where They Are." *Christian Science Monitor*, March 22, 1969.

Hendrikson, Paul. "In a Land of Make-Believe, the Real Mr. Rogers." *Washington Post*, November 13, 1982.

Henry, William A., III. "Mr. Rogers in Person Is Mr. Nice Guy." *Boston Globe*, June 12, 1978.

Hewlett, S. *When the Bough Breaks: The Cost of Neglecting Our Children*. New York: Basic Books, 1991.

H.K. "Growing up with Mr. Rogers." *Parade*, May 9, 1971.

Holston, Noel. "Mr. Rogers: OK to Make Mistakes." *Minneapolis Star and Tribune*, May 4, 1987.

Honig, Alice Sterling. "Television and Young Children." *Research in Review*, May 1983.

Huston-Stein, A., L. Friedrich-Cofer, and E. Susman. "The Relation of Classroom Structure to Social Behavior, Imaginative Play, and Self-Regulation of Economically Disadvantaged Children." *Child Development* 48, no. 3 (1977): 908–16.

Irwin, E. "Puppets in Therapy: An Assessment Procedure." *American Journal of Psychotherapy* 34 (3): 389–99 (1985).

Isenberg, Barbara. "Over Easy: TV Views the Aged." *Los Angeles Times*, September 2, 1977.

Jones, Diana Nelson. "When a Child Has Cancer." *Pittsburgh Post-Gazette*, June 28, 1990.

Jory, Tom. "Children and Divorce." *Boston Globe*, February 14, 1981.

Judson, Bay. "The Art Museum in Mr. Rogers' Neighborhood." *School Arts Magazine*, April 1982.

Kaye, Evelyn. "Kids, TV, and Hospitals: A Search for Balance." *Boston Globe*, November 16, 1978.

Kelly, Marguerite. "Parents' Almanac: Mr. Rogers, the American Family, and Divorce." *Washington Post*, February 12, 1981.

King, Janet Spencer. "Christmas with Mr. Rogers." *Ladies' Home Journal*, December 1988.

Kleiner, Dick. "Mr. Rogers: Views from the Neighborhood." *Baltimore News American*, June 17, 1981.

Klinzing, Dennis R., and Dene G. Klinzing. "Communicating with Young Children About Hospitalization." *Communication Education*, November 1977.

Krasnow, Iris. "Mr. Rogers' Secret: His Message to the Children Makes Him Special." *St. Petersburg Times*, August 4, 1985.

Lapinski, Susan. "Mr. Rogers: A Friend of the Family." *American Baby*, August 1987.

Lardner, James. "Annals of Law: The Betamax Case–1." *New Yorker*, April 6, 1987.

———. "Annals of Law: The Betamax Case–2." *New Yorker*, April 13, 1987.

Laskas, Jeanne Marie. "The Good Life — and Works — of Mister Rogers." *Life*, November 1994.

———. "Mr. Rogers: He Likes You Just the Way You Are." *Applause Magazine*, April 1988.

———. "Zen and the Art of Make-Believe." *Pittsburgh Magazine*, October 1985.

Lawrence, Margaret Morgan, "How Prejudice Begins." *Child Study: A Quarterly Journal of Parent Education* 33, no. 1 (winter 1955–56).

Leo, Peter. "Kids Like Fred Rogers Just the Way He Is." *Pittsburgh Post-Gazette*, April 17, 1979.

Leonard, Vince. "Rogers Goes to Washington — and Does Some Good Deeds." *Pittsburgh Press*, May 2, 1969.

Levin, Doron P. "Loved by Kids for His TV 'Neighborhood,' Mr. Rogers Is a Hit in Boardrooms, Too." *Wall Street Journal*, April 4, 1981.

Linn, S. "Puppet Therapy in Hospitals: Helping Children Cope." *Journal of the American Medical Women's Association* 33 (2): 61–65 (1978).

Linn, S., W. Beardslee, and A. Patenaude. "Puppet Therapy with Pediatric Bone Marrow Transplant Patients." *Journal of Pediatric Psychology* 11 (1): 37–46 (1986).

Lipson, Eden Ross. "Mr. Rogers' Home Video: When Parents Are Away." *New York Times*, October 18, 1981.

Long, Marion. "Paradise Tossed." *Omni*, April 1988.

Manley, Will. "Facing the Public." *Wilson Library Bulletin*, October 1984.

Margulies, Lee. "Mr. Rogers Is What He Is." *Los Angeles Times*, December 18, 1982.

Mark, Norman. "The Perfect TV Shows for Your Children." *Today's Health*, April 1974.

Marsh, Robert. "Growing up with Mr. Rogers." *Focus*, October 24, 1982.

Martin, Judith. "Cheers for Mr. Rogers." *Washington Post*, October 17, 1973.

Maynard, Fredelle. "Mr. Rogers' Neighborhood: Where Small Children Feel at Home." *Image*, March 1974.

McCullaugh, Jim. "Here Comes Mr. Rogers — and There Goes the 'Neighborhood'!" *Billboard*, July 26, 1986.

McFarland, Suzanne L. *Extending the "Neighborhood" to Child Care*. Washington, D.C.: Corporation for Public Broadcasting, Research Report, 1992.

McGrath, David. "Fred Rogers Enjoys All Those 'Mr. Rogers' Neighborhood' Spoofs." *Happenings Magazine*, April 1, 1982.

McNulty, Edward. "Troubador of Grace." *Marriage and Family Living*, June 1988.

Meier, Peg. "Sexspeak Begins with Mr. Rogers." *Los Angeles Herald Examiner*, March 8, 1989.

Menn-Hamblin, Becky. "A Visit to the Neighborhood." *Storytelling*, Spring 1990.

Minow, N., and C. Lamay. *Abandoned in the Wasteland: Children, Television, and the First Amendment*. New York: Hill and Wang, 1995.

Mohler, Mary. "Mr. Rogers on Monsters." *Ladies' Home Journal*, October 1986.

Monkres, Peter. "The Heroism of Nurture." *Christian Century*, December 19, 1979.

Montgomery, K. *Target: Prime Time*. New York: Oxford University Press, 1989.

Moran, Brian. "BK Won't Ruin Mr. Rogers' Beautiful Day." *Advertising Age*, May 10, 1984.

Morris, Norman S. "What's Good About Children's TV." *Atlantic Monthly*, August 1969.

Murphy, Ryan. "Interview with Mr. Rogers." *Miami Herald News*, June 2, 1991.

Nadas, Betsy P. *Danny's Song*. Austin, Tex.: Pro-Ed, 1975. I Am, I Can, I Will series; illustrated by Frank Dostolfo and William Panos.

Neuhaus, Cable. "Fred Rogers Moves Into a New Neighborhood — and So Does His Rebellious Son." *People*, May 15, 1978.

Newell, David. "Memoirs of Speedy Delivery." *Gambit Magazine*, August 15, 1975.

O'Connor, John J. "Dealing with the Aged: How Kin Try to Cope." *New York Times*, August 1, 1980.

———. "Mr. Rogers, a Gentle Neighbor." *New York Times*, February 15, 1976.

———. "An Observer Who Bridges the Generation Gap." *New York Times*, April 23, 1978.

Ogintz, Eileen. "Neighborhood Hero." *Chicago Tribune*, March 6, 1988.

Orlean, Susan. "Hanging Around the Neighborhood." *Boston Phoenix*, February 12, 1985.

O'Toole, James. "Mr. Rogers' Red Sweater Warms Smithsonian Visitors." *Pittsburgh Post-Gazette*, November 11, 1985.

Pae, Peter. "This Neighborhood Hasn't Changed a Bit Over the Decades." *Wall Street Journal*, March 2, 1990.

Palmer, E. L., K. Taylor Smith, and K. S. Strawser. "Rubik's Tube: Developing a Child's Television Worldview." In *Children and Television*. Newbury Park, Calif.: Sage Publications, 1993.

Pilbrick, Linda. *When Your Family Moves*. Pittsburgh: Family Communications, 1981. Let's Talk About It series for parents.

Platte, Mark. "Mr. Rogers Fries Over Ads in Television Burger Wars." *Miami Herald*, May 8, 1984.

Plotsker-Herman, Candace. "Children's TV: A Tool — Not a Toy." *American Baby*, August 1986.

Plutzik, Roberta. "A Special Neighborhood." *TV Record*, August 10, 1986.

Polak, Maralyn Lois. "Fred Rogers: An Honest Adult." *Philadelphia Inquirer*, December 9, 1984.

Postman, N. *Amusing Ourselves to Death: Public Discourse in the Age of Show Business*. New York: Penguin, 1986.

Powers, Ron. "Easy Does It — That's Mr. Rogers' Approach." *Chicago Sun-Times*, February 18, 1973.

———. "Mr. Rogers to De-Horrify the Santa Claus Syndrome." *Denver Post*, February 8, 1973.

———. "The Quiet Man of Children's TV." *Chicago Sun-Times*, February 25, 1973.

Pramik, Mary Jean. "Toys and Their Role in Creative Play." *Good Housekeeping*, September 1985.

The Project on Disney. *Inside the Mouse: Work and Play at Disney World*. Durham: Duke University Press, 1995.

Putka, Gary. "Are Mollycoddlers Turning Our Tykes Into Little Wimps?" *Wall Street Journal*, May 10, 1989.

Rader, P. J. "The Man in the Sweater." *Minneapolis PBS Magazine*, April 1988.

Raymond, Allen. "Behind the Scenes with Mr. Rogers." *Early Years*, December 1982.

Reddicliffe, Steven. "A Neighborly Visit — Straight Talk from Mr. Rogers." *Dallas Times Herald*, May 30, 1982.

Rist, Marilee C. "The Curious Appeal of Mr. Rogers' Neighborhood." *Pennsylvania Magazine*, September 3, 1983.

Rogers, Fred. "Adoption Programs for Young Children." *National Adoption Reports*, September 1985.

———. "Ask the Expert: Mr. Rogers." *American Baby*, September 1985.

———. *Bedtime*. Pittsburgh: Family Communications, 1992. Cassette; performed and produced by Mister Rogers.

———. "Best Children's Toys." *Ladies' Home Journal*, March 1986.

——. "Building Attitudes and Values." *Childhood*, September 1976.

——. "Children and Pets Growing Together." *PTA Today*, April 1982.

——. *Daniel Striped Tiger Gets Ready for Bed*. New York: Random House Books for Young Readers, 1988. Illustrated by Pat Sustendal.

——. *Danny's Song*. Austin, Tex.: Pro-Ed, 1979. I Am, I Can, I Will series; cassette. Performed by Mister Rogers.

——. *Death of a Goldfish*. Pittsburgh: Family Communications, 1970. Video.

——. *A Dentist and a Toothfairy*. Pittsburgh: Family Communications, 1977. Video.

——. *Dinosaurs and Monsters*. New York: CBS/Fox Video, 1986. Video.

——. *Discipline*. New York: Hearst/ABC Daytime, 1982. Video; for adults.

——. *Divorce*. New York: Hearst/ABC Daytime, 1982. Video; for adults.

——. "Family Ties: The Youngest Link." *Working Parents*, September 1988.

——. *Feeling Happy, Feeling Sad*. Austin, Tex.: Pro-Ed, 1979. I Am, I Can, I Will series; cassette. Performed by Mister Rogers.

——. *Feeling Mad*. Austin, Tex.: Pro-Ed, 1979. I Am, I Can, I Will series; cassette. Performed by Mister Rogers.

——. *Francie's Fairy Tale*. Austin, Tex.: Pro-Ed, 1979. I Am, I Can, I Will series; cassette. Performed by Mister Rogers.

——. *Fred Rogers' Heroes: Who's Helping America's Children*. Pittsburgh: Family Communications, 1994. Video; produced by Margaret Whitmer.

——. *Friends Who Fight*. New York: Hearst/ABC Daytime, 1982. Video; for adults.

——. "From Mr. Rogers: When Your Child Goes to School." *Family Circle*, September 8, 1987.

——. *Going on an Airplane*. New York: G. P. Putnam's Sons, 1989. Photographs by Jim Judkis.

——. *Going to Day Care*. New York: G. P. Putnam's Sons, 1985.

——. *Going to the Dentist*. New York: G. P. Putnam's Sons, 1989. Photographs by Jim Judkis.

——. *Going to the Doctor*. New York: G. P. Putnam's Sons, 1986. Photographs by Jim Judkis.

——. *Going to the Doctor*. Pittsburgh: Family Communications, 1976. Video; alternate title, *Going to the Pediatrician*.

——. *Going to the Hospital*. New York: G. P. Putnam's Sons, 1988. Photographs by Jim Judkis.

——. *Going to the Potty*. New York: G. P. Putnam's Sons, 1986. Photographs by Jim Judkis.

——. *Going to Sleep*. Austin, Tex.: Pro-Ed, 1979. I Am, I Can, I Will series; cassette. Performed by Mister Rogers.

——. *Growing*. Austin, Tex.: Pro-Ed, 1979. I Am, I Can, I Will series; cassette. Performed by Mister Rogers.

———. *Growing Up Without Sight*. Austin, Tex.: Pro-Ed, 1979. I Am, I Can, I Will series; cassette. Performed by Mister Rogers and Ted Lennox.

———. *Helping and Loving*. Austin, Tex.: Pro-Ed, 1979. I Am, I Can, I Will series; cassette. Performed by Mister Rogers.

———. "How To Make Christmas Meaningful for Your Children." *Today's Health,* December 1975.

———. *If We Were All the Same*. New York: Random House, 1987. Cassette, with book illustrated by Pat Sustendal.

———. *Imaginary Friends*. New York: Hearst/ABC Daytime, 1982. Video; for adults.

———. "It's Special to Know You." *New York Times*. April 25, 1976.

———. "It's You I Like." *Gifted Children Newsletter*, December 1984.

———. *Johnny Costa Plays Mister Rogers' Neighborhood Jazz*. Pittsburgh: Family Communications, 1985. Record and cassette; produced by Mister Rogers; performed by Johnny Costa, Bobby Rawsthorne, Carl McVicker. Lyrics and music by Mister Rogers.

———. *Josephine the Short-Necked Giraffe*. Austin, Tex.: Pro-Ed, 1975. I Am, I Can, I Will series; adapted by Barry Head.

———. *Josephine the Short-Necked Giraffe*. Austin, Tex.: Pro-Ed, 1979. I Am, I Can, I Will series; cassette. Performed by Mister Rogers.

———. "Kids: The Serious Business of Playtime." *Washington Post,* January 3, 1984.

———. *Let's Be Together Today*. Pittsburgh: Family Communications, 1968. Record and cassette; produced and performed by Mister Rogers.

———. "Let's Help Youngsters Deal with Change." *USA Today*, March 17, 1983.

———. *Let's Talk About Going to the Hospital*. Pittsburgh: Family Communications, 1976. Video.

———. *Let's Talk About Having an Operation*. Pittsburgh: Family Communications, 1976. Video.

———. *Let's Talk About a Visit to the Emergency Department*. Pittsburgh: Family Communications, 1982. Video; alternate title, *Let's Talk About a Visit to the Emergency Room*.

———. *Let's Talk About Wearing a Cast*. Pittsburgh: Family Communications, 1976. Video.

———. "Making Day Care a Success." *Working Parents*, August 1984.

———. *Making Friends*. New York: G. P. Putnam's Sons, 1987. Photographs by Jim Judkis.

———. "Memories of Christmas Past." *Woman's Day*, December 14, 1982.

———. "Mr. Rogers on Men in Child Care." *Childcare Action News*, July 1989.

———. *Mister Rogers' Neighborhood . . . Circus Fun*. New York: CBS/Fox, 1995. Video.

———. *Mister Rogers' Neighborhood . . . Kindness*. New York: CBS/Fox, 1995. Video.

———. *Mister Rogers' Neighborhood . . . Love*. New York: CBS/Fox, 1995. Video.

———. *Mister Rogers' Neighborhood . . . Making Music*. New York: CBS/Fox, 1995. Video.

———. *Mister Rogers' Plan and Play Book: Daily Activities from Mister Rogers' Neighborhood for Child Care Providers*. 3d ed. Pittsburgh: Family Communications, 1991.

———. *Mister Rogers Talks About Childhood Cancer*. Philadelphia: American Cancer Society; 1989. Video; two-part series.

———. "Mr. Rogers Talks About Discipline." *Nurturing News*, December 1985.

———. *Mister Rogers Talks About the Environment*. Pittsburgh: Family Communications, 1990. Video; with twenty-four page activity booklet.

———. *Mister Rogers Talks About the New Baby, Moving, Fighting, Going to the Doctor, Going to School, Haircuts*. New York: Platt and Munk, 1974.

———. *Mister Rogers Talks with Children About Going to a New School*. Harrisburg: Pennsylvania Migrant Education, Pennsylvania Department of Education, 1986. Video; with teacher's guide.

———. *Mister Rogers Talks with Children About Saying Goodbye to Friends*. Harrisburg: Pennsylvania Migrant Education, Pennsylvania Department of Education, 1986. Video; with teacher's guide.

———. *Mister Rogers Talks with Children About Speaking Different Languages*. Harrisburg: Pennsylvania Migrant Education, Pennsylvania Department of Education, 1986. Video; with teacher's guide.

———. *Mister Rogers Talks with Parents About Competition*. Pittsburgh: Family Communications, 1981. Video.

———. *Mister Rogers Talks with Parents About Day Care*. Pittsburgh: Family Communications, 1983. Video.

———. *Mister Rogers Talks with Parents About Discipline*. Pittsburgh: Family Communications, 1982. Video.

———. *Mister Rogers Talks with Parents About Divorce*. Pittsburgh: Family Communications, 1981. Video.

———. *Mister Rogers Talks with Parents About Make-Believe*. Pittsburgh: Family Communications, 1982. Video.

———. *Mister Rogers Talks with Parents About Pets*. Pittsburgh: Family Communications, 1982. Video.

———. *Mister Rogers Talks with Parents About School*. Pittsburgh: Family Communications, 1979. Video.

———. *Mister Rogers Talks with Parents About Superheroes*. Pittsburgh: Family Communications, 1980. Video.

———. "Mr. Rogers Tells How to Get Through to Children." *Family Circle*, July 1973.

———. "Mr. Rogers Wants a Word with Parents." *Detroit Free Press*, August 2, 1991.

———. *Moving*. New York: G. P. Putnam's Sons, 1987.

———. *Moving*. New York: Hearst/ABC Daytime, 1982. Video; for adults.

———. *Music and Feelings*. New York: CBS/Fox, 1986. Video.

———. *Musical Stories*. New York: CBS/Fox, 1988. Video.

———. *Neighborhood Sounds*. Austin, Tex.: Pro-Ed, 1979. I Am, I Can, I Will series; cassette. Performed by Mister Rogers.

———. *The New Baby*. New York: G. P. Putnam's Sons, 1985. Photographs by Jim Judkis.

———. *No One Can Ever Take Your Place*. New York: Random House, 1988. Cassette, with book.

———. "Nurturing Creative Energy." *New York Times Magazine*, August 21, 1983.

———. *Nurturing Creativity*. New York: Hearst/ABC Daytime, 1982. Video; for adults.

———. *Old Friends . . . New Friends*. Pittsburgh: Family Communications, 1977–78. Video; twenty-part series with various guests and performers.

———. "The Parent/Caregiver Partnership." *Child Care Center*, September 1986.

———. "The Past and Present Is Now." *Young Children*, March 1984.

———. *A Place of Our Own*. Pittsburgh: Family Communications, 1970. Record and cassette; produced and performed by Mister Rogers.

———. *Purple Adventures of Lady Elaine Fairchilde*. Austin, Tex.: Pro-Ed, 1975. Video; five-part series with teacher's guide.

———. "Reflections." *Life*, March 1990. Special issue, "The World of Children."

———. *School Experiences*. New York: Hearst/ABC Daytime, 1982. Video; for adults.

———. *Siblings*. New York: Hearst/ABC Daytime, 1982. Video; for adults.

———. *So Many Things to See!* Pittsburgh: Family Communications, 1977. Let's Talk About It series for parents.

———. *Something Broken, Something Fixed. Taking Care*. Harrisburg: Pennsylvania Coalition Against Domestic Violence, 1990. Video; with booklet, *I Do and I Don't*, by Fred Rogers and Hedda Sharapan.

———. *Some Things Change and Some Things Stay the Same*. Philadelphia: American Cancer Society, 1989. Photographs by Jim Judkis.

———. *So Much to Think About When Someone You Care About Has Died*. Pittsburgh: Family Communications, 1991. Photographs by Jim Judkis.

———. *Speedy Delivery*. Austin, Tex.: Pro-Ed, 1973. I Am, I Can, I Will series; illustrated by Richard Hefter.

———. *The Story of Planet Purple*. Austin, Tex.: Pro-Ed, 1979. I Am, I Can, I Will series; cassette. Performed by Mister Rogers.

———. *Talking with Families About Creativity*. Pittsburgh: Family Communications, 1982. Let's Talk About It series for parents; designed and illustrated by Jim Prokell.

——. *Talking with Families About Discipline*. Pittsburgh: Family Communications, 1982. Let's Talk About It series for parents; designed and illustrated by Jim Prokell.

——. *Talking with Families About Pets*. Pittsburgh: Family Communications, 1982. Let's Talk About It series for parents; designed and illustrated by Jim Prokell.

——. "Talking with Leaders About Creativity." *Leadership!* October 1986.

——. *Talking with Young Children About Death*. Pittsburgh: Family Communications, 1978. Video; for adults.

——. "Thoughts on the Establishment of a 'Mister Rogers' Collection at the University of Pittsburgh." ACT *Phaedrus Magazine*, March 1978.

——. *A Trolley Visit to Make-Believe*. New York: Random House Books for Young Readers, 1987. Illustrated by Pat Sustendal.

——. *Trying Again*. Austin, Tex.: Pro-Ed, 1979. I Am, I Can, I Will series; cassette. Performed by Mister Rogers.

——. *Wake-Up Sounds*. Austin, Tex.: Pro-Ed, 1979. I Am, I Can, I Will series; cassette. Performed by Mister Rogers.

——. *What About Love?* New York: CBS/Fox, 1987. Video.

——. "What Do You Bring to TV?" *Saturday Evening Post*, September 1978.

——. *When Monsters Seem Real*. New York: Random House, 1988. Cassette, with book.

——. *When Parents Are Away*. New York: CBS/Fox, 1987. Video.

——. *When a Pet Dies*. New York: G. P. Putnam's Sons, 1988. Photographs by Jim Judkis.

——. *When You Have a Child in Day Care*. Pittsburgh: Family Communications, 1983. Let's Talk About It series for parents.

——. *When Your Child Goes to the Dentist*. Pittsburgh: Family Communications, 1977. Let's Talk About It series for parents.

——. *When Your Child Goes to School*. Pittsburgh: Family Communications, 1977. Let's Talk About It series for parents; photographs by Barry Myers.

——. *When Your Child Goes to the Hospital*. Pittsburgh: Family Communications, 1977. Let's Talk About It series for parents.

——. "Words to Grow On." *Guideposts*, April 1989.

——. *Wishes Don't Make Things Come True*. New York: Random House, 1987. Cassette, with book.

——. *Wishing and Pretending*. Austin, Tex.: Pro-Ed, 1979. I Am, I Can, I Will series; cassette. Performed by Mister Rogers.

——. *Won't You Be My Neighbor?* Pittsburgh: Family Communications, 1967. Record and cassette; produced and performed by Mister Rogers.

————. *You Are Special*. Austin, Tex.: Pro-Ed, 1979. I Am, I Can, I Will series; cassette. Performed by Mister Rogers.

————. *You Are Special*. Pittsburgh: Family Communications, 1994. Record and cassette; produced and performed by Mister Rogers.

————. *You Are Special: Words of Wisdom from America's Beloved Neighbor*. New York: Viking, 1994.

————. "You Can Be a More Sensitive Parent." *Redbook*, April 1987.

————. *You Can Never Go Down the Drain*. New York: Random House Books for Young Readers, 1988. Illustrated by Pat Sustendal.

————. *You're Growing*. Pittsburgh: Family Communications, 1993. Cassette; produced and performed by Mister Rogers.

————. "Your Own Good Neighbor." *Parents*, April 1979.

Rogers, Fred, and Jean Freeman. "Mr. Rogers Talks About Christmas and Your Child." *Woman's Day*, December 18, 1979.

Rogers, Fred, and Earl Grollman. *Talking with Families About Divorce*. Pittsburgh: Family Communications, 1981. Let's Talk About It series for parents.

Rogers, Fred, and Barry Head. "Insight Into Childhood." *Pittsburgh Press*, May 20, 1989.

————. "Josephine the Short-Necked Giraffe." *Focus*, August 1975.

————. *Mister Rogers: How Families Grow*. New York: Berkeley Books, 1988. Illustrated by Jim Prokell.

————. *Mister Rogers' Playbook: Insights and Activities for Parents and Children*. New York: Berkeley Books, 1986.

————. *Mister Rogers Talks with Parents*. New York: Berkeley Books, 1983.

Rogers, Fred, and Claire O'Brien. "How to Break the News." *Working Mother*, March 1988.

————. *Mister Rogers Talks with Families About Divorce*. New York: Berkeley Books, 1987.

Rogers, Fred, and Sheldon Secunda. *Tell Me, Mister Rogers, About Learning to Read, Sleeping Away from Home, Going to the Dentist, Thunder and Lightning, When Pets Die, Nobody Feels Perfect*. New York: Platt and Munk, 1975.

Rogers, Fred, and Hedda Bluestone Sharapan. *My Mom Still Loves Me*. Pittsburgh: Family Communications, 1990. Video, with booklet, *Good Weather or Not*, by Fred Rogers and Hedda Bluestone Sharapan; illustrated by James Mellott. Materials for children whose parents are mentally ill.

————. "Quiet on the Set!" *Children's Video Report*, June 1988.

————. "Seven Ways Parents Can Help Their Kids Cope with the War." *TV Guide*, February 23, 1991.

————. "Talking with Young Children About Death." *Infants to Teens*, February 1985.

————. *When Your Child Has Cancer*. Philadelphia: American Cancer Society, 1989.

Ross, Nancy S. "Make-Believe Opera." *Opera News*, January 13, 1973.

Rubin, Marilyn McDevitt. "Mr. Rogers Reflects on Food, Children, and Giving Thanks." *Pittsburgh Press*, November 4, 1984.

Rubenstein, E. "Television and Behavior: Research Conclusions of the 1982 NIMH Report and Their Policy Implications." *American Psychologist* (1983): 38.

Ruth, Daniel. "Darker Days of Mr. Rogers." *Chicago Sun-Times*, October 1985.

Saline, Carol. "My Dinner with Mr. Rogers." *Philadelphia*, November 1984.

Schaer, Sidney C. "Mr. Rogers: A Corner on Childhood." *Newsweek*, December 27, 1981.

Schlarbaum, Ruthanne. "Mr. Rogers' Neighborhood and Sesame Street." *Colloquy*, September 1971.

Secrest, Clark. "Mr. Rogers Touches Kids' Minds and Hearts." *Denver Post*, December 19, 1982.

Seiler, Michael. "Listening to What Mr. Rogers Says." *Los Angeles Times*, June 18, 1985.

Shales, Tom. "TV Violence a 'Special' Subject for Mr. Rogers." *Chicago Sun-Times*, June 6, 1981.

Sharapan, Hedda Bluestone. *Talking with Young Children About Death*. Pittsburgh: Family Communications, 1979. Let's Talk About It series for parents; designed and illustrated by Jim Prokell.

Shayon, Robert Lewis. "Senatorial Goose Bumps." *Saturday Review*, May 24, 1969.

Shea, Terrence. "Mr. Rogers' Wee World." *National Observer*, August 4, 1969.

Shepard, Richard F. "TV: On Superheroes." *New York Times*, February 4, 1980.

Shipp, Randy. "A Neighborly Visit with Mr. Rogers." *Christian Science Monitor*, August 21, 1979.

Shropshire, Mike. "Rogers' Good Neighbor Policy Assures Him Legion of Little Fans." *Dallas Morning News*, June 7, 1982.

Singer, Dorothy G. "Television's Good Neighbor: A Visit with Fred Rogers." *Newsletter of Parenting*, September 1980.

Singer, Dorothy, and Jerome Singer. "Bugs Bunny — Questionable, Mr. Rogers — Perfect." *TV Guide*, February 13, 1982.

———. *The House of Make-Believe*. Cambridge: Harvard University Press, 1990.

———. "Is Human Imagination Going Down the Tube?" *Chronicle of Higher Education*, April 23, 1979.

Singer, Jerome L., and Dorothy Singer. "Come Back, Mr. Rogers, Come Back." *Psychology Today*, March 1979.

Skalka, Patricia. "Welcome to the Neighborhood." *American Way*, October 1983.

Smith, Cecil. "6,000 Cheers for PTV's Mr. Rogers." *Los Angeles Times*, March 3, 1969.

Smucker, Tom C. "Pop's Culture." *Village Voice*, June 21, 1983.

Spiegelman, Barbara, and Susan Melnick. "Access to the Neighborhood of Mr. Rogers: Creating a Source for Research." *School Library Journal*, November 1985.

Steigerwald, Mary. "The Ministry of Fred Rogers." *Mothering*, March 1984.

Stein, A. H., and L. K. Friedrich. "Television Content and Young Children's Behavior." In *Television and Social Behavior*. Vol. 2, *Television and Social Learning*, edited by J. P. Murray, E. A. Rubinstein, and G. A. Comstock, 202–317. Washington, D.C.: U.S. Government Printing Office, 1972.

Stein, Sara. *A Piece of Red Paper*. Austin, Tex.: Pro-Ed, 1973. I Am, I Can, I Will series; illustrated by Otto D. Sherman.

Stern, Daniel. *Diary of a Baby*. New York: Basic Books, 1985.

Stern, Jane and Michael. *Jane and Michael Stern's Encyclopedia of Pop Culture*. New York: Harper Collins, 1992.

Stevens, Melanie Chadwick. "Mr. Rogers' Neighborhood." *Parents Magazine*, May 1982.

Sucher, Cynthia. "Mr. Rogers: An Insightful Talk with an Extraordinary Man." *Access*, February 1981.

Townley, Rod. "Mr. Rogers — Warm and Wonderful — or Just Plain Dippy?" *Philadelphia Inquirer*, May 19, 1974.

———. "He Reaches Into Kids' Souls." *TV Guide*, March 23, 1985.

Trott, Walt. "Mr. Rogers Delights Small-Fry." *Capital Times*, July 29, 1980.

Wagner, Judith. "When Children Ask About Handicaps." *American Education*, August 1975.

Warburton, T. L. "A Visit with Fred Rogers: A Guided Tour Through a Special Neighborhood." *Journal of Popular Film and Television*, March 16, 1988.

Wardlow, Jean. "Tiny Voices Vote for 'Mr. Rogers'." *Miami Herald*, November 29, 1969.

Wecker, David. "Mr. Rogers Is the Real Thing." *Cincinnati Post*, May 9, 1985.

Weingrad, Jeff. "Rogers Moves His Neighborhood." *New York Post*, December 7, 1977.

Weiskind, Ron. "Fred Rogers Lays Himself Out for TV Critics." *Pittsburgh Post-Gazette*, January 16, 1986.

Wehmiller, Paula Lawrence. *Face to Face, Lessons Learned on the Teaching Journey*. Philadelphia: Friends Council on Education, Tyson-Mason Paper, 1992.

Whelan, Ann. "It's You He Likes." *Baby Talk Magazine*, November 1990.

Whitehead, B. D. "The Family in an Unfriendly Culture." *Family Affairs* 6, nos. 1–2 (1990): 1–6.

Winnicott, D. W. *The Maturational Processes and the Facilitating Environment*. New York: International Universities Press, 1965.

———. *Mother and Child: A Primer of First Relationships*. New York: Basic Books, 1957.

———. *Playing and Reality*. New York: Basic Books, 1971.

Woltman, A. G. "Spontaneous Puppetry by Children as a Projective Method." In *Projective Techniques with Children*, edited by A. I. Rabin and M. R. Haworth, 305–12. New York: Grune and Stratton, 1960.

Wren, Christopher. "Quality Clicks with Kids." *Look*, December 1979.

———. "Work in Progress — Mr. Rogers' Children." *Intellectual Digest*, January 1974.

Young, Mort. "Mr. Rogers, a Realist, Sees No Changes in Children's Shows." *Boston Herald*, June 2, 1974.

Ziaukas, Tim. "Kid Video TV Stars of Yesteryear." *Pittsburgh Magazine*, July 1986.

INDEX

Library of Congress Cataloging-in-Publication Data

Mister Rogers' Neighborhood : children, television, and Fred Rogers /
Mark Collins and Margaret Mary Kimmel, editors.
p.   cm.
Includes bibliographical references.
ISBN 0-8229-3921-5 (cloth : alk. paper)
1. Rogers, Fred, influence.   2. Mister Rogers neighborhood
(Television program)   I. Collins, Mark.   II. Kimmel, Margaret Mary.
PN1992.4.R56M57   1996
791.45'028'092 — dc20   95-48461